Shiny and New

Also by Dylan Jones

Sweet Dreams: From Club Culture to Style Culture

The Wichita Lineman: Searching in The Sun for the World's Greatest Unfinished Song

David Bowie: A Life

London Sartorial

Manxiety

London Rules

Mr Mojo

Elvis Has Left the Building: The Day the King Died

The Eighties: One Day, One Decade

From the Ground Up

When Ziggy Played Guitar: David Bowie and Four Minutes that Shook the World

The Biographical Dictionary of Popular Music

British Heroes in Afghanistan (with David Bailey)

Mr Jones' Rules for the Modern Man

iPod Therefore I Am: A Personal Journey Through Music

Meaty Beaty Big & Bouncy (Ed.)

Sex, Power & Travel (Ed.)

Ultra Lounge

Paul Smith: True Brit (Ed.)

Jim Morrison: Dark Star

Haircults

The i-D Bible

Dylan Jones

Shiny and New

Ten Moments of Pop Genius that Defined the '80s

WHITE
RABBIT

First published in Great Britain in 2021 by White Rabbit,
This paperback edition published in 2022 by White Rabbit
an imprint of The Orion Publishing Group Ltd
Carmelite House, 50 Victoria Embankment
London EC4Y 0DZ

An Hachette UK Company

1 3 5 7 9 10 8 6 4 2

A CIP catalogue record for this book is
available from the British Library.

ISBN (Mass Market Paperback) 978 1 4746 2007 9
ISBN (eBook) 978 1 4746 2008 6
ISBN (Audio) 978 1 4746 2009 3

Printed and bound in Great Britain by
Clays, Ltd, Elcograf, S.p.A

www.whiterabbitbooks.co.uk
www.orionbooks.co.uk

For Oliver Peyton

'Where we're going, we don't need roads'

- Dr Emmett Brown to Marty McFly
in Back to the Future

Contents

Preface

What's Past is Prologue

'I remember the eighties with somewhat of a blush.
No man's hair should be bigger than his girlfriend's.
But that was the time. Dublin in Technicolor. In reality it
was monochrome and in the grip of a recession, but on
video you could be transported.' – Bono

The fourth of May 1987, the centrum Arena in Worcester, Massachusetts: the support band Lone Justice were comfortably ensconced back in the dressing room, safe in the knowledge that the crowd out front had been suitably primed for the main attraction. The house lights were still up, as the U2 faithful returned to their seats, clutching hot dogs and plastic buckets of beer, with big, expectant grins on their faces. Then, slowly, almost nonchalantly, the band walked on from the back of the stage, looking for all the world as though they were walking into church.

Instead of careering into 'Where the Streets Have no Name', one of their new songs from *The Joshua Tree*, the album they were promoting, or a dyed-in-the-wool classic like 'Pride (In the Name of Love)', the band carefully launched into an impassioned version of Ben E. King's 'Stand by Me', the Leiber and Stoller standard that had first been a hit in 1961, over a quarter of a century earlier. Recently it had been a hit all over again because of its use a) as the theme of the Rob Reiner movie of the same name, and b) in a Levi's commercial for their 501 jeans. In January, it had reached No.9 on the *Billboard* chart, while in February it had actually been No.1 in the UK.

By playing 'Stand by Me', U2 were telling everyone within earshot that they deserved to be spoken of in the same breath in the rock and roll hall of fame.

5

'This,' then, 'and now this.'

Throughout the eighties, U2 had made a habit of covering other people's songs, often just dropping a refrain or two into the middle of one of their barnstormers (Bono had a particular penchant for 'Send in the Clowns'). This is what U2 did, paying homage to rock's rich heritage by appropriating what they liked most about it.* On their mammoth 1987 tour - 110 shows and no sleep till Tempe, Arizona - they took this custom to new extremes. On the *Joshua Tree* tour they would play snippets of everything from Lou Reed's 'Walk on the Wild Side' and Them's 'Gloria' to Neil Young's 'Southern Man' and Bob Dylan's 'Knockin' on Heaven's Door', from the Impressions' 'People Get Ready' to Eddie Cochran's 'C'mon Everybody'. Onstage at Wembley in June, before performing 'Helter Skelter', Bono said to the crowd, 'This is a song Charles Manson stole from the Beatles; we're stealing it back.'

But at two concerts in San Francisco later in the year, the band also wove in snatches of Marvin Gaye's 'Sexual Healing', Lionel Richie's 'Dancing on the Ceiling' and the Beastie Boys' 'Fight for Your Right to Party' - signs that the eighties had not only pushed itself into U2's understanding of pop's great legacy, but also that accelerating musical diversity was now something of an inescapable truth. Pop was no longer a series of logically positioned building blocks, but rather a rapidly developing metropolis.

This came with an acknowledgement that pop's kaleidoscopic nature was probably exponential. Pop was now splintering like never before. Pop was now a starburst galaxy, as sub-genre begat fusion-genre, a galaxy big enough for the likes of Madonna, Morrissey and Prince. Even big enough for U2.

Some were even saying that 1987 was going to be something of a vintage year, with Prince's *Sign O' the Times* already vying with *The Joshua Tree* for the mantle of Best Album of the Decade. The year would also see the release of the Smiths' *Strangeways Here We Come*, Guns N' Roses' *Appetite for Destruction*, R.E.M.'s *Document*, Public

---

* This was also expensive, costing the band additional performance royalties for the songs involved.

Enemy's *Yo! Bum Rush the Show*, Tom Waits' *Frank's Wild Years*, the Cure's *Kiss Me, Kiss Me, Kiss Me*, and the Pet Shop Boys' *Please*. The rare groove compilation *Get Your Own*, meanwhile, outsold Michael Jackson's *Bad* in London on its first week of release. Sampling old soul records became a national pastime, both in the UK and the US, with James Brown the most popular victim. Slapping at least a dozen law suits on rappers who had overstepped the mark, the Godfather of Soul intoned, 'How would you like it if someone cut a button off your suit?' In this instance, at least, the past was being used to prop up the present.

U2 were doing their own sampling. As they continued to bounce around the world, further fragments of the decade appeared in their shows, as their appreciation of the eighties grew: Joy Division's elegiac 'Love Will Tear Us Apart', Michael Jackson's slinky 'Billie Jean', the Eurythmics' mechanical 'Sweet Dreams', Simple Minds' stately 'Promised You a Miracle' and George Clinton's frankly libidinous 'Atomic Dog' via R.E.M., Grandmaster Flash, Van Morrison, Tom Waits and more. If U2 appeared to have spent much of the decade trying to distance themselves from the eighties - culturally, politically, psychologically - towards the end of the decade they now looked as though they finally wanted to embrace it.

Finally, it looked as though the eighties were going to last for ever.

Introduction

The Atomisation of Pop

The eighties was not a decade to be trifled with. The eighties took itself seriously. It was big, brash, and tended not to take any prisoners. Of course, there were some who thought that it took itself *too* seriously, a decade that was rather full of itself. And there were others who felt that the eighties didn't pay enough attention at all, that it was callow and trite. The truth, as always, was somewhere in between, but it's also far more complex. In the world of pop, the eighties actually turned out to be one of the most inventive and diverse decades of them all.

'When I die, sprinkle my ashes over the eighties.'
– David Lee Roth

In the run-up to recording *Get Happy!*, his whiz-bang collection of Stax-influenced pop, Elvis Costello was spied leaving the legendary Camden record emporium Rock On with armfuls of sixties soul and R&B albums and singles. As he walked to his car, his shiny black trilby pushed back in a raffish tilt, and sporting his enormous trademark black-rimmed glasses, he looked like he was at least two parts vinyl.

Get Happy! was almost a concept album. Released in February 1980, at the very beginning of the decade, it evoked the heyday of US soul by reinventing it in a completely novel way, mixing muscular musicianship and new wavish chops with articulate, postmodern songwriting – material that was both a celebration of the genre, and a meta attempt to contextualise.

Phew, rock'n'roll! It was a moment.

We saw a lot of this in the early eighties – Costello would do it again, a year later, by recording his country album *Almost Blue*

– where post-punk artists would use their Year-Zero aesthetic as a way of 'interpreting' already existing musical styles: we saw it with 2 Tone (which started in the seventies, but which came of age in the eighties), with ABC's Po-Mo torch songs (disco Sinatra, basically), with Stock Aitken Waterman's synthesised pop (records produced with a deliberately sloppy backbeat, so anyone of any age could dance to them), and with airbrushed heavy metal ('hair metal' – cf. Van Halen), europop, and a plethora of innocent-looking shoegazers dressed in Oxfam raincoats and off-white plimsolls trying to recreate the DNA of classic sixties pop with almost unfathomable conviction.

Yet the eighties would also unleash a fusillade of new musical genres, and a wealth of genuinely unique musical styles. In terms of inventiveness, no other decade can touch the eighties; no other period can boast such a vast archive of originality and intent. It was a decade on steroids, a decade augmented. A decade full of moments. A decade when the rigid stratification of musical spheres suddenly felt very old-fashioned.

There was – go on, deep breath – thrash metal, yacht rock, No Wave, hardcore, death metal, electro, house, go-go, techno, acid house, indie ('college rock' in the US), the burnished 'quiet storm' soul-jazz of Sade (if you tuned in to FM radio any time after 10 p.m. on a Saturday night in the mid-eighties, and you didn't hear 'Smooth Operator' within twenty minutes or so, I think you were legally allowed to claim some kind of international tax rebate), and of course the beginning of the golden age of hip-hop. Then there was goth, synthpop, adult contemporary, new country, hi-NRG, the global anglo-pop of Duran Duran, the Eurythmics, Culture Club, Wham! and Spandau Ballet (funny trousers sweep the planet!), noise bands, and a lot of power ballads that were made instantly more appealing by the addition of a walloping great drum sound (usually an automated drum sound).

The eighties was all about big drums, while the drum machine was one of the key armaments of the decade – almost every song in this collection has an electronic drum sound; the only one that doesn't is 'Bigmouth Strikes Again' by the Smiths, although even the band's producer, Stephen Street, used a drum loop when producing the title track of the album it came from, *The Queen is Dead.*

So while on the one hand, technology was standardising the way music sounded, rounding the corners, straightening the edges and turning the messy and the grandiose into something that worked on the radio, on the other hand it allowed you to be more inventive than ever.

In a sense this explosion of electronic experimentation was not so different from the psychedelic emancipation that sprang up in Los Angeles in 1965; but whereas the likes of the Byrds dropping acid for the first time (in the company of the Beatles) would result in them exploring new influences such as the free jazz of John Coltrane or the music of Indian sitarist Ravi Shankar, so the arrival of machines like the Oberheim DX drum machine, the Fairlight CMI and the Roland synthesisers completely changed how most records were made and produced. The eighties would obviously produce its own drug subcultures, but it was the machinery that brought about radical advancement.

While the Byrds' Roger McGuinn talked about the band's 'jet sound', eighties electronica was actually the real sound of the future.

The eighties also hosted an extraordinarily diverse selection of very contrasting artists: Madonna, Prince, the Smiths, the Stone Roses, ABC, New Order, S'Express, R.E.M., Hüsker Dü, Prefab Sprout (hot dogs and jumping frogs), Guns N' Roses, Scritti Politti, Run-DMC, the Jesus and Mary Chain, George Michael, Tracy Chapman, Bryan Adams, Echo and the Bunnymen, Dinosaur Jnr., Sonic Youth, Black Flag, Cocteau Twins, Aztec Camera, the Beastie Boys, Public Enemy, NWA and more – acts that couldn't have been more different from each other if they had tried (and they tried). The decade saw the likes of Michael Jackson and Bruce Springsteen, who had started out in the seventies, become proper global stars, having honed their image and their sound until they almost became caricatures of themselves, transforming pop in the process. Along with Madonna and Prince, they were big personalities with movie-star-sized heads.

There were some great albums, too, albums which have since become part of the pop pantheon: *Pretenders* by the Pretenders (modern guitar pop); *Sound Affects* by the Jam (post punk pop); *Songs the Lord Taught Us* by the Cramps (goth); *Bass Culture* by Linton Kwesi Johnson (dub poetry); *Dare* by the Human League (peak synth); *Rattlesnakes* by Lloyd Cole and the Commotions (jangly college pop); *Paid in Full* by Eric B. and Rakim (minimalist hip-hop); *Café Bleu* by the Style Council (attitudinal blue-eyed jazz); *Too-Rye-Ay* by Dexys Midnight Runners (attitudinal Celtic soul); *Remain in Light* by Talking Heads (brainbox polyrhythmic rock); *My Life in the Bush of Ghosts* by Brian Eno and David Byrne (egghead sampled vocals and found sounds); *3 Feet High and Rising* by De La Soul (psychedelic hip-hop); *Rain Dogs* and *Swordfishtrombones* by Tom Waits (junkyard rock); *Diamond Life* by Sade (modern coffee-table soul); *Duck Rock* by Malcolm McLaren (world hip-hop); *Arc of a Diver* by Steve Winwood (FM radio rock); *Graceland* by Paul Simon (African fusion); *The Joshua Tree* by U2 (stadium rock); *Sign O' the Times* by Prince (DIY funk eclecticism); *Imperial Bedroom* by Elvis Costello (baroque and roll); *Cupid and Psyche '85* by Scritti Politti (arch blue-eyed sophistipop, or appropriation without consequences); *Sandinista!* by the Clash (three dozen curate's eggs); *Psychocandy* by the Jesus and Mary Chain (feedback on the beach); *Back in Black* by AC/DC (the greatest heavy metal album of all time); *Reckless* by Bryan Adams (described by *Classic Rock* as one of the greatest rock albums of all time, and justly so); *The Nightfly* by Donald Fagen (which immediately replaced Steely Dan's *Aja* as the quintessential example of recording studio prowess, but with slightly less sarcasm); *Let's Dance* by David Bowie (in which Bowie reinvented himself as a civilian); *Thriller* by Michael Jackson (an album which would become the benchmark of modern, sophisticated dance-pop, not least for Jackson himself); *The Dreaming* by Kate Bush (in which commercial heft underwrote studied eccentricity); *Faith* by George Michael (in which a teen idol grew up right before our eyes); *Actually* by the Pet Shop Boys (the debut album by a duo categorised in the music press as the Smiths you could dance to); *Spirit of Eden* by Talk Talk (described by the *Guardian* as 'a doggedly uncommercial musical tapestry'); *I'm Your Man* by Leonard Cohen (in which the singer-songwriter made something of a technological handbrake turn), and *Brothers in Arms* by Dire Straits (if you liked that kind of thing, and lots of people did - it was the first CD to sell a million) and so on and so on.

Everything was so diverse. When the broadcaster and journalist Danny Baker was asked to make a BBC TV programme about the eighties a few years ago, the records he chose were a mix of the expected - New Order, the Clash, the Pretenders and the Smiths - and the contrary: who in their right mind would choose Motorhead, the Fall, Prefab Sprout and the surrealist poet Ivor Cutler to define the musical DNA of the eighties? But then, why wouldn't you?

The eighties were like that.

This was a period when artists were leery of being assigned a fixed creative persona or having the success of their genre become a trap. Pop stars were inventing their reputations but savvy enough to dismantle and reinvent at a whim. Everyone and everything was mutating.

Pop in the eighties developed like no other decade before or since, exploding during a period that had more than its own fair share of political, cultural, economic and sociological upheaval. The eighties was a decade of political innovation - both in the mass privatisation of state-owned industries and the deregulation of financial markets - and collective economic and psychological turmoil. Britain in the eighties wasn't just polarised, it was ideologically divided, with Thatcherism carving a swathe of modernism - and brutalism - through the land, especially the north. On the global stage, politics were binary, too, with Ronald Reagan's existential boosterism creating a two-tiered USA, and the collapse of the Iron Curtain dragging eastern Europe into an uncertain future.

The soundtrack to all of this could not have been more diverse, or more varied. If up until this point pop had been fairly linear, in the eighties it fractured with gusto. Instead of one thing continually following another, it started to atomise.

In the fifties, rock'n'roll defined itself by what it wasn't - and what it wasn't was anything that anyone over the age of thirty was going to like. This was delinquency in overdrive, the newfound generation gap writ large: when Elvis Presley appeared for the third time on *The Ed Sullivan Show* on 6 January 1957, he was famously shot from the waist up, to protect the innocent (and the curious) from his libidinous hips; in reality it made no difference whatsoever because the innocent could still see his hair.*

The sixties was all about gangs, groups that grew in stature as they experimented themselves to death (in the case of Jimi Hendrix, Janis Joplin, Brian Jones and Jim Morrison, all gone at the age of twenty-seven).

The seventies was the first decade where there were signs of splintering, particularly in the incendiary world of punk, and what came soon after.

The eighties, though, was when this splintering went mainstream, where innovation begat innovation, and the charts suddenly became full of the most diverse types of music. You name it, it was popular. Every week, seemingly, pop's vocabulary grew and grew. The charts might have been a cornucopia of inconsistency, but there were diamonds in the dirt. And the more you looked, the more you waited, there was moment after moment after moment.

As the *Guardian*'s Alexis Petridis once said, nostalgia is a form of curation, offering an ability to cut out those parts of the past we no longer like. Taken as a body of work, the eighties produced an

---

* One of the little quirks of the first music to exploit the generation gap was the habit of leaving the 'g' off song titles ('Good Rockin' Tonite', for instance). This had actually happened before. When Irving Berlin was writing the score for *Annie Get Your Gun*, the fictionalised musical based on the life and career of sharpshooter Annie Oakley, he called up Oscar Hammerstein and said, 'I can't write all these hillbilly lyrics.' Hammerstein said to him, 'All you have to do is leave off the g's.'

extraordinary cavalcade of records - records that introduced rap, hip-hop and acid house, records that harnessed and corrupted indie, that kick-started rave and sowed the seeds of grunge and Britpop, and records that invented new forms of electronica, a genre that continues to thrive, almost like a bacterium. Of course, we now cut out the stuff we don't like even more than we did at the time - Men Without Hats, Men At Work, and rather a lot of other seemingly inconsequential men like Phil Collins, Bobby Brown, Chris de Burgh, Kenny Loggins, Jason Donovan et al. - but the eighties was always a lot smarter than we thought it was.

George Michael, whose talent sometimes seemed at odds with how the decade was perceived to be panning out, was occasionally surprised about what he got away with. '"Careless Whisper" was not an integral part of my emotional development,' he said. 'It's sad because that song means so much to so many people. It disappoints me that you can write a lyric, very flippantly - and not a particularly good lyric - and it can mean so much to so many people.'

In this respect Michael was his own worst enemy, believing the decade's own bad publicity.

Of course, there were many old flames who found it hard to adapt. This was the decade where Mick Jagger launched a solo career that stubbornly refused to take off, the decade where Grace Slick sprouted shoulder pads for the 'We Built This City' video, the decade when Bob Dylan not only resorted to using a gated reverb drum sound (on *Empire Burlesque*), but also starred in a film with Rupert Everett. Self-abasement was rife, although there were those like Peter Gabriel who managed to reinvent themselves with ease, his 'Sledgehammer' video giving him the kind of cultural ubiquity unavailable to the likes of other seventies superstars such as Robert Plant, Paul Rodgers or the Bee Gees.

After all, with the death of John Lennon in December 1980, the pop continuum had broken. It had already been fractured in 1977, when Elvis Presley died, but by then he was already a parodic, almost alien being, feted and pitied in equal measure, his death seen almost in isolation. And even though he had been a househusband for five years, rearing his son Sean and baking bread – he had 'got tired of waking up in the papers' – Lennon was a Beatle, and Beatles were meant to last for ever.

What would we do now that one of them had gone? As Martin Amis said at the time, the past would never be the same again.

And what of the long tail of the world's biggest group? When John Lennon was shot, the three remaining Beatles were thrown back into the group's narrative, forced to address it in deed and in song, Paul McCartney with 'Here Today' and George Harrison with 'All Those Years Ago'. McCartney in particular had spent a decade in denial about his former band, as he ploughed on with Wings, publicly spooning with his beloved wife, Linda, determined to control his legacy. All three would improve their currency in the eighties – McCartney with solo work that would occasionally rival his work in the Beatles, Harrison in the Traveling Wilburys, and Ringo as the voice of Thomas the Tank Engine.

The Rolling Stones would return, too. After the enormous success of *Tattoo You* – which Mick Jagger had cobbled together from various old recordings he had found, including what would turn out to be one of their most enduring hits, 'Start Me Up' – they would stumble for a while before returning at the end of the decade with their *Steel Wheels* album, containing at least two new Stones classics, 'Rock and a Hard Place' and 'Slipping Away'.

Even the music press grew up. In 1985, *Rolling Stone* launched their hugely influential 'Perception, Reality' campaign, designed to alert potential advertisers that the magazine's readers were no longer hippies, but rather affluent and mainstream. Yuppies, by any other name. One of the ads read, 'To those of you who are still shortchanging the buying power of a *Rolling Stone* reader, deposit this in your information bank: over two and a half million *Rolling Stone* readers are card-carrying capitalists, last year spending more than thirteen billion dollars in department stores and other retail outlets. Cash in on the action in *Rolling Stone*.'

In terms of publishing, the music industry had probably never been so well-catered for. In 1985, Bob Guccione Jr. – the son of the

Penthouse publisher - launched *Spin* as a kind of hipper alternative to *Rolling Stone*, focusing on college rock and hip-hop.

'At the time, there was a radio station on Long Island with a weak signal, which played new music,' says Guccione Jr., 'the kind you couldn't hear anywhere else on the dial, but which was all my friends and I were listening to - relying on records and tapes we found and told each other about, a handful of clubs and those restaurants hip enough to play it. Reception was tough in Manhattan and only possible to get in my apartment at night. When I left the city, I would drive up the east side of Manhattan rather than the much closer west side, in order to pick up the signal. This is where we heard, like magic seepage from an alternative universe, the Smiths, R.E.M., Nick Cave, the Replacements, Hüsker Dü, the Cult, Tears For Fears and U2, before any of them had a hit.'

• • •

In the UK a year later, the publishers responsible for *Smash Hits* launched a grown-up music magazine called *Q*, aimed at those hundreds of thousands of people - millions, probably - who had enjoyed the 'legacy' acts at Live Aid, the Queens, Elton Johns, David Bowies and Status Quos of this world, and who were tired of reading about increasingly obscure bands in the *NME*. Rock nostalgia was born, legitimised at last.

The British music press had expanded to include new style magazines such as *The Face*, *i-D*, *Blitz* and *New Sounds New Styles*, along with wildly successful teen magazines like *Number One*, *Just Seventeen* and the aforementioned *Smash Hits*, while the *NME*, *Sounds*, *Melody Maker*, *Record Mirror*, *Zigzag*, *Echoes*, *Black Music* and *The Wire* were still largely forging ahead. As an example of the atomisation of the music press, in 1988 a small group of passionate journalists and designers launched *Straight No Chaser*, a London-based magazine devoted to the ever-expanding world of acid jazz and electronic soul.

All this activity not only showed how catholic we were all becoming in our tastes, it showed how tribal we were - tribal to the extent that we were being so particular, we would often be in a tribe of one. In the eighties there was a music for everyone.

The cultural expansion of the decade was so rapid, there was often a misguided sense that in order to stay relevant, artists had to modernise. This resulted in many stars succumbing to a design orthodoxy in order to keep up. For instance, if you looked at the cover of Paul Simon's 1983 *Hearts and Bones* (actually one of his very best, though largely ignored at the time), you see a man uncomfortable in this new milieu – trapped by inappropriate clothing, trendy photography and 'eighties' graphics. The cover of his next record, 1986's sumptuous, if controversial, *Graceland*, was far more fitting – stately, confident and more befitting Simon's status. The music it contained was a stunning example of how technology and creative ingenuity were pushing the decade forward.*

All this divergence and experimentation didn't help Neil Young's career. In 1983, the legendary singer-songwriter was served papers from his then record label, Geffen Records, for producing 'unrepresentative' and 'uncharacteristic' albums, essentially saying that Neil Young no longer sounded like Neil Young. Considering that he'd been making records that incorporated vocoders, synthesisers and electronic bears to no great effect, it was easy to side with the record label. To confuse matters, his next venture would be a swift sashay into the world of rockabilly. So diversification didn't work for everyone.

It was a time when it became acceptable to properly design your records, and where preparation and graft became as important as divine intervention. I'm not talking about graphic design, but overall design. I remember Bryan Adams telling me one night how the creation of his 1984 monster album *Reckless* was based on little but

---

* When *Graceland* was released, Simon faced accusations that he had broken the cultural boycott against the apartheid regime in South Africa, a controversy that would rage for years. In 2012, the journalist Andrew Mueller wrote in *Uncut*, 'Apartheid was of course a monstrosity, but it would be absurd to suggest that Simon's introduction of South African music to the world prolonged it and quite plausible to suggest that it did some small amount to hasten its undoing.'

persistence, attention to detail and a painstaking search for the right songs. Adams knew he had an opportunity to create a niche for himself - a young Bruce Springsteen - and after three successful albums, felt he had an opportunity to move it all up a gear or two. With unrelenting focus - and the help of the producer Bob Clearmountain - he achieved it. *Reckless* produced six hit singles, including 'Run to You', 'Summer of '69' and 'Heaven' (a song that would later, in various different forms, become a chill-out classic in Ibiza).

It was also a time - perhaps the first time - when it became acceptable to want to be famous for no other reason than a desire to be famous. Fame in the eighties was a legitimate career choice, a choice exemplified by a nondescript but big-bosomed personality called Angelyne, who came to some sort of prominence in Los Angeles in 1981. Desperate for attention and employment - both of which she inevitably eventually got - she leased a series of billboards in and around Hollywood on which she appeared, clothed only in wraparound sunglasses and the very skimpiest of tops. 'I am famous for doing nothing,' she said, proudly.

But you didn't have to move to Los Angeles to escape yourself. In the eighties, the best route to reinvention was the decade itself. All you needed to do was cut your hair, hire a stylist and buy a drum machine. Lo and behold, any old prog rocker, punk or disco diva could be revamped as a bona fide MTV rock god. Or not. Just look at how ZZ Top reinvented themselves through video.

Lifestyle, which had previously been a concept that had its roots in the rampant individualism that sprang up in the fifties, sixties and seventies - often in the form of subcultures and youth cults - became one of the big marketing tools of the decade. In fact, for many, lifestyle became everything. And because lifestyle needed a soundtrack, so music became commodified, which meant that the music industry became attractive to a lot of people who didn't have the necessary aptitude. In this climate of possibility, aspiration was a key factor, one which often overrode talent.

Consequently, the eighties is often maligned as the decade of style over content, a time of image ruling reality, a period of homogenous, monotonous pop. In essence, the decade seemed to have a 'kick me' sign on its back.

But the eighties was actually one of the most inventive periods of pop culture, especially where music is concerned, a period which exploded in a kaleidoscopic splay of self-determination. As the new decade detonated, so pop exploded with it, no longer linear, no longer modernist, but fractured, postmodern, multi-channelled, multiplied. And very often brilliant – pushing on into the future, all graphite and glitter.

'Punk rock was eventually condensed by slack media consensus into one convenient storyline – "Hairy Prog Dinosaurs Killed Overnight By Safetypin-Pierced Heroes" – which was wholly unoriginal and several yards from the truth,' said esteemed music journalist Mark Ellen, before lamenting that the same reductive packaging is always applied to the eighties:

'Interminable television programmes still suggest the whole episode was nothing but a calamitous mistake, a cultural cul-de-sac full of rotten records by shameful individuals with orange skin and espadrilles. But as someone who spent seven of the available years editing music magazines – *Smash Hits* and *Q* – I'm here to tell you this couldn't be further off the mark.'

In fact, the decade was one great experiment, when technology and ambition conspired to produce music that was genuinely revolutionary. As instruments became unrecognisable, so did the traditional pop genres.

The eighties was a decade when everything and everyone was different.

'In a really bizarre way, everything seemed possible in the eighties,' said Claire Grogan, the singer with Altered Images – a band whose debut single, 'Dead Pop Stars', was championed by John Peel, but who will always be remembered for their extraordinarily successful 'Happy Birthday'. '[The eighties seemed] genuinely inspiring and passionate and extreme. There was freedom. Things just seemed possible.'

Artifice was everywhere. Talking about *Rattlesnakes*, his breakthrough record with the Commotions in 1984, Lloyd Cole says,

'The landscape for the album was my imagination. I'd been to Europe once, but my romantic imagery was from books or films. I stumbled on a way of creating images with very few words. Everyone knows exactly what a "Grace Kelly car" looks like, and it's probably in the south of France.'

'We sampled a neighbour's VW Golf and the group saying "Money" played backwards,' says the Art of Noise's Anne Dudley about their 1985 single 'Close (to the Edit)'. 'To our amazement it got to No.8.'

For Jim Kerr, who fronted Simple Minds, the decade possessed 'a level of individualism and imagination that was almost overwhelming'.

These were all moments.

Then of course there were U2 themselves, a band who convened during punk, but who came of age and prospered in the very stadiums punk was meant to kill off. They reinvented the stadium by personalising it, connecting with their audiences in the way they used to when they played pubs and clubs. U2 went out of their way to include the audience in their journey, delivering messages of hope and redemption among all the flag-waving and pyrotechnics. When they started playing larger venues, video was still frowned upon, thought to be impersonal, cheating almost. U2 nevertheless co-opted the medium, almost bringing the MTV experience to life, and reinventing themselves in the process. In an era of mass communication, when scale started to mean so much more than secrecy, U2 became the lords of all they surveyed – which, from their vantage point, was a hell of a lot.

What the decade gave the band was ambition, a representation of both sincerity and success. 'I always thought the job was to be as great as you could be,' says Bono. 'If it is not absolutely the best it can be, why bother?'

Critics liked to say that one of the underlying issues of the decade was scale. Big was very much 'in' in the eighties, and there was an alternative consensus that considered this detrimental to the culture. How could you still represent whatever ideals you started out with if you were now filling stadiums and appearing on breakfast television? How could Big be anything less than a sell-out? Ever mindful of the kind of contradictions that made it impossible for many post-punk bands to embrace success, U2 grabbed the Make Me Big Machine with all eight hands. They pushed their pennies into the Zoltar machine just like Tom Hanks did in *Big*. And they asked for the same thing. To be Big. (On their 1988 album *Rattle & Hum*, they pushed this too far, and were diminished by their attempts to be thought of as American.)

In the fifties, sixties and seventies you could have worn a frown, a button-badge or a T-shirt that said QUESTION AUTHORITY. In the eighties the message was far more likely to be DEFINE AUTHORITY.

That's not to say that good old-fashioned rock'n'roll excess was confined to the archives. As the bells sounded at midnight on New Year's Eve in 1979, rock stars didn't suddenly put away their vials of cocaine, leather dildos and pornography. In fact, the vast amount of money swilling through the industry in the eighties actually enabled and encouraged bad behaviour. Just look at what Van Halen got up to. And Ozzy Osbourne certainly didn't slow down. In 1981, during a meeting with CBS executives, drunk and angry at one of the label's publicists, he bit the heads off two live doves; in 1982 he famously stuck a bat in his mouth and took a bite out of it onstage (something that sobriety and Covid-19 have probably ruled out for good); and in 1984 he snorted a crawling line of ants in front of heavy metal disciples Motley Crue.

Judging from their own accounts, the members of Motley Crue actually behaved worse than any of their seventies forebears. In the eighties, even excess was more bloated than it had been before.

• • •

If music in the eighties was a series of random, disconnected moments, these moments were epitomised by the unlikely success of Madonna, a so-so talent with a furious ambition who was able to bounce between pop and R&B, and between the catwalk and the disco with both commitment and grace.

They were also epitomised by the likes of Prefab Sprout, not that there was anyone else like them - they sounded like no one or nothing that had come before (which was sort of the point). This wasn't surprising when you learned that when he first started writing songs, Paddy McAloon, the band's leader, thought he had to invent his own chords in order to do so; which is why their early records sounded so odd. One journalist said they made the kind of noise a jazz band might if they were entertaining themselves at a cocktail party before the guests arrived. Once McAloon mastered sophistication, the band's records became rich, colourful and cinematic, while still giving the impression they were written and recorded with no specific consumer in mind. Like Steely Dan - to whom Prefab Sprout were not completely dissimilar - they sounded as though they were making music for themselves and themselves only.

Virginia Astley's 1983 mini-masterpiece *From Gardens Where We Feel Secure* came complete with its own natural soundtrack in the shape of field recordings of birdsong and sheep. There was a little light piano, some woodwind and some ambient vocals, but mainly this was the sound of the countryside, an instrumental accompaniment to a typical British summer's day.

Elsewhere, the Jesus and Mary Chain sounded like Suicide and the Beach Boys duelling with miniature chainsaws, Tracy Chapman sounded like a gap year pen pal, while the Beastie Boys sounded not unlike a spring break house party (with spraying beer cans an optional extra). Guns N' Roses meanwhile sounded like Led Zeppelin if they had convened in the back room of the Roxy on the Sunset Strip in the early eighties rather than Soho in 1968 (the band came complete with lashings of eighties arrogance, too: in 1989, the band's singer, Axl Rose, kept the Rolling Stones waiting for three hours for the rehearsal of a Rose/Jagger duet).

Drum machines and sequencers didn't just make it easier for traditional rock groups to embrace the 12-inch remix - and thus making it easier for the likes of Bruce Springsteen and ZZ Top to be played in nightclubs - they also allowed the entire family tree of R&B to branch out in ways hitherto unimaginable. The eighties may have been a binary decade, but it also called time on those old-fashioned ideas of rock music and 'black' music. Seriously, what colour was a New Order record? What colour were Hall and Oates, or ABC come to that?

In addition, Madness sounded like an Ealing comedy, Simple Minds like Olympic prog rock, and R.E.M. like campus radio. And the noise Michael Jackson made with Quincy Jones sounded like dance music that had been created – over centuries, it would seem, but including the most sophisticated and contemporary technological nuances available – in a laboratory. It was sublime.

Quincy had already had a storied career – working with Dizzy Gillespie, Ray Charles, Lena Horne, Sarah Vaughan, Duke Ellington, Frank Sinatra, Miles Davis and George Benson – but even so, in many people's eyes his career was defined by his work with Jackson. When the Jackson 5 singer decided to make his first proper grown-up solo album, there was one man whose advice he sought first. He had worked with Quincy on *The Wiz* – a disco version of *The Wizard of Oz* that was never going to age well – and had started to put his trust in him. The two met on the set on the day Jackson had to rehearse a scene in which he read a Socrates quote. When the crew started stifling their laughs when he spoke – he pronounced it 'Soh-crates', to rhyme with 'low rates' – he knew he'd screwed up. It was Quincy who whispered the correct pronunciation in his ear. And when Jackson asked Quincy to recommend someone to produce his record, the producer naturally suggested himself.

They started making the record in earnest in LA at the very end of 1978, with Quincy indulging his protégé, taking his ideas seriously and making sure he was comfortable in the studio. He also surrounded him with experienced, non-confrontational musicians, and offered Jackson hundreds of songs to choose from. Weirdly, their work ethics dovetailed almost perfectly. 'Now I'm a pretty strong drill sergeant when it comes to steering a project,' said Jones, 'but in Michael's case it's hardly necessary.'

When *Off the Wall* was eventually released, in August 1979, the extraordinary collection of songs - 'Don't Stop 'Til You Get Enough', 'Rock With You', the title track and Stevie Wonder's 'I Can't Help It', etc. - showed an entertainer coming of age, wrapped in the kind of sophisticated packaging (Jackson was wearing a tuxedo on the cover) that was automatically going to appeal to an older, wider and whiter demographic than before.

This demographic turned out to be a lot broader than either of them imagined, although the album's success was nothing compared to the success of its 1982 follow-up, *Thriller*, which would go on to become the bestselling album of all time, with sales estimated in excess of 50 million copies worldwide. Containing some of the most famous songs of the eighties - 'Billie Jean', 'Beat It', 'Wanna Be Startin' Something' - the album still resonates. These were the first 'black' records to be played on MTV, being so successful that mainstream media couldn't afford to ignore them. (Perversely, Quincy initially didn't want to include the album's second single, 'Billie Jean', on the record - it was once eleven minutes long - not least because he thought some people might think Jackson was singing about the tennis player, Billie Jean King.) The songs were beautiful and polished, warm and effusive.

They worked together on *Thriller*'s successor, *Bad*, released in 1987, an inevitable disappointment that still ended up selling over 30 million units. (Barbra Streisand was offered the album's big duet, 'I Just Can't Stop Loving You', but allegedly turned it down on account of the age gap between her and Jackson, something that hadn't occurred to the singer.)

Jackson's best music was for the ages, timeless floor-fillers that have outlived the vagaries of fashion. Since the fifties, dance music had been created with built-in obsolescence, but like Nile Rodgers' Chic, Jackson's greatest records would never go out of style. He himself obviously has, and the complexities of his predatory sexual behaviour have meant that while we still like to dance to his music, the Jackson brand is toxic. A lot of dance music is so closely co-ordinated that it's difficult - sometimes impossible - to separate it from the time in which it was made, but *Thriller* in particular seems to exist in a perfectly sealed vacuum, impervious to everything except the noise surrounding the indulgences of the man who made it.

According to Philip Larkin, sexual intercourse began in 1963, between the end of the Lady Chatterley ban and the Beatles' first LP. The eighties actually began between the release of Jackson's 'Don't Stop 'Til You Get Enough' in July 1979 – a record that hinted at the limitless possibilities of gentrified R&B – and 'Rapper's Delight', released two months later, the world's first rap single, and a record that would change pop for ever. It would unquestionably change the eighties.

There was a lot about the eighties that was shrill, indifferent and callow, but a lot of the music – and there was a *lot* of it – was very good indeed. In the eighties it felt as though there was a new genre every week, although sometimes this inventiveness was just too much: 'I was walking down the street the other day and I heard this sound,' said Reeves Gabrels of David Bowie's Tin Machine, in 1989. 'I thought it was a great new band playing something intriguing. It turned out to be an air conditioner unit in an elevator.'*

· · ·

You can almost imagine the office of a large weekly music paper in the mid-eighties, full of fifty or so pale, beleaguered rock hacks (resoundingly white and male), many of whom would have been perched on cheap metal desks arguing over the relative merits of the Pixies, the Wedding Present or Cactus World News (although the enthusiasm in their case would have probably been rather

---

* As a snapshot of the incongruities of the decade, transport yourself to a typically soggy March mess of a day in Manhattan, in June 1984. *Rolling Stone*'s Kurt Loder is about to interview Bob Dylan. 'As his long nails raked the strings of his Martin guitar,' wrote Loder about Dylan, 'he began huffing softly into the harmonica racked around his neck, and soon a familiar melody filled the air. Could it be? I moved closer to cock an ear as Dylan cranked up the chorus. Yes, no doubt about it – Bob Dylan was running down the first-ever folkie arrangement of "Karma Chameleon", the Culture Club hit.'

more muted). As the door to the main editorial office swings open, and a stormtrooper-style courier enters the room carrying a large cardboard box, with a ROUGH TRADE stencil on the top, a thin, helpless voice can be heard from behind the subs' desk: 'Oh no, duck! Here comes another genre!'

Take 'Made of Stone' by the Stone Roses, from 1989, a single that reminded many of us that guttersnipe, jingle-jangle pop still had the power to transfix - whether it came in the form of the Byrds, the Flamin' Groovies or the Smiths. It also came soon after the Second Summer of Love, when acid house swept over the UK, kick-starting Madchester in the process.

The fundamental switch in club culture during the decade was the move from exclusion to inclusion. In 1980, status revolved around the lifting of the velvet rope; but by the decade's end, the only VIP rooms that mattered were the mini-cab offices which were going to ferry you to a field next to the M25.

The Stone Roses epitomised everything that was good about Madchester, and they were the first band to signal the end of the eighties, an end to the decade when everyone's favourite prefix was 'designer' (designer funk, designer folk, designer country etc). The year 1989 would turn out to be theirs, when 'Made of Stone' reminded many that pop was often at its best when it went hand-in-hand with insurrection. Refreshingly uninterested in anything much around them, the Stone Roes were genuinely imperious. They consolidated their brand when, one minute into a live TV performance on *The Late Show*, an arts programme on BBC2, the power failed, prompting singer Ian Brown to repeatedly roar 'Amateurs!' at the presenter Tracey MacLeod. Oh, how we giggled! The Roses were belligerent, full of spunk and wildly imaginative. (When Pete Townshend saw an early Roses performance, he said that Reni, their drummer, was the most naturally gifted drummer he had seen since Keith Moon.)

Like the songs I've chosen to build the narrative around in this book, 'Made in Stone' was a moment in time that resonated long after it was made, and long after you first heard it. There were many such moments in the eighties, because the decade spent much of its time expanding in order to fit them all in.

Shiny and New attempts to frame the decade in a new light, by focusing on ten extraordinary records, showing how they not only disrupted the decade, but also how they redefined and altered it to suit their own narrative: rap, noir ska, New Pop, electro, indie, acid house and more, ten extraordinary records – by the Sugarhill Gang, the Specials, ABC, New Order, Madonna, Bruce Springsteen, the Smiths, Prince, S'Express and Public Enemy – that changed our understanding of pop. These are not only ten of the most important records of the decade, they're also clear indicators of what it meant to actually live in the eighties. You can look at the songs here as co-ordinates that realigned the musical sat-nav of the decade, songs that created new genres and kick-started many more.

There are many counter-narratives, of course, and my list is obviously subjective. I could, for instance, have focused on the biggest commercial hits of each year. If I had done, we would be reading instead about 'Don't Stand So Close To Me' by the Police; 'Tainted Love' by Soft Cell; 'Come On Eileen' by Dexys Midnight Runners; 'Karma Chameleon' by Culture Club; 'Do They Know It's Christmas?' by Band Aid; 'The Power Of Love' by Jennifer Rush; 'Don't Leave Me This Way' by the Communards; 'Never Gonna Give You Up' by Rick Astley; 'Mistletoe and Wine' by Cliff Richard and 'Ride On Time' by Black Box.

Some of these would have produced their own narratives – both Soft Cell and Culture Club were formed in the environs of the nascent club culture of the time, while both the Communards and Black Box were indicative of certain kinds of new dance, Eurobeat and Italo House respectively (and on their cover version, the Communards were simply adapting hi-NRG). However, the Police were fundamentally a seventies phenomenon, Dexys Midnight Runners were an idiosyncrasy, and Jennifer Rush and Cliff Richard could have had hits with their songs in almost any decade. The Band Aid record meanwhile is at the core of a much bigger development (mainstream global aid), although I don't think even its architects would say that it's a sonic masterpiece.

So here they are, my choices - ten moments of pop genius that defined the decade. Ten songs that altered the narrative of the decade, ten records that genuinely represented change.

Pop would continue to fascinate, confound and challenge, but it would never be as big as it was in the eighties, it would never be as pervasive, nor as diverse, and it would never be so shiny or new.

1980

Hello
Hip-Hop

'Rapper's Delight' by the Sugarhill Gang

Released at the tail-end of 1979, 'Rapper's Delight' helped launch hip-hop as a multi-billion-dollar phenomenon. The opportunistic fourteen-minute track also revived the career of its producer, a smart R&B veteran – but managed to infuriate the true pioneers of rap in the process. Who the hell were the Sugarhill Gang anyway?

> *'Do not let any record company disturb your creative flow. You are not writing for the record company. You're writing for the public.'*
>
> *– Grandmaster Flash*

When the huddle broke, you could see a '98 Oldsmobile bouncing up and down, as four excited teenagers – two on the back seat, two sitting up front – rapped along to the amped-up sound of Chic's 'Good Times' pouring out of the dashboard speakers. This was August 1979, and a group of gawkers on the sidewalk opposite a New Jersey pizza parlour were witnessing the very first audition by the very first rap group. The scene could have come from a Tom Wolfe book, a telling little vignette destined to be read aloud to hip-hop scholars for decades to come.

As the car sat on the asphalt, bobbing up and down, its doors wide open, history was being made.

Tick, tock.

On the other side of the Atlantic, in Britain, where the radio stations and nightclubs were still dominated by the sounds of post-punk and disco, the decade was turning, as the country started to transition from the grey breeze-block seventies into the Technicolor plastic eighties, walking into a decade where pop culture would be swiftly transmuted into a lifestyle culture fuelled by new media and new money, accelerated by the onslaught of Thatcherism, privatisation, fashion, television, and a generation of pop stars who weren't remotely embarrassed about ambition. As one wag commented, it was just like punk had never happened.

What the eighties also brought was a completely new recognition of black music, of dance music in particular, and this started with rap – specifically party music in the ruins of a bankrupt New York.

And it was all kick-started by four teenagers sitting in a 1998 Oldsmobile.

Even though it was released at the very end of 1979, the Sugarhill Gang's 'Rapper's Delight' became a Top Three hit over Christmas in the UK, and had a long tail throughout 1980. It wasn't the first rap recording, but it was the first to introduce the genre to a wide audience.* By the end of the eighties, dance music would be genuinely kaleidoscopic in its variants, but in 1980, as disco started to wane, it was suddenly all about rap.

Boastful but benign, early rap celebrated success and overt style, while its social commentary was initially passive in the extreme. It would soon morph into something far more combative and confrontational, but in 'Rapper's Delight' rap found its springboard. This fourteen-minute monster hit immediately shifted the centre of gravity from hip-hop as a live form in which DJs and rappers shared equal billing, to one that gave primacy to rappers and (soon) their recordings. It was also the catalyst for what would arguably become the most important development in popular music since punk.

. . .

---

* The first proper rap record was actually 'King Tim III (Personality Jock)', the novelty B-side of a single called 'You're My Candy Sweet' by the Fatback Band, released in 1979 on Spring Records. A fairly unremarkable record, it nevertheless introduced what would soon become standard rap devices such as the invitation to clap one's hands, self-aggrandising boasts, spelling ('I'm the K-I-N-G the T-I-M'), brand calling ('Burger King'), references to the microphone, and the heavy use of slang.

The antecedents of hip-hop go back a long way, but what few of the (mainly white) professorial critics who embraced the genre in the early eighties knew was that it had one of its births in Washington DC, back in the mid-fifties. When hip-hop exploded on the cusp of the decade, its narrative arc was soon articulated back to the West Bronx neighbourhood block parties of the early seventies, to the spoken-word albums of Gil Scott-Heron, Jamaican toasting, doo-wop, and even to field hollers and work songs. No one thought to mention Bo Diddley.

According to legend, backstage at a concert at the Howard Theatre in Washington in the spring of 1956, the R&B duo Mickey and Sylvia heard the blues guitarist Jody Williams play an Afro-Cuban riff that he had played on 'Billy's Blues', the debut single by the R&B pianist Billy Stewart. The legendary guitarist Bo Diddley was also on the bill, who then used the riff as the basis for his own song, the classic 'Love is Strange' (due to a publishing dispute, credited to his wife, Ethel Smith), which was soon covered, coincidentally, and with enormous success, by Mickey & Sylvia.

Twenty-three years later, Sylvia Robinson launched Sugarhill Records, and co-wrote and produced its debut release, the first successful iteration of New York's avant-garde party music, 'Rapper's Delight', by the Sugarhill Gang. Robinson didn't know anything about 'rap' or 'hip-hop' – the catch-all term for the world that was coalescing around breakdancing, scratch DJ-ing, graffiti and beatboxing – and yet she would be the first person to give it a platform.

Having had a successful career as Mickey & Sylvia, in the late fifties she set up a record company with her new husband, Joe Robinson, before retiring in 1962 to look after their three sons. Towards the end of the sixties, she sprang back into action with a new label, All Platinum, and was happy to stay behind the scenes until she wrote a song that she hoped would be covered by Al Green, 'Pillow Talk', which she eventually recorded herself when Green said it was too raunchy and compromised his religious beliefs. It was a massive hit in 1973, both in the US and the UK; its moaning and heavy breathing predated Donna Summer's 'Love to

Love You Baby' by two years. Around the same time, she was also responsible for marshalling other huge disco hits such as 'Girls' by the Moments (and Whatnuts) and 'Shame Shame Shame' by Shirley & Company. But by the end of the decade, the hits had stopped, and she was floundering.

Robinson's Damascene moment came on the night of her forty-fourth birthday party in Manhattan, on 29 May 1979, at a fancy uptown club called Harlem World. She says she had a vision. Her teenage son, Joey Jr., had hired some local DJs to provide the music for her party, one of whom, Lovebug Starski, already had a strong local following. During the evening he started talking over the records, whipping the crowd up by embellishing the tunes with his own catchphrases and rhymes.

'I saw him talking to the kids and saw how they'd answer back,' she said. 'He would say something every now and then, like "Throw your hands in the air," and they'd do it. If he'd said, "Jump in the river," they'd have done it.' Having never heard anything like it before, Robinson wondered why no one had thought about putting this new music onto a record. Her once great family record business was in trouble, she was unsure about what to do next, and this new 'rapping' thing seemed like a reasonable gamble. 'It was God that was showing me, you see,' she said.

And so, having spent several months setting up a new label, Sugar Hill (named after the historic district in Harlem that was once home to Duke Ellington and Cab Calloway), she started auditioning 'singers' to make her first record – although most rappers (a new word to everyone at the time; Robinson continued to call it 'talking real fast') were reluctant as they thought it was something that only worked in a live environment. Not even Lovebug Starski could see the potential in it ('I wasn't interested in doing no record back in them days, because I was getting so much money for just DJ-ing,' he said). The answer to her problems lay closer to home.

She asked Joey Jr. if he knew anyone who could do what Lovebug did. After various false starts, they auditioned one of his friends, 380-pound Henry 'Hank' Jackson in the back of Robinson's

1998 Oldsmobile, in front of the New Jersey pizza parlour where he worked, Crispy Crust Pizza. Jackson was also managing a popular club act called the Cold Crush Brothers, whose tapes he'd often rap along to while making his pizzas. Robinson had already decided to use Chic's 'Good Times' as the basis of the backing track, as it had recently been a massive hit and was already being used by DJs for breaks and beats in the clubs, so this was the song that Jackson was asked to rap to.

As Jackson was rapping, another of her son's friends, Mark Green, approached them, while waving a friend of *his*, Guy 'Master Gee' O'Brien over to the car. 'He's all right,' said Green, pointing at Jackson, 'but my man's *vicious*,' pointing at O'Brien. The sound of 'Good Times' booming out of the open doors of the Oldsmobile started to attract a small crowd, and soon another putative rapper – Michael 'Wonder Mike' Wright – squeezed himself into the car, and started hollering along.

And so, as the town car bounced up and down, and the voices rang across Englewood's Palisade Avenue, the Sugarhill Gang was born. All were told to turn up at Robinson's studio the following Monday, when, in less time than it took to make a pizza, they recorded the fourteen-minute single in one take. The record cost just $750 to make, and as Steven Daly said in a piece about the song for *Vanity Fair*, 'As befits any history-making pop breakthrough, from Elvis Presley's inaugural sessions at Sun Records to the Ramones' first LP, the recording of "Rapper's Delight" was over in an evanescent blur.'

In a few weeks, however, it would be selling 50,000 copies a day and changing the face of pop. Not only was it the first commercial hip-hop record, it also gave the genre a name: 'hip-hop, and you don't stop,' spoken, almost incidentally, by Wonder Mike.

'When somebody calls you, somebody passes the mike, you do like an entry, a warm-up,' said Guy O'Brien in 2019. 'For example, with me, I'll say, "*On and on and on, on and on.*" I'm using that to set up what I'm going to say. "*Hip-hop, you don't stop*" – that was Mike's entry. He used to do that at parties.'

'No one has ever been able to ascertain whether Lovebug Starski or the Furious Five's Keith "Cowboy" Wiggins came up with the term hip-hop,' said Wonder Mike. 'But I'd heard the phrase through my cousin and just started going: "hip-hop, hippie to the hippie, to the hip-hip-hop and you don't stop." The part where I go, "To the bang-bang boogie, say up jump the boogie to the rhythm of the boogie, the beat" is basically a spoken drum roll. I liked the percussive sound of the letter B.

'At parties, guys would pass mics around for hours, so rapping for twenty minutes in a studio seemed like nothing. When we made the record, we kept coming up with clever things and the producers never stopped us. The finished recording was nineteen minutes long, all the rap done in one take, but we cut it to fourteen, making the intro shorter and cutting out some party noise.

'My rap was part planned, part spontaneous. I wanted the start to be powerful and was inspired by that old sci-fi show *The Outer Limits*, which began: "There is nothing wrong with your television set. Do not attempt to adjust the picture." So my introduction went: "Now what you hear is not a test, I'm rappin' to the beat." And, because I wanted to appeal to everyone, I said: "I'd like to say hello to the black, to the white, the red and the brown."'

If disco was a world of fantasy and illusion, hip-hop was a world of bravado and realism. If disco was all about dress codes and sculpted hair, hip-hop was all about the street. If disco was all about upward mobility, then hip-hop was all about downward nobility.

Ironically the song was built on the bones of one of the most famous disco bass lines of them all - Chic's 'Good Times'. When it was released, 'Rapper's Delight' immediately caused controversy because initial pressings didn't contain any reference to the fact that the bulk of the instrumentation had been written by Chic's Nile Rodgers and Bernard Edwards, who, unsurprisingly, promptly called their lawyers. When Rodgers first heard it - one night in the midtown discotheque Leviticus - he was incensed, as to him it appeared as though some over-zealous upstarts were grandstanding over the top of his record - jumping up and down on the upper deck as all his hard work was driving the bus. 'When I heard "Rapper's Delight" I thought the DJ was doing it live ... Then I looked around and saw no DJ – he was standing right in front of me.'

'We felt amazed that somebody could actually do that,' said Alfa Anderson, who was one of the original singers with Chic. 'Just take a track and use it as their own. They dropped the track when we were out of the country, touring England. I thought it was clever, but I thought it was really sneaky. We appreciated the artistry, but the fact it was done the way it was, was a little unscrupulous. But look what it started!'

In the UK the record had immediate ubiquity, as suddenly it was everywhere – in nightclubs, on the radio, on pub jukeboxes (at least the 7-inch version), in cars: all of a sudden it became the sound of the winter. Everywhere you went you heard 'Everybody go hotel, motel, Holiday Inn ...' Even though it was something of a transformative record, a new kind of beat, it possessed the universality of Donna Summer's 'I Feel Love', Sylvester's 'Mighty Real' or indeed 'Good Times' itself. There was something familiar about it, colloquial even, as it referenced Superman, Holiday Inns, even the embarrassment of having to endure your best friend's mother's cooking. The Sugarhill Gang were not exactly trying to overthrow the government, nor encouraging anyone else to.

Which is one of the reasons the already established hip-hop community took against it. Even though Sugar Hill Records would soon have a virtual monopoly over New York's most prodigious hop-hop acts – Grandmaster Flash, Spoonie Gee, Funky 4+1 More and Treacherous 3, Mean Machine and Positive Force – the Sugarhill Gang themselves were generally considered to be interlopers, a cobbled-together group no different from the Monkees, inadequate ambassadors of a scene which had yet to find its real voice.

By the time 'Rapper's Delight' was scaling the charts, what soon became known as hip-hop was already entrenched in New York's subcultural terrain. Largely unmediated, nevertheless the scene already had its stars: DJ Kool Herc, a Bronx youth who had arrived from Jamaica in 1967 as Clive Campbell, and who in the early

43

seventies started using obscure funk instrumentals as 'breaks' between songs, and who initiated 'merry-go-rounds', playing two copies of the same record on parallel turntables at neighbourhood parties; former gang member Afrika Bambaataa (born Lance Taylor), who started organising South Bronx block parties in 1977; and Grandmaster Flash (Joseph Saddler), another Bronx DJ who was one of the first pioneers of scratching. Working with MCs who started honing boisterous interjections, they had all developed their own followings ... and none of them was especially pleased when the Sugarhill Gang took off in the way they did. Like Lovebug Starski, none of them thought what they did would transfer to vinyl; indeed, they thought making records might actually contribute to the demise of their parties. Sure, tapes recorded at block parties would be circulated and shared, but surely no one would buy an actual record? Grandmaster Flash later said this was a 'huge error', while Afrika Bambaataa was aghast: 'We said, "Who the hell is this, coming out with our stuff on records?"' There was also a lot of talk about misappropriation of lyrics and rhymes, of the Sugarhill Gang borrowing material from established MCs.

'DJ AJ, Grandmaster Flash, Afrika Bambaataa, Kool Herc – all of these guys were local DJs who would do local shows here in New York,' Bronx rapper Kurtis Blow said. 'So when the Sugarhill Gang made it, the guys who had been doing this thing sort of felt like they were being ripped off — or, you know, "These guys are not a part of the Bronx, and they didn't struggle to bring hip-hop to this point to 1979." And so there was a lot of animosity toward the Sugarhill Gang in the beginning.'

They were accused of being the Bill Haley and the Comets of hip-hop, and yet they had green-lit a whole new world of pop.

'Musically, the record was less thrilling,' wrote David Toop, one of the first British critics to appreciate rap. 'In the early days of the 12-inch single, records used the available time to the full. Ten minutes of Lolleata Holloway, Melba Moore or Bettye LaVette was an emotional epic; fourteen minutes ten seconds of non-stop rhymes from the Sugarhill Gang was more like listening to farming news or stock market reports. Although nobody knew it at the time, their verses were recycled from groups like the Cold Crush Brothers; they were to Bronx hip-hop what the Police were to the Sex Pistols, the difference being that the Bronx originals had yet to find a Malcolm McLaren figure with a stack of confrontational tactics to help them out.'

'All the other rappers didn't consider the Sugarhill Gang to be real rappers,' said Sugar Hill's house drummer, Keith LeBlanc, who would go on to play with Tackhead and Little Axe, while also having his own hit with Malcolm X's 'No Sell Out'. 'They just got lucky. They hadn't lived the life, they hadn't invented anything. They took what people were already doing in New York and Sylvia got her son to find some kids to imitate what was going on in New York. There wasn't so much resentment towards the Sugarhill Gang as jealousy that they got to be the first group out. I think the Sugarhill Gang is the only group that was manufactured – the others all had their own material.'

• • •

As the seventies slipped into the eighties, New York had a conflicted image for those who didn't live there, especially for those of us abroad. In the popular imagination, the city promised a mixture of both excitement and fear, as people's impressions were clouded by the dystopian images we saw in films like Martin Scorsese's *Taxi Driver*, Walter Hill's *The Warriors*, Daniel Petrie's *Fort Apache The Bronx*, Sidney Lumet's *Prince of the City* and John Carpenter's science fiction masterwork, *Escape From New York*. Carpenter's film (as he co-wrote it and co-scored it as well as directing it, this was one of the shining examples of the way in which American directors greedily aped the auteur approach during the seventies) imagined a Manhattan set in the near-future world of 1997, reinterpreted as an atmospherically grimy futuristic metropolis. Due to uncontrollable crime rates following a Soviet gas attack, the island has been converted into a Federal maximum-security prison colony for prisoners serving life sentences. All the bridges and tunnels have been mined, and a huge wall lines the shoreline. Trapped in their own custodial nightmare, the inmates have formed gangs which control the crumbling, garbage-strewn city, a city that many at the time saw as a thinly veiled metaphor for Manhattan itself, a giant island-prison inhabited by humanity's dregs – murderers, terrorists, thieves, swindlers, perverts, petty criminals and the permanently disoriented – a human zoo without bars. There are no services, no government, no work, and the town is nothing but a Po-Mo trash heap. Life is a permanent scavenger hunt, with villains monitored from a central command post on Liberty Island, with guards and radar stations on the facing shores and continuous helicopter patrols. Once a month there is a food-drop into Central Park. Manhattan has become, in the words of the *New York Times*, 'a sort of super Roach Motel: the inmates check in but they don't check out. The film works so effectively as a warped vision of ordinary urban blight that it seems to be some kind of hallucinatory editorial.'

It was easy to believe in this beleaguered city. Because while elsewhere Manhattan was still being portrayed as a kind of urban middle-class fantasy island in films like *The Goodbye Girl*, *Superman*, and Woody Allen's two love letters to the city, *Annie Hall* and *Manhattan*, this was a view that was increasingly thought to be fiction. To some they were the modern American equivalent of the Italian 'Telefoni Bianchi' films of the thirties, representing a version of the city that didn't really exist.

The consumers of funk and R&B had never believed this fairy tale anyway, as for the last ten years or so they had been listening to Marvin Gaye, the O'Jays and Gil Scott-Heron, black musical heroes who had been painting a very different version of the urban experience. If you had existed on a diet of *What's Going On*, *Ship Ahoy* and *The Revolution Will Not Be Televised*, you would have already been very aware of the inequities of the modern urban existence, something echoed by Curtis Mayfield, Billy Paul, Parliament, the Isley Brothers, Stevie Wonder and hundreds of other black artists in the seventies.

Increasingly, there had been a focus on New York as the nucleus of this attrition, and while Washington DC, Detroit and Los Angeles were also generating their fair share of musical agitprop, it was New York's urban jungle that was being painted as the gilded metaphor: urban racial deprivation. Ironically, it was 1977's strangely upbeat 'Let's Clean Up the Ghetto' by the Philadelphia All Stars which best encapsulated many people's feelings towards the city. It almost sounded like a local council public service advertisement, using the strike by the city's sanitation workers as a way to chart the city's decline, encouraging a sense of civic pride.

Things started to peak in the summer of 1975. In June, travellers arriving at New York City's airports were greeted with pamphlets with a hooded death's head on the cover, warning them, 'Until things change, stay away from New York City if you possibly can.'

'WELCOME TO FEAR CITY' read the stark headline on the pamphlets, which were subtitled 'A Survival Guide for Visitors to the City of New York'. Inside was a list of nine 'guidelines' that just might allow you to get out of the city alive with your personal property intact. At the time, New York Mayor Abe Beame was on less-than-friendly terms with his police department. Faced with an enormous budget deficit, he publicly considered laying off more than 10,000 uniformed officers, and so this pamphlet was the way for the unions representing the police, the firefighters and other city employees to fight back. The guidelines painted a nightmarish vision of the city. Don't take the subway, it advised; never leave midtown Manhattan; stay inside after 6 p.m., no matter what neighbourhood you were in. Visitors were instructed to clutch their bags with both hands, to hide any property they might have in their cars, and not even to trust their valuables to hotel vaults. 'Hotel robberies have become virtually uncontrollable, and there have been some spectacular recent cases in which thieves have broken into hotel vaults.'

Over a million Fear City pamphlets were printed for distribution, with a further million on order if those ran out.

By August 1977, things had reached fever pitch, as the city's rising poverty and economic downturn were exacerbated by a sweltering heatwave. It seemed like the streets were continuously full of people, as often the streets were cooler than people's homes. The cinemas and restaurants were full, too, as many of them had air-conditioning. Anywhere cool was popular.

For weeks, the city had resembled something from a pulp thriller, hot and frustrating in the daytime, crowded and tense at night. The city was so hot it made you dizzy. So hot that some downtown tenants had taken to standing on chairs under their ceiling fans, having put towels under door slats to trap the cool air inside. When you went to Central Park, there were so many people sitting on the grass it looked as though a concert was about to start. People were actually sick of going out. For the first time in years, the town felt dangerous as soon as the sun went down. Times Square and the streets around it in midtown felt like an unpoliced and irreligious no-go zone full of hookers, pimps, muggers and panhandlers. This was *Last Exit to Brooklyn*, in real time, and in 3D.

The city was just recovering from the July blackout, when an electricity power failure had turned the city into darkness for forty-eight hours. As the city had been going through a severe economic downturn, the blackout encouraged looting on a massive scale. Stores all over the boroughs were affected (the only neighbourhoods that weren't were in southern Queens, and parts of the Rockaways), but the behaviour in Manhattan was particularly bad: thirty-five blocks of Broadway were destroyed – 134 stores looted, 45 of them set alight. In the Bronx, thieves stole fifty new Pontiacs from a car dealership, while in Brooklyn, many stores had their fronts pulled off by youths tying ropes to backed-up cars. During the blackout, a number of looters stole DJ equipment from electronics stores. It has been claimed that as a result, the hip-hop genre, barely known outside of the Bronx at the time, grew at a remarkable rate.

All in all, 4,500 looters were arrested, and 550 police officers injured. The *New York Times* reported that the most-quoted words used by New Yorkers to describe the looters were 'animals', 'rabble', 'parasites' and 'piranha'. Race was uppermost in people's minds, and the looting caused the kind of tension the city had always tried to ignore. The *Times* even criticised the writer George Will, 'a columnist ordinarily notable for his sensitivity and sophistication, [who] drew from the blackout looting the proposition that, "The United States has within its urban population many people who lack the economic abilities and character traits necessary for life in a free and lawful society."'

To visitors, the city felt like one big red-light district. Prostitutes openly walked the streets, movie theatres screened porn around the clock, and Times Square was full of live sex and peep shows. You could, if that was your thing, watch a bodybuilder listlessly masturbate on a revolving stage, or see a stag film of a young woman fucking a horse. There were endless potholes in the roads, the trains didn't run on time, and subway cars were filthy, covered in graffiti inside and out. There were card sharks on the sidewalks scamming tourists, pickpockets in the train terminals, and beggars outside the fancy Upper East Side hotels. One of the most popular T-shirts on sale in Times Square had 'Welcome to New York' printed on it, along with an image of a .45 handgun and the instruction, 'Now Hands Up, Motherfucker!'

After a decade of benign neglect, white flight had sent the middle classes out to the suburbs. Places like Alphabet City and the Bowery were no-go zones after dark, even if you were a local. Eighth Avenue on the West Side was called the Minnesota Strip due to the high volumes of hookers. You could rent hotel rooms by the hour, often for as low as $5. In one hotel at the junction of West 54th Street and Eighth Avenue, 100 pimps lived under the nonchalant watch of the police precinct opposite. Drug dealers roamed Canal Street, offering 'loose joint, ludes and black beauties'.

The city was also recoiling from the denouement of one of the most notorious serial-killing sprees in American history. David Berkowitz, better known as Son of Sam, started murdering people in the New York area just before Christmas 1975, and had killed six people and wounded several others before he was finally caught in the summer of 1977. His crimes became legendary because of the bizarre content of the letters that he sent to the police and the media and his reasons for committing the attacks: 'I am a monster,' he wrote. 'I am the "Son of Sam". I am a little "brat". When father Sam gets drunk he gets mean. He beats his family. Sometimes he ties me up to the back of the house. Other times he locks me in the garage. Sam loves to drink blood. "Go out and kill" commands father Sam'. Berkowitz was caught at the beginning of August, and although the city enjoyed a collective sigh of relief, the attacks had gone on for such a long time, they had dramatically increased everyone's sense of paranoia.

New York felt as though it had had enough. Everyone was looking forward to the autumn, to being at home, without having to resort to wandering the streets looking for somewhere cool and quiet. Even the DJs and MCs who had been hosting block parties all summer were eagerly anticipating scaling things back. The city would start to crawl its way out of recession, but by 1980, when the local economy was on the rise, the perception of New York outside the island was still one heavily laced with negativity.

Which is why the emergence of rap had such a powerful effect outside the US. Not only was rap a completely new musical genre, but it was also geographically explicit – it came from New York and nowhere else, emanating from a city that was at once exhilarating and frightening, which from a cultural perspective made it extremely attractive.

It was an intoxicating time to be in the city, where 'edge' could be found on almost any street corner, at least any street corner south of the Upper East Side. There were independent art galleries, crack dens, nightclubs, pop-up restaurants, East Village bars in burnt-out buildings, coffee stalls in empty lots in Hell's Kitchen, performance art and street cabaret, off-Broadway theatre, parties in lofts in the meatpacking district, people rushing home to watch their VCRs, rooftop drinks parties, and Andy Warhol and Jean-Michel Basquiat everywhere you looked.

Still, a misdemeanour or felony took place every forty seconds, and 1980 would turn out to be the city's worst year for crime on record. It was also the year AIDS came to the city. More than any other place in the US, including San Francisco, New York would be affected most by the AIDS epidemic, the first cases of which were reported at the end of 1980.

'When I first moved to the city, there was a garbage strike. I was hustling,' said Sonic Youth's Kim Gordon, who, like many aspiring musicians, had gravitated towards New York. 'I had a horrible grave-yard shift at a coffee shop, one of the only places to eat in Chelsea, open twenty-four hours – super crickets, deserted. I worked part-time for gallerist Annina Nosei. She and Larry Gagosian had this space, it was a condo loft in a building on West Broadway. [By 1 a.m.] I'd be somewhere like [the TriBeCa No Wave club] Tier 3, seeing [the electronic Berlin band] Malaria!, and then walking over to Dave's Luncheonette. A lot of the alternative spaces – Franklin Furnace, A-Space – had music, too. Hearing hip-hop on the street, minimalist new music, free jazz – it all added to this fabric that was a landscape.'

The streets were full of boom boxes blasting out hip-hop, car radios blaring out post-punk, and radios in Central Park pumping out the big hits of the year: 'Bette Davis Eyes' by Kim Carnes, 'Endless Love' by Diana Ross and Lionel Richie, 'Lady' by Kenny Rogers and of course 'Rapture' by Blondie, which was released at the very end of 1980, on their *Autoamerican* album, and which would be the first rap record to reach Number One in the US.

Great extravagance, then, toe-to-toe with poverty. The yin and yang of the city was starting to appear: great wealth abutting appall-ing devastation. While New York offered a kind of refuge from the euphoria surrounding Ronald Reagan's new presidency, it was still a troubled state, and hip-hop certainly reflected the abiding dissonance of the city. Parts of New York were pivoting out of bankruptcy – 'peacocking towards boom times' – and parts were still broken. Downtown you had the emergence of fancy new nightclubs, while uptown the neighbourhoods were full of crack dens. According to the activist Al Sharpton, it was very much a tale of two cities: 'People say that Manhattan was dirty and dangerous in the early eighties, and I just have to laugh. Do you even think about what it was like in Brooklyn? I mean, that's when Brooklyn was *Brooklyn*, not some extension of the West Village or a place with good coffee. Things were fifty times as bad in Brooklyn as they were in Manhattan.'

Hip-hop was all about everything. It was collage, bricolage, montage, a space where any form of music could work as long as the DJ splicing it all together had their watchful eyes on the movement of the crowd. If disco had celebrated its audience, the dancers, with hip-hop the power moved back to the DJ, the great Svengali in the glass booth (like Larry Levan at Paradise Garage or David Mancuso at the Loft) who could alter the mood of a room by switching from an instrumental break on a James Brown record to a disco remix of a Van McCoy 12-inch, even something from a Spaghetti Western, Billy Squire's 'The Big Beat' or Steve Miller's 'Take the Money and Run'.

'Myself, I used to play the weirdest stuff at a party,' said Afrika Bambaataa. 'I would play *The Pink Panther* theme ... "Honky Tonk Women" by the Rolling Stones [which he did regularly at the Bronx River Community Center] ... Grand Funk Railroad ... I'd throw on "Sgt Pepper's Lonely Hearts Club Band" - just that drum part. One, two, three, BAM. I'd throw on the Monkees' "Mary Mary" - just the beat part where they'd go "Mary Mary, where are you going?" - and they'd start going crazy. I'd say, "You just danced to the Monkees." They'd say, "You liar. I didn't dance to no Monkees." I'd like to catch people who categorise records.'

· · ·

What the denizens of the South Bronx didn't know was that their party juxtapositions were already being mirrored in New Romantic clubs in London - where seemingly incongruous records would be blended together seamlessly - and on the city's catwalks, during fashion shows by some of London's cooler young designers.

The music you hear at fashion shows is never incidental, and can often be the most important aspect of the entire exercise. More than any other social barometers, fashion designers live in the moment, and their choice of music - particularly the way in which it is juxtaposed - can help determine how their brand is interpreted. In a world where nuance is all, the seemingly indiscriminate blips and squeaks that accompany a designer's clothes as they are sashayed down the catwalk in front of the world's press can - crazy as it may seem - be zeitgeist-determining. And in the early eighties, fashion-show DJs in London were as important in the development of modern pop as the Bronx House Party DJs. Grandmaster Flash (later dubbed by *Life* magazine 'the Toscanini of the turntables') and DJ Kool Herc may have mixed hip-hop beats with the likes of Queen and Kraftwerk, but at the same time, DJs at London's fashion shows were mixing Dvorak with George Clinton, children's TV themes with Irish jigs, heavy metal with Beethoven, Gregorian chants jumbled up with deafening hi-energy. Models would career down the runway accompanied only by bird noises or the sound of a typewriter, by machine-gun fire and orchestral explosions, by Shostakovich and the Sex Pistols, as the catwalk DJs experimented with their aural bouillabaisse. Soon they would be mixing hip-hop tunes in with the rest, using the modern dancefloor rhythms as a sonic glue.

For a while, the fortunes of the Sugar Hill label mirrored those of rap itself, as the label released a cavalcade of great 12-inch singles, everything from 'The Message' by Grandmaster Flash and the Furious Five (with its famous 'Don't push me 'cos I'm close to the edge' earworm) to 'White Lines (Don't Don't Do It)' by Melle Mel, records that encouraged the kind of social commentary the genre would become famous for. The label's signature hit, and the record that would define rap for some years, was 'The Adventures of Grandmaster Flash on the Wheels of Steel' from 1981, an extraordinary and profound sound collage that again used 'Good Times' as its foundation, probably making many casual observers think all rap records were based on the Nile Rodgers classic. It also included samples from 'Another One Bites the Dust' by Queen, Michael Viner's Incredible Bongo Band's 'Apache', and the group's own 'Freedom' as well as Blondie's crossover hit, 'Rapture'. This remains the high-water mark for early rap, the hip-hop equivalent of 'Bohemian Rhapsody' or 'Hey Jude'.

'I think [Flash] is the most significant person in bringing a certain approach to collaging music, through DJ methods, into a popular sphere,' says David Toop. 'Those techniques had been done before by composers like John Cage, and used in electronic music, and in fringe, marginal areas of rock music and what have you. But they had never really been done quite so openly in party music. And hip-hop was party music. Never mind all the other stuff that we now know about, like the sociology, the politics and so on; it was party music, primarily, but party music that was also avant-garde.'

'Good Times' continued to be the pizza base for rap, something acknowledged in June 1981 when Chic jammed with the Clash during their residency at Bond's Casino in New York. They started playing 'Rapture', which then turned into 'Good Times', which turned into a version of Queen's 'Another One Bites the Dust' before finally segueing into 'Radio Clash', which in a way was the punk stars' own homage to the song (the song's promo video, viewed now, with the band mucking about with spray canisters and ghetto blasters, being a classic example of rock'n'roll cultural appropriation).

'It was like a live version of "The Adventures of Grandmaster Flash on the Wheels of Steel",' says Rodgers. It was no surprise that the Clash had taken to hip-hop so enthusiastically, as they were constantly pushing the boundaries of what was deemed acceptable for them to record. Their single 'The Magnificent Seven' was recorded in New York in April 1980 (several months before Blondie's 'Rapture'), and was a decent enough fusion of punk sensibilities and dance aesthetics.* Mick Jones had become hooked on breakbeats,

---

* Even though Blondie had already had a national Top Ten hit with 'Rapture', in 1981 the *New York Times* still found themselves having to describe what rapping was: 'a kind of rhythmic versifying with skeletal instrumental or unrecorded accompaniment. Rapping is probably familiar to most New Yorkers as an intrusive noise on the subway or in the park – the noise that comes out of blaring cassette players and portable radios.' When David Toop published his book *The Rap Attack: African Jive to New York Hip-Hop*, in 1984 – a book which detailed the microcosmic elements happening in New York City that would eventually meld together to form what would become known as hip-hop – the concept was still so new that at the time of the book's printing, it had to be described with the signifier '*New York* hip-hop', suggesting it hadn't yet even reached the pulse of other countries.

having discovered Grandmaster Flash and Afrika Bambaataa in a music store in Brooklyn (and had taken to carrying a huge boom box around with him, earning him the nickname 'Whack Attack'), and Joe Strummer became fixated with rapping – so many of Strummer's lyrics were shopping lists of rebellion, and he quickly picked up on rap's astringent possibilities. One reviewer said the bass on 'The Magnificent Seven' (played incidentally by the Blockheads' Norman Watt-Roy, stepping in for an absent Paul Simonon) sounded like Chic at a cockney knees-up, and that's not far wrong, as its slightly robotic groove makes it innately British. Nevertheless, this was not only the first major white rap record, it was an early example of a rap record with genuine political and social content. 'These groups were radically changing music and they changed everything for us,' said Strummer.

Sugar Hill's upbeat stylings would begin to falter as other artists and labels sprouted up around them, many of which claimed to be more authentic, and most of which were eminently more political. Soon rap would become more strident, more aggressive, more pertinent, with the arrival of the Profile and Def Jam labels and tough-talking acts like Ice-T, Run-DMC, LL Cool J and the Beastie Boys (whose *Licensed to Ill* became the first rap album to hit Number One on the pop charts, in 1986). In a heartbeat it had become the CNN for (mainly) black people. The genre didn't fancy giving up its adherence to the luxury world though, and while gangsta rap would soon start celebrating the 'Thug Life', there were just as many rappers who were happy to wang on about their designer sneakers.

'The motivation for "My Adidas" came from Run's brother Russell, who was high, and was just seeing the impact that Run-DMC and hip-hop were having on Adidas,' said Darryl McDaniels, the DMC in Run-DMC. 'He was like, "Yo, you need to make a record about your sneakers." This guy called Doctor Ds was known for writing these newsletters, once a week, and one of the newsletters was about felon shoes. He made out trainers were for wrongdoers. We put him in his place.'

As rap developed, it would establish its own way of dealing with sex, notably by extolling a hyper-sexualised world swarming with bitches and hos, almost as though misogyny were part of hip-hop's DNA. Towards the end of the decade, and as gangsta rap became a dominant force, women were often referenced only as objects of status or as sexual accessories, as they had been for years in heavy metal. And like metal, rap didn't really do 'love', didn't acknowledge vulnerability or affection. Early rap was self-involved, self-referential, too bound up with braggadocio and skills. Early rap was all about party people.

Perhaps the biggest party record of all, and one of the most important from hip-hop's first imperial phase was 1982's 'Planet Rock' by Afrika Bambaataa & the Soul Sonic Force, a Franken-stein's monster of a record incorporating samples from Kraftwerk's 'Trans-Europe Express', which had been a South Bronx block party staple since the record's original release in 1977. If some said it sounded like an orchestra being rocketed into outer space, others said it sounded like the future in reverse.

'I don't think they ever knew how big [Kraftwerk] were among the black masses in '77 when they came out with [the album] *Trans-Europe Express*,' Bambaataa said. 'When that came out I thought it was one of the weirdest records I ever heard in my life. I said, excuse the expression, this is some weird shit. Everybody just went crazy off of that.

'I guess they found out, when they came over and did a per-formance at the Ritz [in 1981], how big they was. They had four encores and people would not let them leave. That's an amazing group to see – just to see what computers and all that can do. They took like calculators and added something to it – people pressing it and start playing it like music. It was funky. I started looking at [the] telephone – the push-button type – they really mastered those industrial type[s] of machines.'

Grandmaster Flash says it was one of the few records he didn't often mix in with anything else: '"Trans-Europe Express", that was one record you couldn't cut too much – it was cutting itself. That shit was jumping off – leave that shit alone – smoke a cigarette. You can go cool out – go to the bathroom.'

The same year, 1977, Kraftwerk's Ralf Hütter heard another of the album's songs, 'Metal on Metal' (itself a version of the title track) in a New York nightclub. 'So I thought, "Oh, they're playing the new album," but it went on for ten minutes and I thought, "What's happening? That track is only something like two or three minutes." Later I went to ask the DJ and he had two copies of the record and was mixing the two.'

Like many DJs since the sticky New York summer of '77, Bambaataa had been using various passages on the album in his nightly sessions, compounding the music of the future by making it *even more* futuristic. Culturally the Kraftwerk record had forged a new European identity as well as a German one, although Bambaataa's appropriation of *Trans-Europe Express* created a new music identity – one that would inform almost all the electronic pop that came in its wake. Electro pop, techno, you name it, most of it came from Kraftwerk. Soon the idea of using machines to make electronic music would be commonplace, a new normal, invented by Kraftwerk and nudged along with delicate complexity by Afrika Bambaataa.*

As for the Sugarhill Gang, they quite quickly faded into the night. In the statuary of hip-hop heroes, they were never exactly front and centre. Not being particularly telegenic, they didn't become stars in the way Grandmaster Flash or Afrika Bambaataa would, but faded like a cartoon version of something far more profound.

For a while they owned 1980, but it would soon start to own them.

---

* Bambaataa was a great bear of a man, and he looked like George Clinton might have done if he'd swallowed a large fridge. Softly spoken, direct, and quite mad-looking in his octagonal sunglasses, big old hoodie and 'tennises' the size of small boats, all Bambaataa really needed to assume the disposition, if not the mantle, of an African potentate was a throne. He was treated like royalty too, until the summer of 2016, when the Bronx political activist Ronald Savage accused Bambaataa of molesting him in 1980, when Savage was fifteen. This led to a series of other child abuse allegations dating as far back as the 1970s, although no charges were ever made due to New York state's statute of limitations.

1981

Too Much Fighting on the Dancefloor

'Ghost Town' by the Specials

If the country thought it had surrendered itself to a cavalcade of New Romantic careerists, it only had to look at the Specials to see a band intent on reflecting what was going on on the other side of the velvet rope, in those parts of the country where Thatcherism was having its worst effects. Soon, Jerry Dammers' band would be accompanied by a series of real-time live events, with riots from Brixton to Birmingham, and from Liverpool to Bristol. And as the country exploded, so the strains of 'Ghost Town' could be heard, disappearing wearily into the night.

> 'I was a very young mod. The older mods at school used to like me because I brought in a copy of Mad magazine every week and let them read it. I think Mad magazine is the biggest influence in my life. At the age of ten, I decided I was going to have a band, one of the best in the country.'
> – Jerry Dammers

If the decade had started with a fanfare of coloured disco lights, fancy dress costumes and a seemingly collective, nationwide objective to 'move on' - in other words, dressing up and dancing while ignoring the fact that the country was going to the dogs - the riots that started in the spring of 1981 certainly made many people sit up and realise we actually weren't all living in a pop video. In Brixton, in the early summer, after days of rising tension and years of social deprivation, relations between the Metropolitan Police and the local community suddenly sparked a riot. On the evening of 11 April there were 450 injuries, the destruction or burning of over 200 vehicles, and 150 damaged buildings. Even though the police's stop and search powers were about to be curtailed by a government who could see they weren't working, many in the force had become almost institutionalised, especially in their attitudes towards black youth. This situation was particularly fraught in Lambeth, where over a quarter of the population were black, while 40 per cent of those were under nineteen. So the level of anger was huge.

Although there were only eighty arrests during the first riot, over 5000 people were involved, representing a massive groundswell of anger. One policeman said it 'looked like World War III. Cars blazing, people running everywhere', while another said it was 'like Beirut, not London. It was like another country.' At one point a double decker bus found itself weaving into the rioters; its conductor was promptly assaulted, its driver dismissed, and having been commandeered was then driven at speed right into the police line.

Then, a few weeks later, came the predictable, inevitable sequel, a riot in Toxteth, Liverpool, followed by copycat riots in Southall in west London, Manchester's Moss Side, Handsworth in Birmingham and Chapeltown, Leeds. The police were accustomed to low-level civil unrest, but nothing had prepared them for confrontations involving rioters using axes, sledgehammers and even cars as weapons. All of a sudden the country appeared to be spiralling into an endless cycle of violence, framing Prime Minister Margaret Thatcher as the principal villain.

In the days after the first riot, Brixton was a paradoxical postcode: furious and violent at night, and completely empty and silent during the day. I was living there at the time. When we all woke, to survey the damage, most people quickly squirrelled back to their homes, appalled and embarrassed by the carnage, and by lunchtime the streets were empty again. Completely. It felt as though everyone had been shipped out to the country, as the city shimmered with silence.

And breaking that silence wasn't just the sound of petrol bombs and broken glass, it was the sound of 'Ghost Town' by the architects of the recent 2 Tone revolution, the Specials. Not only was this one of the most important records of the early eighties, it remains one of the most evocative, provocative singles of all time, a prime piece of agitprop that still has the power to shock. With its melancholic wailing, its hypnotic lope, its ominous organs and 'The people getting angry' chant, there was no better mirror to the societal privations of 1981, a year in which society often felt on the brink of collapse. It's one of the most baleful records ever to make Number One.

While punk was largely a cultural insurrection, repeatedly using thematic working-class imagery – the brutalist modern tower block being the most obvious manifestation of this, a symbol of post-war progress that very quickly became a totem of social deprivation – 'Ghost Town' was a direct response to the urban distress the Specials' leader Jerry Dammers saw around him. The band had already experienced huge success as the standard-bearers of the multiracial 2 Tone organisation (which included the likes of Madness, the Selector and the Beat), with hits like 'Gangsters', 'A Message to You Rudy' and 'Rat Race', among others. Inspired by punk, they had their own grudges to articulate, and they were doing it through the medium of ska.

'Britain was falling apart,' said Dammers. 'The car industry was closing down in Coventry. We were touring, so we saw a lot of it. Glasgow were particularly bad.' In Liverpool he saw shops closing down, more beggars on the streets, little old ladies selling their cups and saucers on tables outside their homes, and he started to see the frustration and anger in the young faces of those who came out to see his band. He felt there was something very wrong with the country. 'The overall sense I wanted to convey was impending doom. There were weird, diminished chords: certain members of the band resented the song and wanted the simple chords they were used to playing on the first album. It's hard to explain how powerful it sounded. We had almost been written off and then "Ghost Town" came out of the blue.'

The Specials were advocates of late-seventies postmodern ska, the inventors of 2 Tone, and – for the briefest of times – one of the most important British bands of the post-punk period. They were a gang – five white men, two black – who dressed well, spoke sharply, and didn't look like they wanted to be messed with. In the space of just two years, from 1979 to 1981, the original Specials managed to embody the new decade's violent energies, morals and conflicts – though always with an ironic and often sardonic detachment that kept the band cool as the eighties became increasingly heated. Their records defined a slice of a generation who weren't sure they wanted to be defined in the first place. They were slightly yobby – the *NME* called their debut album 'a speed and beer-crazed ska loon' – but they had an underlying social conscience. They would turn out to be temporal, but they left their mark in the same way the Clash did, or the Undertones, by connecting. Sure, the band were earnest, but they were studiedly sarcastic, too, which endeared them to everyone from ageing punks to their younger siblings. Not only that, but they came from Coventry, Britain's very own answer to Detroit, the epitome of the post-war urban wasteland, the quintessential concrete jungle; they had a right to protest, especially against the determined onslaught of Thatcherism.

Nineteen-eighty-one was a desperate year in the UK. Youth unemployment was rife as the country felt the bite of Thatcher's economic cuts, and riots were erupting all over the country, riots that appeared, with eerie synchronicity, at the same time as 'Ghost Town'. It even felt like a riot, or rather how a riot felt just before it kicked off, or maybe just after it, when all the dust had settled. Dammers' record was an apocalyptic portrait of inner-city oppression set to a loping beat offset by an unsettling and vaguely Middle Eastern motif. The single sounded like the fairground ride from hell, a snake charmer of a song, complete with strident brass, madhouse wailing, and dub-style breaks. The video was just as bleak, featuring a road trip through some of the least salubrious streets of central London. Three weeks after the song was released – bingo! – there were riots and civil disobedience all over the country.

The genesis of the song started back in 1980, after Dammers had witnessed the St Pauls riots in Bristol. For most of the seventies, St

Pauls – a predominantly black and white working-class area – had been the victim of deteriorating housing, poor education services and an increasingly strong police presence. Racial tension was high, as the African-Caribbean community felt victimised. Although the exact cause remains unclear, in early April, a riot erupted, involving nearly 2000 people. It was this event that started Dammers thinking of 'Ghost Town', a song that would go on to define him, his band, and 2 Tone in general.

'St Pauls was the first riot, so I was aware of the situation,' he says. 'I was aware that things were deteriorating. "Ghost Town" was obviously referencing the situation. Unemployment was heading for three million, and it was a very worrying time.'

'It wasn't a surprise when it went to Number One – most things 2 Tone became hits,' said Pauline Black, the lead singer of fellow 2 Tone band, the Selector. '"Ghost Town" epitomised the 2 Tone idea that black and white can operate in the same unit and speak to the youth. And its sense of melancholy spoke clearly: there was the "sus" laws [the informal term for the "stop and search" law that enabled the police to stop, search and potentially arrest suspects], inner cities not functioning, racism dividing the working class. There was fighting at our gigs; there were lots of National Front people around. There was frustration about 2 Tone falling apart. We were seventies bands in a time of two-man synth bands. The record companies were happy to leave 2 Tone's problems behind.'

Weren't they just. Surrounded by a burgeoning New Romantic movement, 2 Tone felt very council estate, very rough, and very monochromatic.

'Ghost Town', though, felt properly revolutionary, the kind of record that no one had the right to expect any more. Tantalising, mesmeric, it feels as unprecedented now as it did then. The riots were domestic experiences, the kind that visitors to the UK just wouldn't understand. Which was why 'Ghost Town' was such a perfect soundtrack. Musicians love to use the word 'cinematic', although this usually comes across as vague or as a reminder that they hired a string section, or stole something from a John Barry record (often when musicians drop 'cinematic' into their conversations this is usually *all* they mean). But Dammers was different: he wanted to create his own legacy rather than forage around in someone else's.

The most poignant moment in the record happens at 1min 52sec, when the song moves back from the bridge into the verse, and when the organ starts to tip-toe through the tune again. At this moment in the promo, which basically showed the band squeezed into a classic Vauxhall Cresta, patrolling empty, crumbling streets, you can see Dammers' gurning face peeking out of a backseat window. The record, like its recording, was a three-ring circus, presented munificently so that you could choose what to listen to. And Dammers was there in the centre of it all, the ring-master, as he had been through the Specials' short career, a narrative arc that lurched quickly from iron-clad intent to weary – and eerie – disillusionment. In essence, the Specials' career looked like this: stratospheric peaks, experimental detours, and as much disarray as mastery.

'Seventeen months separate the Specials two Number One singles and a million musical miles,' wrote Simon Price of the *Independent on Sunday*. 'Their first, a live recording of "Too Much Too Young", was essentially the Sex Pistols' "Bodies" gone ska, but the intervening year saw the Specials ditch that punky-reggae template. Jerry Dammers experimented with lounge-noir on their second album, causing intra-band friction. "Ghost Town" initiated a strand of spooked British pop that has lived on in Tricky and Portishead's trip-hop and the dubstep of Burial and James Blake.'

Realism? This was urban decay writ large, accompanied by a kick drum and a muted horn. The kaleidoscopic 'Ghost Town' didn't offer balm for a world-weary pop-culture; rather it was a political exhortation. 'For those of us who were not part of Thatcherism's good life, for those of us who were excluded, then "Ghost Town" spoke to our bruised hearts,' says Tony Parsons, who was still writing for the *NME* at the time.

The song was about the dissolution of the band as much as deindustrialisation and the toxicity of the streets. There had been internal fights within the Specials almost from the off, as Dammers was always trying to push the band in an experimental direction. The recording of 'Ghost Town', which was the last time the original band were in a studio together, was so fraught, and so obviously frustrating, that the guitarist Roddy Byers tried to kick a hole in the wall. As the studio was so small, each band member recorded their part separately, adding to the sense of separateness; and when they were together, there was bickering, scowling. It was this tense environment that produced the extraordinary sound of 'Ghost Town'.

'The aural landscape is so vast that each member sounds disconnected from the next,' says Dorian Lynskey, in his history of protest songs, *33 Revolutions Per Minute*. '[Singer Terry] Hall's chirpy memories of the "good old days", Rico Rodriguez's long elegiac trombone solo, and that ghastly chorus of taunting wraiths. The record does not so much end as lose the will to go on, sinking back into the fog. Like all great records about social collapse, it seems to both fear and relish calamity. The ghost town is theirs to haunt.'

'When I think about "Ghost Town" I think about Coventry,' said the band's drummer, John Bradbury, who grew up in the city. 'I saw it develop from a boom town, my family doing very well, through to the collapse of the industry and the bottom falling out of family life. Your economy is destroyed and, to me, that's what "Ghost Town" is all about.'

. . .

The riots would eventually end, although not before the Specials themselves collapsed. As they were due to appear on *Top of the Pops* to promote the record, Terry Hall, Lynval Golding and Neville Staples told Dammers they were going to leave, appearing a few months later as Fun Boy Three (weren't they just) with their debut single, 'The Lunatics Have Taken Over the Asylum', a record which owed much to the lyrics and orchestration of 'Ghost Town'.

In some respects, 1981 was defined by the riots as much as by the music they inadvertently inspired. Yes, there was a royal wedding, in sharp juxtaposition to inner-city decay, a wedding that would produce a genuine royal superstar, yet the riots – the worst for a century - would resonate throughout the country for years. Motivated by racial tension, a perception of inner-city deprivation, and heat, the defining factor was the ongoing war of attrition between the black community and the police. The four main riots occurred in Brixton in London, Handsworth in Birmingham, Chapeltown in Leeds and Toxteth in Liverpool, although there were disturbances in at least twenty other towns and cities, including Derby, Bristol and, almost unbelievably, High Wycombe.

The worst were in Brixton, on 10-12 April. Dubbed 'Bloody Saturday' by *Time* Magazine, the main riot took place on the 11th, and resulted in a mass confrontation between the mob and the Metropolitan Police. There were forty-five injuries to members of the public, and nearly 300 to the police; over 5000 rioters were involved, many of whom had simply come out to fight as they had nothing better to do, and nowhere better to do it.

'We were watching a live TV broadcast of the Brixton riots and saw this bloke smash a camera shop window, and grab the biggest camera he could find, which looked like a Nikon with a motor drive,' says my friend Chris Sullivan, the former owner of the Wag Club (which would launch in Soho a year later). 'He ran off with it, but then as soon as he passed an off licence, he stopped, turned around, and then threw it through the window. He nicked as many bottles of booze as he could carry. He then ran away leaving the camera behind. The camera was probably worth two grand, while the booze probably wasn't worth more than £100 tops. That summed it up for me.'

In Toxteth, eyewitnesses recalled the 'brazen calmness' of the looters, who were almost using the rioters as a human shield. They turned up with supermarket trolleys, safe in the knowledge they would never be caught. 'Refrigerators, dryers, you name it,' said one observer. 'I even saw one lady hold up a piece of carpet and ask if anyone knew whether it was 6ft by 4ft.'

The riots were more than a collection of urban disturbances, they were a media flashpoint that drew international attention to the huge rift in ideologies between the left and the right in the

UK, as well as the gap between perception and reality in terms of how the government were coping with the economy. There was also a growing sense that the Tories had no understanding of, and no pastoral interest in, the have-nots under their care; those who hadn't and wouldn't benefit from financial deregulation, privatisation or Thatcher's changes to the welfare state. While she would always say that she was empowering those who had previously been beholden to the state, Thatcher was criticised most often for having no idea what to do with communities when the safety net had been withdrawn. Especially as she was the one who had withdrawn it. The resulting report into the riots concluded that they were due to complex political, social and economic factors that had created 'a disposition towards violent protest' due to racial disadvantage, inner-city struggles and the attrition between the local communities and the police.

The forgotten riot is the one in Brixton that started on 28 September 1985. It was sparked by the shooting of Dorothy 'Cherry' Groce by the police, while they were looking for her son Michael Groce in relation to a suspected firearms offence. They thought he was hiding in his mother's home, raided it, and accidentally shot Mrs Groce, paralysing her from the waist down. As news of the attack spread, so hostilities began, and the police lost control of the area for two days, during which time dozens of fires were started and shops looted. Photojournalist David Hodge died a few days later, after a gang of looters he was trying to photograph attacked and beat him. The Broadwater Farm riot in Tottenham, in north London, a week later, was dominated by two deaths. During a police search of her home on 5 October, an African-Caribbean woman called Cynthia Jarrett died of heart failure, triggering a sequence of events which resulted in a full-scale riot the following day on the Broadwater Farm council estate, involving youths throwing bricks, stones and Molotov cocktails, as well as using firearms. At 9.30 p.m. Police Constable Keith Blakelock was trapped by a gang of local balaclava-clad boys, blowing whistles and ringing bells, who tried to decapitate him using knives and machetes. He was butchered to death. According to a man watching from his second-floor flat, the mob was relentless, like 'vultures tearing at his body'. When he was examined later Blakelock had 42 different wounds. Winston Silcott, Engin Raghip and Mark Braithwaite were convicted of murder and sentenced to life imprisonment, although all three were cleared by the Court of Appeal in 1991 after it emerged that evidence had been tampered with (Silcott remained in prison for the separate murder of another man, Tony Smith, finally being released in 2003).

. . .

I spent the years between 1981 and 1987 knocking about in south London, living in various housing association flats in Brixton, Peckham, Herne Hill and the Oval. The 1981 riots happened just a quarter of a mile from where I lived in the Oval, while the 1985 riot happened right outside my front door. On Saturday 28 September I had just come back from a trip abroad. I spent the whole day indoors, transcribing tapes, writing, listening to music and cleaning the flat, not bothering to go outside for a paper, or turn on the radio or TV. The flat was right behind the Ritzy cinema, just off Cold-harbour Lane, a first-floor, two-bedroomed housing association flat that backed onto a small courtyard, and faced Brixton's Front Line. The first I knew something was up was around five o'clock in the afternoon, when I started to hear screaming, windows being smashed, and the sound of accelerated running past the window. I looked through the vast, seven-foot-wide venetian blind that faced the street and saw dozens of local residents – almost exclusively young black men – running by my window carrying stolen record players, televisions, CD players, radios, amplifiers, microwaves, small fridges, speaker systems, anything they could carry. They'd been looting in and around the shops in Brixton market, and in a second I realised I was in the middle of a full-scale riot.

Now I was attuned to everything, including the sound of looters breaking in through the front door of our building. They steamed into the four ground-floor flats and took anything they wanted that they could carry (again, audio equipment, vinyl, TVs). I had already barricaded our own front door with various pieces of random furniture, although this was largely to try and appease my girlfriend, as I knew that any concerted push from the other side would have caused them to come tumbling down the corridor as the door flew open. The looters (even though they were ostensibly rioting all they were really doing was stealing) did actually run up to the first floor, although they immediately headed back down again as the sound of sirens approached. Police ran into our building but by then most of the looters had run off in the direction of Railton Road, and safe havens.

These were small gangs, little groups of boys who had grown up together, becoming disenfranchised together. When I rang my friend Robin, who lived up the road on Brixton Hill, and told him about the dozens and dozens of people still running by my window with enough stereo equipment to start their own branch of Curry's, he laughed and rather unhelpfully suggested that I nip out and find something for myself ('Don't you need a new stereo?'). We had both lived in Brixton for some time and had become almost immune to the attritional nature of the place. It was our version of gallows humour, as we were no longer surprised by break-ins, muggings or harassment from the locals.

The next morning, Brixton looked as though it had been turned inside out. Everything that was usually inside someone's house appeared to be outside, all the household detritus that looks so pathetic and parochial when removed from its natural habitat. And it wasn't quiet, so much as mute. No noise. No sound. Nothing. The area soon went back to normal, although the fact that there were even more boarded-up windows in the market and along the high street just made you think that whatever forms of gentrification were taking place, Brixton was never going to get any better as every time it did, there would always be those who would find a way to destroy it (most of whom lived there).

As we eventually moved on – shipping out to Shepherd's Bush, in west London – so others took our place, and a gentrification of sorts did occur, the kind that increasingly appealed to those who couldn't afford to get onto the housing ladder anywhere else. By the end of the eighties, those pockets of gentrification that had started to pop up around central London would become so oversubscribed that those on the bottom rungs were pushed further and further out, to those previously out-of-bounds areas east of the city villages that promised the sort of luxurious loft-living the young bankers in docklands had been promised decades before. Some thought this was progress, although what was rarely advertised in the *Sunday Times'* Home section was the fact that most of these new developments were nothing less than gated communities. They didn't need to say anything, as it was implicit. The gentrification of London was continuing at an unusually fast pace, one that reflected the new money swirling around and rushing into the city, and the way in which it was being used as an architectural hothouse; but what was rarely discussed was the divisive way in which we were all now being forced to live, the rich rubbing up against the poor, and neither of them appreciating it very much.

London wouldn't experience riots again for another twenty-six years, when the looters couldn't even be bothered to swathe their frustration with their own plight with anything tangible; the looting in 2011 was simply an excuse to steal some new trainers. The gangs were bigger, more organised, more vicious, more resigned to living outside of society; no explanations or excuses were needed nor offered. Compared to the two-speed society of the tweenies (as economists are still trying to describe the second decade of the twenty-first century), 1985 seemed almost quaint.

The riots of the eighties were devoured so much by the international media that the burning oil drum became as much a part of modern British iconography as the white suits in the 1981 television adaptation of Evelyn Waugh's *Brideshead Revisited* – and for a while seemed to appear in any film about the British underclass, surrounded by a gang of RADA-trained professional cockneys and a smattering of generic gangsters, drug dealers and punky molls in fishnets. To the outside world it looked as though rioting was what any youth cult worth their salt did when they'd grown tired of posing for style magazines or making bad pop records.

Living in London you certainly had the feeling you were somehow living under siege. In south London, conflict gave an edge to every transaction in a corner shop, every late-night walk home from the Underground. Walk into a Brixton pub and you felt eyes upon you. Television coverage of the riots painted them clearly as battles between residents and police, although what they really did was create even more racial tension on the street, between neighbours of different ethnic backgrounds, between people who knew each other and of course those who didn't. I had a friend who was chased down Gresham Road near Brixton Police Station by some of his black neighbours just because he happened to be white at the wrong time of day. He sought refuge in the house of a (black) neighbour, who promptly called out to the gang giving chase. They ran in and kicked the living daylights out of my friend. Police aggression made everyone paranoid; people who had previously lived quite happily side by side turned against each other because it seemed like the safest thing to do.

The morning after the first 1981 riot was almost as bad as the riot itself, as the mess and the devastation made you feel as though you were living in a place that was never going to improve, that was only ever going to get worse. Back in 1981, walking around Electric Avenue and Atlantic Road after the first night's disturbance was nothing if not surreal. Coldharbour Lane always looked like a fairly unforgiving place at the best of times, but for weeks after the riots it felt as though it had been transported directly from some post-apoc wasteland, a tunnel of terror. Walking down the Lane at night you felt a little like Orpheus walking out of the underworld, too anxious to turn around and see what might be behind you.

Everywhere there was tension. One afternoon that autumn, a few months after the 1981 riots, I had walked from a squat in Peckham up to the Oval, and was just about to enter the Underground when I was approached by a gang of about a dozen skinheads. They were all over the place at the time, although they tended to leave Brixton and its immediate environs alone, so whenever you saw them in the area you suspected there might be trouble. I assumed that my dyed hair, red bandana and Chinese slippers had probably caused my shorn-haired friends to think I was a lily-livered liberal with a penchant for African-Caribbean culture, so as soon as I saw one of them reach into his pocket for his knife as he mentioned something I was meant to have said to his 'sister', I turned on my slippered heels and ran. All the way to Brixton. And, unlike Orpheus, without looking back.

The late summer of 1981 was a wake-up call for so many people I knew, as we had all finished college, and were experiencing the inevitability of signing on the dole, looking for work while juggling the day-to-day existence of a life without structure or support network. For me and for so many others at the time, my support network was the black economy, acting as a cocktail barman at Brixton's chi-chi nightclub the Fridge one minute, and bunking the tube the next. On Tuesdays doing the door at a West End nightclub (where essentially you let in your friends for free, and drank the profits), and on Wednesdays waking up with just enough time to sign on. Odd jobs were essential to supplement what you got from the government: film extra work, a spot of photography, retail conference stewarding, modelling for friends who couldn't find anyone else, DJing, drumming in bands who were never going to get signed, running a Sunday market stall in Camden Lock, having spent the early hours buying up bric-a-brac and tat in Brick Lane ... Anything for cash. Seriously, what have you got, when does it start? This was the time of *Only Fools and Horses*, of *Minder*, of *Boys from the Blackstuff*, of the nefarious and the naughty, the second-hand and the underhand. In our world, the economy was driven by nightclubs, as this was a completely cash economy. Club owners, club runners, DJs, bands, doormen, barmen, waitresses, bouncers, small-time drug dealers. Everything was based on cash, as there was no other currency. Having no safety net meant we encouraged each other to be more entrepreneurial than perhaps we would otherwise have been, although we were none of us the kind of people who would have ever pursued jobs for life.

Urban deprivation for us was a backdrop to a new world, one in which we knew we were going to have to fend for ourselves.

When Mrs Thatcher first arrived in Downing Street in 1979, there were many who thought she would become as much a prisoner of the Whitehall machine as her predecessor Edward Heath, yet she quickly used abrasiveness to slap down the mandarins. 'She gives the civil servants hell,' said one observer soon after she became prime minister. 'She writes these brusque, caustic notes accusing them of woolly thinking, and they are absolutely terrified of her.' The Cabinet were terrified too, as her treatment of her colleagues was appalling. There would be no woolly thinking in Mrs Thatcher's government. Elected against a background of rotting refuse and unburied bodies following the Winter of Discontent, she took her mandate for governing as a mandate for change.

Thatcher had a habit of invoking the pernicious legacy of the so-called Permissive Society whenever she was confronted with something she didn't understand. It was easier for her to stand back, aghast. Equally, Thatcher dismissed the idea that racism, heavy-handed police tactics and unemployment were behind the Brixton disturbances – even though police brutality and continual harassment of young black men had been one of the prime motivators behind the riots – saying, 'Nothing, but nothing, justifies what happened ... What aggravated the riots into a virtual saturnalia was the impression gained by the rioters that they could enjoy a fiesta of crime, looting and rioting in the guise of social protest. They felt they had been absolved in advance.' She was criticised for this outburst, but she wasn't entirely wrong. She was, though, when she claimed that money couldn't buy either trust or racial harmony. What many forgot about the peace process in Northern Ireland was that it was as much to do with prosperity as political and sectarian will. Of course, large-scale investment would have helped Brixton, although the more disquiet there was, the more unlikely any investment seemed. However, it was to come sooner than anyone thought, as Tesco bought a site on Acre Lane the day after the 1985 riots. Gentrification eventually came to Brixton, inadvertently moving it upmarket; not by much, but by enough. Pride followed prosperity, and in the summer of 2011, when opportunistic revellers attending a street party used the excuse of the riot in Tottenham a few days earlier to loot and burn a string of shops in Brixton, local residents were incensed, calling the thugs 'pathetic ... It's just an excuse for the young ones to come and rob shops. We are going to get people blaming the economy and what happened last week but that's not the real reason this happened. This is costly for our community reputation.' It would have been difficult to imagine the residents displaying the same sentiments in 1981, or indeed in 1985.

· · ·

Almost forty years after the riots, if you had been reading the small ads in the arts pages of your favourite national newspaper, you would have seen that revival tours were all the rage. The Human League, the Who, Lloyd Cole, Ultravox, Deep Purple, the Eagles, Golden Earring and Simply Red were all treading the boards again, seemingly regardless of how these opportunistic outings would ultimately affect their legacies. And who could blame them? They were gigs, after all. People at the time would pay good money to see bands they enjoyed in their youth, sometimes regardless of how many original members they contained. That weird little band from 1983 whose only hit you once devoured as though it were the essence of life itself? Yup, well they were probably back too, playing the Shepherd's Bush Empire the night after Joe Jackson, and probably supporting Orchestral Manoeuvres in the Dark, or the Happy Mondays. With all the original members, too, strangely - apart from the drummer, who had no doubt died in a bizarre gardening accident in what the rest of the band at the time thought was a misguided, if not completely unfunny, homage to Spinal Tap.

Back then, as far as music was concerned, there was nothing quite so *au courant* as nostalgia.

And if you looked carefully, you would have seen that the Specials were back too, churning out the old hits as though they were a human jukebox. They were greeted with open arms by the critics and public alike, only they weren't really the Specials at all, because the most important member, Jerry Dammers, the man who invented them, who gave the band their political edge, who wrote most of their songs and who was responsible for making them truly memorable, was not encouraged to participate in the reunion ('I founded the Specials, and now they've excluded me,' said Dammers when the band first reunited, in 2008). There had always been friction between Dammers and the group's singer, Terry Hall, one of the most (self-proclaimed) miserable men in pop, and that friction continued; obviously to the extent that they found it impossible to work together.

Dammers was the creative genius behind the Specials, the man who gave them their idiosyncratic musical tropes, and who set them apart from the likes of the Selector, the Beat, or Bad Manners. The Specials without Dammers were like the Doors without Jim Morrison, Queen without Freddie Mercury, or Morecambe and Wise without Morecambe or, er, Wise. I saw the re-formed Specials support Blur at their gig in Hyde Park in 2012, and the band looked like a bunch of fiftysomething cab drivers and sounded like the musical equivalent of a Sunday morning football match. They didn't play 'Ghost Town', but then how could they? The man who wrote it wasn't there.

I knew Jerry extremely well for about five years in the eighties. I would regularly hitch up to Coventry to sit in sullen working men's clubs with him and his extraordinary circle of friends and acquaintances, discussing socialism (we often differed), the provenance of Prince Buster and the validity of Heaven 17. We went clubbing together, spent a few memorable New Year's Eves in Bristol (where Jerry's parents were from; and singing our own versions of 'Ten Green Bottles'), spent birthdays together, and once DJ'd together at a miners' benefit at the Wag Club in 1983 with the comedian Harry Enfield and various members of Madness (he played politically correct funk while I largely played right-of-centre disco). I even sat through some of the tortuous recording of the 1985 album *In the Studio* by the Special AKA (which is what the Specials morphed into), containing Jerry's defining moment, the monumentally influential 'Free Nelson Mandela'.

Inspired by Live Aid, this song ultimately led to the Mandela Seventieth Birthday Tribute concert at Wembley Stadium in 1988, and helped add to the groundswell of support that led to Mandela's release from Robben Island in February 1990. As a piece of agit-prop, 'Free Nelson Mandela' was peerless, a political pop record that managed to achieve even more than it set out to do. Written as a call to arms, a marketing tool almost, it set in motion a chain of events that changed history. And you can't say that about most pop records. The music he started recording with the Special AKA was uncompromising to say the least; their first single, 'The Boiler', was a first-person account of a rape, complete with actual screams, while the follow-up was called 'War Crimes'. Dammers famously told the *NME* that pop music was about giving people what they want to hear. 'We're giving people what they don't want to hear.' But although with Nelson Mandela he had found a cause, the song itself wasn't a misery-fest; rather it was exuberance personified, a joyous happy ending. Dammers recruited Elvis Costello to produce it (he had done the honours on the Specials' first album, after all), and he did a sterling job, drafting in former bandmate Lynval Golding and the Beat's Dave Wakeling and Ranking Roger to sing its life-enhancing, relentlessly upbeat chorus. As proof that perhaps he wasn't the right kind of person to marshal pop hits from such unlikely material, Dammers started playing an indulgent piano solo towards the end of the recording, before, that is, Costello turned the tape off. Furious that his musings had been cut short, he said, 'Elvis, that's jazz!' Costello shot back with, 'It's bollocks.' Nevertheless, between them they created one of the most successful protest songs of all time. 'It ends with the thing of "I'm begging you" and then "I'm telling you",' Dammers said. 'It is a demand but in a positive way; it brought some sort of hope that the situation could be sorted out.'

When the Special AKA eventually split, not long after *In the Studio*, its members went on to solo careers of limited distinction. And after Fun Boy Three fell apart, all Terry Hall really had was his voice. It was a distinctive voice, but he didn't have the surface smarts to properly interact with pop. Dammers wasn't much good at being a pop star either, but he had his dignity, his talent, and his own, very particular idea of creative ambition. If 'Ghost Town' sometimes obscured his lesser achievements, it also upstaged his greatest disasters: despite the eccentricity, the fall from grace, and the inelegant fights with the rest of the Specials, that song was always louder. More reverent, more audacious.

Dammers was always a genuine bohemian, and in a way it was no surprise to me the way his career panned out (DJ-ing, production, forming various esoteric dance orchestras). However, I also thought he might turn out to be our generation's John Barry, scoring important movies with solemn yet iconic orchestral themes, balancing Jacques Derrida with Francis Lai, Scott Walker with Dr John. To me, Dammers was the Lennon and McCartney of ska, and one of the most important voices of the post-punk generation, a man who always appeared to be carrying his generation's hopes and dreams on his shoulders, as well as his own. That he didn't turn into John Barry was a disappointment to me, but probably not to him.

I was thinking about 'Ghost Town' during the dark days of 2020, moments before Prime Minister Boris Johnson issued his lockdown, telling people - quite rightly, but far too late - that the only way to protect themselves as well as other people was by staying indoors, and keeping themselves to themselves. A few days previously, having been encouraged to be more circumspect with their movements, people were still flocking to London's parks, presumably because they assumed they were immune to infection.

Having spent the previous week working from home, trying to marshal the troops via Zoom, a few days before the lockdown I walked into the office to pick up some material I needed for a project our magazine had just successfully moved to the autumn. In the end I spent most of the day there, doing emails, making more video calls and – mostly – cancelling things. After a brief trip to the Pret at the top of our square, I finished up and started to walk home. But, compelled by the inactivity around me, I took the long way, turning right instead of left, striding along Regent Street on my way down to Piccadilly Circus, where I was going to dart right, along Piccadilly itself, and stroll home via Hyde Park Corner.

And the faster I started to walk, the slower I became. I found myself being transfixed by the silence, alone in the vast city, padding around my own private video game. It certainly didn't feel empowering, as the sensation of being alone was intensified by being in the city. It was as though I'd been walking around at night, and someone had suddenly turned the lights on.

Weird, just weird.

The first thing I felt was guilt, being outside when I probably should have been indoors, but as I was completely alone this was a pretty futile emotion. The streets weren't just empty of people, they were empty of life. As I walked south, I may as well have been self-isolating, because I was completely, *completely* alone. I felt as though I'd stepped out of one of those British TV science fiction programmes they made in the sixties – back in a land of bowler hats, umbrellas and red phone boxes – those austere black and white ones when London had been the target of a neutron bomb, the ones that killed all the people but left the buildings intact. For a short while, I felt as though I could have been the last person in the capital, the last person alive, lost in reverie, but oh-so-aware of everything around me. I knew the enemy was out there, just as it had been nearly forty years ago. I couldn't see it, couldn't smell it, but I knew it was coming.

And all the while I was thinking about 'Ghost Town', as it was the only appropriate soundtrack I could think of, the one song that seemed like a suitable soundtrack to the malevolent solitude around me. A few days later, I called Jerry Dammers, essentially to talk about the crisis, and how he thought it might relate to his most famous song. He was in the middle – or thereabouts – of recording a new album, down in his studio in Streatham, in south London.

He had hours of material 'in the can', as he said, but needed time to get it into shape. With all his DJ-ing work cancelled for the time being, he was wisely using this period to try and finalise work he'd been tinkering with for years. 'I'll get there in the end,' he said. 'I'm not a perfectionist but I want this to be good. I think it is good, but I want to give it my best shot. Once and for all.' When I spoke with him, he was as disconcerted by the crisis as all of us. Up until the lockdown he had been working late most nights, regularly seeing the crazies who still stalked the streets in the early hours in those desperate times, and still freaked out by the desolation. 'It's quite spooky walking about at night. I would come back from the studio in the middle of the night and worryingly there would be the odd lunatics walking the streets. It's only the most extreme people who appear to still be out there. It's strange times.'

Maybe so, but 1981 was a pretty strange year too.

1982

Men in Hats

'The Look of Love' by ABC

In the UK, as the New Romantics started to mutate, and as the likes of Duran Duran, Spandau Ballet and Boy George began to occupy the front pages of the tabloids as well as the style press, a new genre started to rear its ironic-bequiffed head: New Pop, as exemplified by Sheffield's ABC, a swanky, postmodern version of the perfect pop group, fusing modern dance tropes with retro Rat Pack cool and terrific tunes. 'The Look of Love' was their calling card, *The Lexicon of Love* their legacy.

> *'I wanted a name that would put us first in the phone directory, or second if you count ABBA.'*
>
> *– Martin Fry*

Nineteen-eighty-one had been a vintage year for pop, a year when the confluence of radical disco, post punk and white funk produced the likes of Was Not Was, the Human League, Kid Creole and the Coconuts and the Tom Tom Club, and when every good new record seemed directed at the same mythical dancefloor. But while the year was best italicised by Grace Jones's *Nightclubbing*, Martin Fry's ABC evinced the perfect mix of celebration and irony. ABC pre-empted the entire eighties New Pop Deal, creating a thoroughly convincing pop property with a light sense of irony - earnest backing vocals, gold lamé suits and snarky lyrics. On 'The Look of Love', when Fry sings, 'Sisters and brothers, should help each other,' you just knew his tongue was firmly in his cheek.

'It was like disco, but in a Bob Dylan way,' said the record's producer, Trevor Horn, although in reality it was actually much better than that. With 'The Look of Love', 'Poison Arrow', 'Tears

Are Not Enough' and 'All of My Heart', ABC managed to create totally modern-sounding records that celebrated the very idea of pop itself. If the Buzzcocks' Pete Shelley had written songs for Motown they may have sounded like this. In a way ABC were doing what Roxy Music had done ten years previously, which was create a shiny pop micro-climate, slightly at odds with the temperature of the times, echoing the past. In ABC's world, men wore suits and women were grateful. The defining quality of their music was its intelligence, driven by a desire to elevate the pop genre, rather than simply turn it into a commodity.

But there was a time before all this, a time when pop consumers – or at least the ones I knew – were only imagining ABC.

Imagine a house party in Stoke Newington, north London, a few months before Christmas. It is 1979, and the decade is soon to end. The party isn't in one of those long, Soviet-style council blocks that fan out from Manor House Underground Station, but in a run-down Stamford Hill flat above a Jewish greengrocer in a Victorian terraced street, squeezed between a laundromat and a newsagent. The flat is largely full of students from St Martin's School of Art, and the music on the turntable is ironic mid-sixties fare: 'Promise Her Anything' by Tom Jones, 'Hoots Mon' by Lord Rockingham's XI, 'You Don't Have to Say You Love Me' by Dusty Springfield, and the first half-dozen Supremes hits, along with a lot of other early Motown singles. The girls at the party are dressed in art school approximations of go-go dancers – accessorised by massive hoop earrings, big-buckled slip-ons and white gloves – while the boys are dressed in Oxfam suits and ties, many sporting Trilbys and Homburgs.

We are not listening to guitar bands, as we appear to have deliberately ignored them, temporarily banished them to the fringes of experience, focusing instead on the neutrality of female-heavy pop. There is a bit of Northern Soul, some Manfred Mann, but almost nothing contemporary.

In the same way that the mods – a decade and a half earlier – were assuming the status of their 'superiors' by dressing like them, so we were appropriating the styles of the stockbroker, the crooner, the spiv and the politician. By using childish gimmicks – dressing up, inexpertly – we were attempting to be adults by very carefully looking to the past.

The room felt as though it was really trying, as the crowd was doing its best to throw the same shapes another crowd had thrown in the Ad-Lib back in the sixties. There was barely fifteen years between the two experiences, and yet the second was already meta, an experience that was already a homage. We were playing the same music, wearing the same clothes, but we were looking at our present from a distance. We weren't a social transformation, we were a style.

Which was very ABC. At least it would be soon – trying to escape the present by moving into the future by looking like the past. By the end of 1979, there was a large student body in London that had started to dress like Frank Sinatra, or at the very least the kind of men who surrounded Sinatra when he burst into song on film. We were moving forward by pilfering from the past, by scouring charity shops and second-hand stores, looking for old demob suits and broken-in Oxfords, searching for the kind of clothes our parents had worn when they were our age. We were sick of dressing like punks (there was no punk music played at our party that night), so we started dressing like film stars – OK, film extras – complete with double-breasted suits, kipper ties (many of which appeared to have floral patterns that had sunk into a jungle gloom, like very old wallpaper), old man hats and watch fobs. Cary Grant had nothing on us. We were the look of the past, the look of the future.

I'm not sure where all this came from. I just think we were tired of looking poor, and perhaps wanted to look like grown-ups, but only in a way that articulated our ambivalence; we weren't sure we really *did* want to be adults, but we didn't mind looking like them for a while, until we worked out what we were really going to do with our lives.

I was one of these young men, someone who wanted to look like someone I wasn't. And by the end of 1981 (which is when

ABC released their first single, 'Tears Are Not Enough'), like a lot of my compadres, I looked rather a lot like the members of ABC. Or rather we all thought they had started to dress like us. Honestly, didn't they know we'd been dressing like this for *ages*?

In a way we were already looking for ABC, or at least something like them, as we were starting to affect the lifestyles of those who'd been here before us, fifteen years ago. We were already at art school – the lucky ones among us, anyway – and we were already plotting careers in the applied arts, in graphics, or photography, or writing, or something – anything! – that was going to flatter our taste rather than our aptitude.

We were certainly intrigued by the idea of New Pop. A slew of music paper journalists (encouraged initially by the *NME*'s Paul Morley, who at the time – a time when his paper was read by 250,000 people each week – was nearly as famous as some of the people he wrote about) were getting sick of miserable 'Northern' groups with Penguin Modern Classic indulgences. They thought it might be fun to listen to music again that was, well, *fun*. Then a bunch of groups – ABC, Scritti Politti, Haircut 100, the Teardrop Explodes, the Human League, Orange Juice, OMD and the Associates included – started thinking that the past might not be a terrible place to live, as long as it could be adapted for the future.

New Pop was based on a genuine love of pop's great legacy, and a respect that was newly contextualised, by punks and post-punks clearly obsessed with the classic British pop single, and who were sick of having been turned into tourist attractions by the tabloids. New Pop thought it was fine to blur the Beatles with the Buzzcocks, thought it perfectly OK to marry ambition with transgression. New Pop was all about retrofitting the future, trying to be contemporary by using imagery and systems from the past.

Sheffield's Martin Fry was equally intrigued by this potentially new way of doing things. In ABC he wrote postmodern torch songs, fully orchestrated love bombs festooned with clever wordplay and ironic key changes. The sassy producer Trevor Horn took Fry's B-movie melodramas and gave them a widescreen presence, using grandiose production techniques to give ABC an awkward glamour that made them instantly, strangely appealing.

Horn had previously been a member of the chart band Buggles, who had a huge global hit in 1979 with the slightly naff 'Video Killed the Radio Star' (which became the very first video to be aired on MTV when it launched in August 1981). Rather incongruously he was then asked to join the progressive rock behemoths Yes, along with his partner in the Buggles, Geoff Downes. After a year of this bizarre mismatch, he left, and then fell into production, recording some startling progressive singles for the previously bafflingly successful pop duo Dollar.

'After playing with Yes I was at a point where I didn't know what to do next,' said Horn, 'and my late wife said to me, "You should forget being an artist because it's not your thing at the moment, but if you went into production you could be the best producer in the world." So that's what I did. I worked with Dollar, and made "Give me Back my Heart", "Mirror Mirror" and "Hand Held in Black and White". That's what led me to ABC, as Martin Fry was a big fan of "Black and White".'

Fry and Horn were chalk and cheese, but the combination worked wonderfully well. Fry introduced Horn to New York records by Defunkt and James Chance and the Contortions, while Horn introduced Fry to the wonders of the recording studio. 'He gave us the keys to the candy store,' said Fry. 'Trevor would say to us: "If you want pizza, I'll get you pizza; if you want a string section, I'll get you a string section. Tell me what you want your records to sound like, and I'll try and help you." We both knew we didn't want ABC records to sound like anyone else. At least no one else British.'

Demos were made using a Mini-Moog, a sequencer and a drum machine, with the band recording over the top. 'It was like tracing, producing something electronically and then getting the band to copy it over the top,' said Horn. 'Which meant that we got it really spot on and snappy and in your face.' Fry, meanwhile, was the lonely mountaineer of the heart, writing arch love songs that were then turned into mini-epics by Horn.

'To me, ABC sounded like sophisticated dance music, but a lot of my friends heard their early demos and thought it was just disco,' said Horn.

'I said, "Listen to the lyrics!" The lyrics were like Bob Dylan, but we made the record the kind of Bob Dylan songs you could dance to. I suppose ABC basically wanted me to a make a record they could play in the local club they went to! They wanted it to compete with the American records they heard in their club in Sheffield. It was all about the sophistication of American dance music. But they were great people to work with because they were all bright guys. It really makes a difference when you work with bright people. They were intelligent and funny. Martin said that if I worked with them I would become the most fashionable producer in the world as they were the most fashionable band – and he was only half joking.'

Fry was only half right, because when they first started working together, his ambitions overrode his talent.

'When we started making "Poison Arrow", we got it to a certain point, and they were still sounding like an English indie band,' said Horn. 'I asked them if they were happy with it, or whether they wanted to make something better. They said better, so that's what we did, completely stripping everything out and starting from scratch. We made *The Lexicon of Love* sound American. By the time it was finished we'd already had hits with "Tears Are Not Enough" and "Poison Arrow", and the record company were waiting for the album. Even when it was finished I went back and remixed four of the songs because I didn't think they were quite right. We were trying to get it to sound as slick and as tight as we could, we were trying to get it to sound American. We spent so long on it that after a while I couldn't tell if it was any good or not. I was asking the guys in the white coats at the pressing plant if it was any good because I just didn't know any more.'

The Lexicon of Love was very much anti-rock (as all good post-punk needed to be), but also very much post-disco (acknowledging the importance of dance music but snootily making sure that everyone knew you were saying this for ideological reasons, not because you actually liked it – God forbid!). The record was the sound of the amateurs being produced by the professional, the rubes being marshalled by the professor, the broken-hearted guttersnipes being finessed within an inch of their lives. And, of course, this luscious, idiosyncratic dance music was juxtaposed with Fry's impossibly bleak lyrics. The subject? The illusory nature of love.

In very base terms, Martin Fry was updating Bryan Ferry and Roxy Music for the New Romantic era, transforming the charts in the process, by reclaiming the dance floor for the empathetic.

'Our music was definitely escapism, not just a generation sipping cocktails in a newly opened wine bar and voting for Thatcher,' said Fry. 'It was the opposite. This was a generation that had seen the Sex Pistols and the Clash and wanted to create something very different for themselves. We were definitely a product of the times – and I guess our music had a romantic edge, but I wasn't up there in a Pierrot outfit.'

So Fry was pretending to be Bryan Ferry, who to his generation had been pretending to be someone back in the Roaring Twenties. By the time Ferry became a man, the men he based himself on had long gone. By the time Martin Fry was pretending to be Bryan Ferry, the Roxy Music singer had almost ceased to exist, at least in any meaningful way.

What Fry and his band were trying to do was trade what little indie credibility they had for chart success. With Trevor Horn's opulent production, Anne Dudley's lush orchestrations and Fry's Elvis Costello-like wordplay, ABC announced themselves as a pop entity that took pop's history and legacy seriously. Some thought *The Lexicon of Love* was an overstuffed chocolate box of a record, while others thought it was rather too knowing; what it actually did was raise the competitive bar. Fry could certainly write. In 'Date Stamp', he managed to encapsulate the transactional nature of eighties romance into a single sentence: 'Looking for the girl who meets supply with demand.'

The band's image was not just all-important, it was crucial. As full-colour magazines such as *i-D*, *The Face* and *Smash Hits* started putting greater emphasis on the way groups looked, developing something sartorially original gave you an immediate entry point. If a band looked interesting in the pictures sent into magazines and newspapers, the editors would take notice. Nobody wanted moody punks staring at them any more. There was emotion, ambition and drama in the way the band presented themselves, as well as the way they sounded. ABC didn't have to dress up as country squires in order to promote 'All of My Heart', the fourth single from *The Lexicon of Love*, but by then their audience expected it. The conventions of their post-Oxfam, pre-Savile Row style were mutating to such an extent that if they had decided to embrace the whole *Brideshead Revisited* schtick (a TV adaptation of Evelyn Waugh's famous novel had been a big hit in 1981), no one would have been either surprised or concerned. *The Face* critic Jon Savage said the band had a 'knowing synthesis' and this applied to their style as much as their music.

The band wanted to look like they came from Las Vegas, so they went to Carnaby Street and hired a tailor who used to make clothes for T. Rex's Marc Bolan. He made a gold lamé suit for Martin Fry, and equally sharp evening attire for the others. The idea was to look as though they were in a film. The cover of *The Lexicon of Love* showed Fry as the hero of a racy fifties melodrama; the back cover revealed the fallacious nature of the picture: like the music, it was all an act. ABC proved that they were a commodity after all, a deliberate irony considering that a lot of Fry's lyrics treated love and romance as commodities too.

While some like to say that irony was invented by Plato, as far as the entertainment industry was concerned, it reared its knowing head in the mid-to-late eighties, roughly between the first sighting of Bruce Willis's smirk in *Moonlighting* and Jack Nicholson's ya-gotta-love-me grin in Tim Burton's *Batman*. Irony seemed the natural conclusion to most postmodern experimentation. And what wasn't to like? It was designed to be playful, funny, diverting. In terms of pop culture it had actually started much, much earlier, almost as soon as the eighties began, as each new pop genre made a nodding reference to the past. And you only had to look at ABC to understand just how tongue-in-cheek had become brass-in-pocket. Suddenly inverted commas were being put around inverted commas.

Actually, irony was purposefully the product of post-war leisure culture, but it only started to become annoying in the sixties, when an obsession with consumerism started to inspire comic book parodies and pop art metaphors. It was in the eighties that it really started to gather speed, though, when it quickly became an epidemic. It was in the music we heard on the radio, on television, in the shops, on our backs and in our bellies (are you trying to tell me that nouvelle cuisine wasn't ironic?). At one point Graydon Carter's *Spy* magazine devoted an entire issue to the problem, enthralling ironists in the eighties' register of socio-economic cults. To paraphrase the extraordinarily ironic eighties pop star Huey Lewis, it was no longer hip to be square, it was cool to be ironic.

Back then, 'irony chic' meant revival tours, Chevy Chase, Bill Murray, *The Monkees' Greatest Hits*, Paul Smith shirts (the 'classics with a twist'), illustrated socks, vogueing, junk fetishism, books such as *Roadside America*, vintage clothing, Homemaker dinner services, Jean Paul Gaultier, sixties Hawaiian shirts, Madras sports jackets - anything, in fact, that made a virtue of its archness or naffness. *Vanity Fair*'s James Woolcott - more than an expert on the subject - put it another way: 'It's the approach of postmodernists from David Letterman to David Byrne, putting ironic quotation marks around stupid so that "stupid" becomes smart. Kitsch is king - yesterday's obvious is today's pop sublime.' Once the domain of the cognoscenti, irony, like sushi, was everywhere. To hell with postmodernism, all we wanted was a snark and a smirk.

'"All of My Heart" for me was saying skip the hearts and flowers and wash your hands of this whole sentimental glop, you know,' said Fry. In this respect he was really no different from his hero, Bryan Ferry, who mined a similar vein back in the early seventies. But unlike Ferry, Fry wasn't a social climber, and neither were the band's fans.

'The look of ABC came from jumble sales,' said Fry. 'It came from going to shit bars full of old guys, in Sheffield and Manchester and thinking, God, there's a world out there somewhere, so a lot of it was pursuing a fantasy, a Vegas fantasy about what show business could be like. It wasn't on your doorstep, so you had to find it. When people think of *The Lexicon of Love*, they'll see the red velvet curtains. I really liked Jerry Lewis in *The Nutty Professor*, when he transforms, and I wanted that kind of feel. The reinvention. All those bands and all those musicians, they were seeking attention. It was escapist and there was a lot to escape from.'

. . .

One thing it looked like they were escaping was the Falklands. For three months in 1982, the UK was at war with Argentina over the sovereignty of the Falkland Islands, in the south Atlantic. The conflict began on 2 April, when Argentinian troops invaded and occupied the islands, ending on 20 June, when the Southern Thule Garrison eventually surrendered, and declared an end to the hostilities. The conflict acted as a flashpoint between Margaret Thatcher's supporters and her enemies – you were unlikely to waver in-between – making the bilateral political landscape in the UK even more pronounced. The optics of affiliation were as important in the entertainment industry as they were everywhere else, as to express any enthusiasm for the invasion immediately labelled you an enemy of culture. Critics on papers like the *NME* or the left-wing London listings magazine *City Limits* were quick to condemn, assuming that if you were a pop star who had enjoyed the trappings of success via the pages of *Smash Hits*, *i-D* or *The Face* then you were probably somehow complicit in the aggression. It might seem preposterous to think people would ever have been so facile, but in 1982, if you ironically wore a suit and tie (even a suit bought for less than the cost of a cocktail in a West End nightclub), you were automatically regarded with suspicion.

Having said that, there were many on the left who actually felt very gung-ho about the government's response to the invasion. I remember going to parties at the time when already quite famous musicians were grudgingly expressing their admiration for Thatcher, not that they would have dared say anything in public or in print. The Falklands immeasurably strengthened Thatcher's own position in the country, and in the Cabinet too. She was cast as the new Boudicca, even the new Britannia, ruling the waves eight thousand miles away from Downing Street. Her toughness in war had been vindicated, winning a new kind of supporter at home, some of whom even wore ironic suits and hats.

Martin Fry's nickname for ABC when they started was the 'Radical Dance Faction', a perverse disco band whose ambitions were mirrored elsewhere by the likes of the Pop Group and Pigbag in the UK, and James Chance and the Contortions, and ESG in the US. In their early days they would even issue manifestos: 'ABC represents ... respect for inbuilt obsolescence and inbuilt adolescence. A Technicolor flag. High-tech, low-tech, and discotheque. Respect for the single. Revolutions happen at 45 rpm.'

Cute. But ABC wanted to be popular with consumers outside the world of the *NME*, or indeed *The Face*.

'All the bands that came through just before and just after ABC – Duran Duran, Spandau Ballet, Depeche Mode – there was a whole generation itching to make dance music, populist music,' said Fry. 'I don't think it was any accident that all those bands became internationally known.'

In 1979, Fry had been to interview the band Vice Versa for his fanzine, *Modern Drugs*. He spoke to band members Steve Singleton and Mark White – 'They were kind of a fledgling Human League, only younger and less revered.' They were going on a train to Middlesbrough to open for Cowboys International; they didn't have a drummer but instead a holdall full of synths. Intrigued by Fry's interest, they invited him to stand onstage with them. 'We got bottled off by these skinheads who didn't get us. We were mohair sweaters and post-punk and ironic, but I loved it. After that, they let me join the band.'

Sheffield at the time was full of experimental bands: there was the Human League, Cabaret Voltaire, art school groups whose audiences tended to be other putative musicians. 'Sheffield was entirely subsidised,' said Fry, 'so you could get on a bus for 10p and go anywhere in the city. It was a great place to be poverty stricken and function. That's why the band was able to change and develop.'

With Fry on board, ABC's USP became blind ambition, having neither the expertise nor the ability to learn to play to the same standard as the people they admired, the polished musicians who played on hits by Chic, Kool and the Gang and Earth, Wind and Fire. In a way, what they aspired to was sci-fi music, because they were projecting into the future, trying to make music that actually wasn't achievable – not in the UK, anyway. Of course, using Trevor Horn's talents they got somewhere close to where they wanted to be, but then they would hear something that had been produced by Quincy Jones ('Stomp', for instance, by the Brothers Johnston), and realise how far they had to go. When Fry and the band eventually heard Michael Jackson's *Thriller*, which was probably the most sophisticated example of modern, polished R&B (as well as containing a near faultless example of what would one day become known as Yacht Rock, 'Human Nature'), they realised their dream of perfection had actually been realised by someone else.

The group were also worried as they kept hearing that other bands were trying to do something similar, fusing dance music with contemporary ideologies. Every week in the *NME* they would read about Spandau Ballet or Stimulin or A Certain Ratio or Duran Duran or someone else juggling art and funk.

'We were frantically writing songs,' said Fry. 'We wanted to be a step ahead. It felt like we were running to a place we wanted to be. I look back and it was like a mania. Everybody had their manifesto, and everybody had a big mouth back then. I used to do interviews and tell people we were going to conquer the world. It all boils down to wish fulfilment, making it a self-fulfilling prophecy.'

Fry believed he was like a boxer, like Muhammed Ali, psyching himself up for the battle ahead. 'It was mildly irritating when Gary Kemp said Spandau Ballet were the best band in the world, or when Simon Lebon said the same thing about Duran Duran. But then at the time we all said it, and we all believed it.'

'Tears Are Not Enough', ABC's first single, was a fairly decent stab at a musical manifesto, but the record wasn't as funky as they needed it to be, wasn't as slick as they wanted it to be, and so they solicited Trevor Horn in the hope of becoming slicker, more soulful, more, well, *sophisticated*. When they recorded 'Poison Arrow', the follow-up, Fry channelled Clark Gable instead of Johnny Rotten, thought Nile Rodgers rather than Mick Jones. And the result was better: it sounded like a song from the forties that had been made by a British band informed by both Chic and A Certain Ratio. But mainly Chic.

ABC may have existed in isolation, yet their influence started to seep as soon as they became successful. The Human League's Phil Oakey performed something of a volte-face after hearing *The Lexicon of Love*, signalling the end of the band's reliance solely on new technology. 'They've changed my opinions enough to say I don't even think we'll be doing all-synthesiser records any more,' he said. 'We can't just do it with the gimmicks of synthesisers. We've got to compete in the areas of great string sections [and] great horn sounds. Like they're doing.'

This was the push-me pull-you of modern pop in the eighties, a culture that zoomed forwards and backwards with alarming alacrity. One minute we were digging back into the past, the next we were pushing on into the future, or perhaps our old-fashioned idea of what the future might look like. The left started to paint all pop consumers as agents of the right, happy to absorb the gentrification of popular culture as though it were a malevolent way of turning us all into passive worker bees, our revolutionary spirit having been turned into a lifestyle. In truth, the likes of ABC were far more concerned with using their fifteen minutes of fame wisely, constructively, moving the culture along.

'The instant success was terrifying,' said Fry. 'We knew we'd stumbled across something – a vision of the pop future. One minute John Peel was phoning to tell us he was playing our single, the next we were off to Studio 54 to meet Andy Warhol.'

Fry and his band were caught in the headlights, and they were stronger than they had imagined.

One of the journalists who had advocated New Pop was the *NME*'s Paul Morley, and he kept a close eye on how the market was changing.

'Things were intellectually and spiritually tightening up inside the iron grip of Thatcherism, and at the same time loosening up economically and socially,' he said. 'Music magazines turned glossy, gossipy and colourful, requiring new sorts of fairytale cover stars, a backlash against the highfalutin weekly inkies containing thousands of intense words about Cabaret Voltaire. All New Pop then made by those interested in being the latest thing had to be influenced by punk, if just the look, the clothes and the expression. One consequence was an experimental sonic elaboration of punk's ideological spirit and aesthetic vision but a rejection of the safety-pinned visual cliché; this became known as post-punk. Another consequence was more theatrical, with dandy tabloid-labelled New Romantics looking back longingly over the spiky heads of the harsher, angrier punk to the showy costumes and window dressing camp of glam, when pop stars looked like pop stars. Some groups could float, sometimes self-consciously, sometimes serenely, between those two camps – Human League, Japan, Depeche Mode, ABC – and others occupied a more purist, thoughtful zone, advocating mental glamour – Gang of Four, New Order, Associates, Magazine, the Smiths.'

'ABC seemed to be appreciated both by *Smash Hits* because we were popular, and by the *NME* because of what we were trying to do,' said Fry. 'We played the A to Z club in Bayswater some Sunday night, and a lot of journalists from the *NME* were there prior to us getting a recording contract. I think one of the reviews, maybe by [*NME* hack] Ian Penman, said our songs were like the lexicon of love, and that's where the title of the album came from. The beautiful thing about selective memories is that you remember the good stuff, but there was a lot of stuff around at the time that we didn't like. To be honest, Duran Duran and Spandau were better at the *Smash Hits* stuff. It was hard to do that stuff with a smile on your face.'

It wasn't that Fry was deliberately aloof, he just felt that what ABC were doing was on a different plane. 'It was never like a pop community. But we were very competitive. It was like the Premier League, where there are only four places to play Champion's League football. And it's only one act that can get to Number One. That's how I saw it. There was also competition between north and south, although in the end everybody ended up in London anyway. If you are really honest, as soon as you have success, it's not so regional, is it? You're all in the lounge at Heathrow having a drink.'

Those who never warmed to ABC found them shrill and devoid of genuine emotion, just like the other torpid excesses of the decade that were starting to make themselves apparent elsewhere. The apotheosis of this kind of eighties culture would be Julien Temple's 1986 disaster movie *Absolute Beginners*, the high watermark of ironic/meta cool, starring everyone from David Bowie and Patsy Kensit to Sade and Lionel Blair, the old song and dance man. It was meant to be the film that validated the decade's much-maligned designer culture, although it would go down in history as the film that almost destroyed the British film industry. Based on the famous novel by Colin MacInnes, Temple's glorified pop promo attempted to hold a mirror up to the eighties as well as to 1958 (the year in which the book is set), and overloaded his cinematic version of Soho and Notting Hill with so much hipster fizz, it quickly became Exhibit A in the case against the eighties as the decade of all style and no content. The few who championed the film felt it simply suffered from the same ailments as Francis Ford Coppola's *One From the Heart*, namely an inability to marry the narrative with its grandiose surroundings. Everyone else just thought it was a self-conscious mess. Hyper-stylised, forced, but bristling with colour and pace, it was very ABC. Perhaps we should have known: in 1983 Temple directed an equally stilted secret agent spoof for the band called *Mantrap*. It was, in a word, terrible.*

Like many acts at the time, ABC put a huge amount of effort into their promos. 'Every video was a one-day shoot,' said Fry. 'And that one day would last forty-eight hours.' The band threw themselves into them, taking great care with the storyboarding, the clothes, the performances and the shoots themselves. 'The record companies weren't pressuring anyone to look a certain way. That came later. For "The Look of Love" we wanted to cross the visual style of Benny Hill with *An American in Paris*. I don't think Kurt Cobain would have put on a striped blazer and sung to a wooden crocodile. There's a parrot on my shoulder at one point. We were

---

* The eighties was the first decade in which promo videos became as important and as memorable as the records they were advertising. This means that music from the decade is now so interlinked with the promos directed for them that often it's difficult to remember one without the other, which often does the music a huge disservice. Rarely would a video be invested with the kind of thought and expertise that went into the record they were promoting. They would often have panache and an obvious sense of cool, and yet they were sometimes so reductive they made the records themselves seem inconsequential. This is certainly true of ABC, because while their music still seems clever and timely – for its time – the videos make the band look like even more of a commodity. In one way, ABC were designed as an ironic commodity, and yet their videos manage to diminish them to such an extent that they call into question the reason for making the records in the first place, amplifying the wrong kind of irony.

'I looked on YouTube and found myself watching the promo video [for "I'm on Fire"] in which Bruce Springsteen plays a mechanic flirting with a dame with an expensive car,' says the music journalist David Hepworth. 'Like almost all videos, it's kitsch and absurd, demeaning the song by making everything explicit. I interviewed him around this time. In those days, videos were still novel and you always asked questions about them. I remember he said he struggled with them because you either had to illustrate the story of the lyrics, which seemed a bit obvious, or impose an entirely different narrative on that song, which seemed unsatisfactory. Of course, nobody really minded because they were a way you could reach audiences. They were adverts. I wonder if that's the reason why so much music from the eighties gets no respect.'

pushing it to the limit, seeing how embarrassed we could get. Art is what you can get away with.'

The band made the mistake of not believing their own publicity, and instead of following up *The Lexicon of Love* with something similar – which is what everyone at the time wanted – they changed tack completely by making *Beauty Stab*, a hard-edged record that appeared to – rather sullenly, actually – deflate everything they had built with *The Lexicon of Love*. Their fans quite rightly felt insulted. Just because Martin Fry didn't want to wear his gold lamé jacket any more didn't mean they all had to follow suit. So they didn't.

'It had all started to get very competitive, with Culture Club, Duran, Spandau Ballet, all the big bands,' said Fry. 'When it was time to record *Beauty Stab*, we wanted to work with Trevor Horn again, but he was back working with Yes. He took me to meet Malcolm McLaren, but then we decided we wanted to change our sound completely. Now is that arrogance or naivety or both? We saw David Bowie reinvent himself, and film directors did it all the time, so why not us? Bowie did it in increments in a funny kind of way and he wasn't always successful. It's all there in the song "That Was Then but This is Now", which was the first single from *Beauty Stab*. But the reception to the album really shocked me, and not in a good way. It was a disaster.'

'After *The Lexicon of Love* I had the opportunity to work with ABC again, but the thought of working with Malcolm McLaren was just so enticing,' said Horn. 'Malcolm played me something in our first meeting and it totally blew me away. He had some scratching sampler, which I had never heard before. Scratching! Imagine. When he said the DJs pull the needle across the record I was like, get the fuck out of here, really? I suggested he might want to produce ABC, but we went our own way.'

The follow-up to *Beauty Stab* wasn't all beer and skittles either. For 1985's *How to Be A ... Zillionaire!*, Fry reinvented the band yet again, this time as cartoon characters (his idea was a kind of post-modern Archies). The music became electronic (which by then seemed in itself somewhat retrogressive), and their counter-intuitive social commentary just looked out of step with a decade that was already getting used to its inconsistencies. Again, Fry had misinterpreted the market, as he later conceded:

'It seems stupid to have to describe it as that now, but that's very much what we were trying to do,' he said. 'Electronics and cartoons. It was all about deconstructing what a successful pop group was at the time, leaving no trail. All the band members were animated, and this was decades before Gorillaz. But I don't know, would it have been better just to have been in Status Quo or something? I do look back upon those records we made in the eighties with some pride though, because some of them have stood the test of time. It would have been better to go out in a blaze of glory early on, but instead we got longevity. What came afterwards I call the flatpack years, where I spent most of my life in IKEA. One minute I'm in Shoom dancing on a podium and the next minute I've got kids and I'm in the queue on Tuesday morning returning the flatpack furniture that I can't put together on Monday night. The Shoom and Hacienda membership cards had been replaced by B&Q, and it's like that lovely Duran Duran song "Ordinary World", it's like suddenly after ten years there's a world out there, and that's what it was like for me.

'I loved the eighties, though, loved *The Lexicon of Love*, loved working with Trevor Horn, and while a lot of people accused us of fiddling while Rome burned, I don't actually subscribe to that, as a lot was improving around us, a lot was opening up, a lot of things were becoming more liberal. Clubs were leading the way - when you went to Area in New York it was like a utopia, it was like a way of saying it doesn't matter if you're gay or straight or black or white for a couple of hours. These days you'd probably be accused of cultural appropriation, playing funk, playing R&B, but in the eighties that wasn't the case, as it felt as though people were becoming united. You know, George O'Dowd wearing dreadlocks, does that mean he's trying to become a Rastafarian? No, he was showing people what the future was about. Maybe that's an over-exaggeration, but that's what I felt.'

While the diamond dust was swept up long ago, and though Martin Fry's gold lamé suit probably languishes in a dry cleaners in a forgotten postcode somewhere, ABC's moment of glory lives on in the hearts of the formerly afflicted (lovelorn, circa 1982), on Spotify, and in the grainy, third-generation promos you find on YouTube. The aura of the band's specific magic persists, a band who, albeit fleetingly, recast the landscape of the Top Ten.

All Martin Fry had really wanted to do was jazz up the torch song, from the safety of his own personal Hollywood musical set in an imaginary nightclub in the sky. A pretend jaded lounge lizard, he channelled his own version of Bryan Ferry to a new constituency that a) had never heard of Roxy Music, b) had deliberately forgotten about them, or c) were too preoccupied to notice the similarity.

'I'm enormously proud of *The Lexicon of Love*, as it's a great record conceived by a great many people,' said Fry. 'It was a wonderful collaboration. Every molecule was conceived. It's very focused, so each bar something seems to happen lyrically, melodically or sonically. I was really into the barbed love song. I loved Joy Division's "Love Will Tear Us Apart", as I thought that was like a revolutionary Sinatra song. When Ian Curtis hung himself it was a tragedy, not just personally, as I thought they were going to go on making records like that for ever. I suppose we were doing the same thing simultaneously. "The Look of Love", "Poison Arrow", "All of My Heart", they are love songs but there's a lot of hate in them. I suppose we were trying to give the love song some dignity. I loved Sinatra, and all those wonderful songwriters like Sammy Cahn and Jimmy Van Heusen, and it just felt right not to be singing about electric pylons – other people could do that.

'There was a lot of material about the future at the time, but ours was a more emotional future. That's what *The Lexicon of Love* is about. It did seem shiny and brand new at the time, but it could almost have been a country and western album. When we did "All of My Heart", we demoed it and it was like a country and western song. In the sense that it's a bit of a tearjerker but obviously we wanted to make it sound more grandiose, widescreen and cinematic. That was the name of the game.'

In essence, *The Lexicon of Love* is a retro concept album about the death of love. Fry's character was surrounded by everything that popularly represented pleasure, and yet none of it had the effect it was meant to have. He was in torch song torment, and he wanted us all to know. Here was desire, love and disillusionment, pretty much in that order.

Listening to the record, you sensed Fry was deliberately lost, immersed in a common chaos of signs, emotions and sensations, and somehow detached from it, too. He avoided easy sentimentality by favouring images over confessions, using his wordplay to paint pictures that painstakingly showed how heartbroken he was.

· · ·

ABC would leave a mark on my life, although not in the way I expected. As a boy I'd often casually thought I'd like a little Action Man scar, a straight one-inch cut lying diagonally across the cheek. Nothing scary or particularly disfiguring, just a small battle scar, something to indicate I'd been around.

Later, in my teens, I briefly considered a tattoo, but luckily realised that self-inflicted scars didn't carry the same cachet (while the girl who would have been the subject of my inking soon disappeared from my life). By the time I was twenty, I didn't want either.

Then, all of a sudden, I didn't have any choice.

It happened towards the end of 1981, on a cold November Saturday night (everything seemed to happen on a Friday or Saturday night back then) in a London dead zone, just behind Kings Cross, an area which at the time seemed resolutely immune to any kind of gentrification. There was my Belgian friend, Pascal Gabriel (who would soon become a record producer), future Swing Out Sister singer Corinne Drewery, plus our friends Jill and Stella, and some other girls whose names I forget.

It was around 11.30 p.m., chucking-out time. We'd just fallen out of The Hemingford Arms, where we'd been all night, and were on our way to a party down the road. All night we had been playing ABC's 'Tears Are Not Enough' on the jukebox. We alternated between 'Tears' and Elvis Costello, Dollar and Pigbag, but it was ABC who we found the most intriguing. They were modern (or at least had been relentlessly championed by the *NME*), they had soul (or what we were rapidly understanding was a new kind of European soul), and they appeared to understand fashion, or more accurately, 'dressing up'. How could a gang of fancy-pants Motown-friendly art students not like them? I've no idea whose party it was we were en route to – no one ever knew in those days; you just pitched up and clocked in, a six-pack of something or other swinging in a plastic carrier bag. As we strode along, five girls and two boys, searching for street numbers, seven or eight lads in their late teens came towards us, shuffling along the pavement. They were wearing training shoes, tracksuits and floppy fringes: soft shapes disguising hard fists, hearts and minds.

When they got parallel, one of them punched Pascal hard and full in the side of the face. I turned around and started towards him as the girls stood in fright. But before I'd taken two paces I was kicked from behind and pushed onto the road. Someone immediately jumped on my back. I was too drunk to be scared, and the adrenalin was pumping so much that I wasn't really aware what was going on. I knew the situation was dangerous, but the only logical thing to do seemed to be to punch and kick as hard as I could. Which I did.

But then I felt something sharp and wet in the back of my neck, swiftly followed by something similar in the middle of my back. I was being cut – slashed, stabbed, call it what you like – with what felt like a cut-throat razor (having never been stabbed before I wasn't sure about this – but I soon found out). I didn't feel pain, as such, just shock. Because I could tell that my skin had been broken in at least three places.

My mind raced as the actual attack seemed to unravel in slow motion. And the sounds from the pub kept whirling around my head – jokes, Pascal's command of the English language, the rush for last orders, words pouring out of the jukebox ... Tears, souvenirs ... 'Tears are not enough ...'

I responded immediately, jumped up, threw the tracksuited troll off my back and sprinted fifty yards down the road, following the girls, only turning round to make sure he wasn't following. And as I turned, I saw the razor dangling in his hand. He stood and stared at me, legs spread, chest pounding. Seconds later I was running towards Kings Cross with Pascal and the others, the pumping blood in my head blocking out the ricocheting plastic soul of ABC.

We ran for what seemed like ages, and then stopped. There was a fuss, of course, because no one knew if I was badly cut. I still couldn't feel much, and I didn't think I was in serious danger but as I couldn't see the wounds, I began to worry.

Hell, Hunter S. Thompson had said it plain enough once: 'It is one thing to get punched in the nose, and quite another to have your eyeball sprung or your teeth shattered with a wrench.' Violence takes a great leap when it involves daggers, knives, barstools, or indeed wrenches.

For me, being stabbed was enough. I was inspected: I had been slashed on the back of the head and right along my spine. Neither cut was particularly deep, though the one in my back was bloody and long enough (six inches) to cause alarm. We eventually made it to the party, where I was inspected some more (at the time it didn't seem so bad with half a dozen girls staring at my half-naked torso in a small kitchen), and where it was decided that I should be taken to hospital.

Although the stabbing had sobered me up somewhat, I was still drunk enough to be cavalier about the whole thing. I was wearing a brand new silver-grey zoot suit, and made a big deal of the fact that it was ruined, and how it had cost me over £100 and so on. We had joked in the pub that I looked like a cut-price Martin Fry, as my suit wasn't a million miles away from ones he was wearing at the time. His was gold, and mine was silver, which I suppose had a certain logic to it.

And so off we went to hospital. Pascal with his (considerable) bruise, the girls still with a Waitrose bag of Holsten Pils, and me with my torn suit, wounded ego and bleeding back.

As I sobered up in casualty, it soon sank in how potentially serious the situation had been. I should have been scared; if I had been sober, I would have been petrified, and frankly would have been worried if I hadn't been. I can't remember whether or not I gave the police a statement; I probably did, but none of us was under the impression that anyone would ever be caught, let alone prosecuted. I do remember getting a tetanus jab in the backside (which was inordinately more painful than anything else that night), and over a dozen stitches. Waiting to be discharged, I tried getting drunk again, but by now my heart really wasn't in it. When I thought about the attackers, it was in the abstract – I didn't know them, and certainly couldn't remember what they looked like. They were out for blood, and mine just happened to be in the vicinity. The attack was territorial and was in many ways predictable: we were walking through the wrong part of town at the wrong time wearing the wrong kind of clothes. Shit, as they say, happens.

I made a point of going out the following night, knowing that I was unlikely to get stabbed again, or, come to that, have my eyeball sprung, or my teeth shattered with a wrench. Thankfully, I was right, although for years, that part of Islington remained one of my least favourite parts of London. And as for ABC, whenever I hear the synthesised strings, over-produced drums and plaintive, heartbreaking lyrics of 'Tears Are Not Enough', 'Poison Arrow' or 'The Look of Love', I think of running down a Kings Cross backstreet in a silver suit, with blood pouring from my back.

1983

How Does it Feel?

'Blue Monday' by New Order

One of the most influential songs of the decade was hatched in the nightclubs of New York in 1981, when New Order started to envisage what it would be like to fill a dancefloor with their own Mancunian version of electronic pop. They saw an opportunity and, in the process, completely reinvented the very idea of indie, and the very idea of electronica, made with an Oberheim DMX drum machine (in an age when buying a sequencer would cost the same as buying a semi-detached house). In doing so, New Order brought about a direct change in our relationship with pop, being an imperfect, mordant convergence of rock and dance.

'New Order emerged from crashes of Joy Division playing a music that was the missing link between Kraftwerk and everything electronically great that came afterwards, and overcame the loss of their lead singer by, in a way, replacing him with space, and time, the time and space you find, beautifully, between electronic beats.'

– Paul Morley

'"Blue Monday" was the one,' says New Order's singer Bernard Sumner. 'I remember someone coming up to me and saying, "What have you done? It doesn't sound like New Order." It was such a radical move, but the thing was, at that particular time, there was an opportunity to do something new with music. Such a shift only comes along very, very rarely. Rock'n'roll in the fifties was probably the last real seismic shift. There's constantly been reinterpretations, but not seismic shifts. Electronic music, dance music - that was a seismic shift.'

117

If the opening snare-shot of Bob Dylan's 'Like a Rolling Stone' can immediately evoke the sixties – like a flare, conjuring up images of sun-drenched insurrection all over America – so the stuttering drum pattern that introduces New Order's most famous song can just as quickly whisk us back to the early eighties, when electronics were still genuinely transgressive, and when the cultural centre of gravity was very much in Manchester rather than either New York or Los Angeles.

In 1983, New Order's drummer Steven Morris had brought an Oberheim DMX drum machine to the studio where they were recording the song, but as they were still relative amateurs in the world of electronics, they couldn't get their sequencer to talk to it. After various trials and errors, one of the engineers designed a circuit that could make them speak to each other, and it started chattering away.

'Rob [Gretton, New Order's manager] thought it was witchcraft,' said the band's guitarist, Bernard Sumner. 'He really did, he really thought it worked by magic.'

In some ways, he was right. It was magic ... magic straight from the future.

The journey from 1981's 'Ceremony', the first New Order record – which was really the last Joy Division record – to 1983's 'Blue Monday' was a transformative one, taking them from concrete underpass guitar rock to a weird electronic melange that had its roots in a variety of esoteric dance tracks, including Sparks's 'Beat the Clock' and Sylvester's 'You Make Me Feel (Mighty Real)' – from raincoats to ironic sequins in a twenty-four-month scoop. Being at a Joy Division gig was a bit like being in a huge Lowry painting, surrounded by stooping young men with intense looks, choppy fringes and Doctor Marten shoes; New Order, however, always attracted their fair share of tearaways, and their gigs were often raucous affairs, with their fair share of fights. Many of which were caused by 'Blue Monday'.

For a band who are so closely associated with the austere idealism of the post-punk years, it is also interesting to note that the inspiration behind 'Blue Monday' chimes in part with *The Wall* by Pink Floyd. When Floyd toured the album, a twelve-metre wall of cardboard bricks was gradually built between them and the audience, before collapsing at the end of the show. This gave the impression the band had disappeared, which was not a million miles away from the concept behind 'Blue Monday'. When playing live, New Order tended not to do encores, as they felt the process was corny and old fashioned. 'We respected our audience too much to have them waiting around like mugs for us,' said bass player Peter Hook. Bernard Sumner just thought they should add another song to the set list. Everywhere they went, their audiences reacted the same: they were disappointed, irritated, and gigs often ended in violence. So, the band came up with the idea of recording a largely instrumental song that could be played instead of them having to do an actual encore. The band would walk onstage, press 'play' and then immediately leave again.

'It was done because we were sick of people asking us to play encores, so the idea was to get the machines to play the encore while we were drinking in the dressing room,' said Peter Hook. 'What happened was that it turned into a great song – not our best song, I might add, but it turned into one.'

'We were trying to create a sort of Frankenstein-monster song,' says Morris. 'Where you just press a button and the song comes out.'

'"Blue Monday" was meant to be robotic, the idea being that we could walk on stage and do it without playing the instruments ourselves,' says keyboardist Gillian Gilbert. 'We spent days trying to get a robot voice to sing "How does it feel?", but somebody wiped the track. Bernard ended up singing it.'

'We always thought encores were a bit predictable, and a bit of a fake,' says Sumner. 'The two things we made a point of not doing when we started out was signing autographs and playing encores. We caved in on both in the end because we realised it was harder work not signing autographs and then explaining to people why, than to actually sign the autographs in the first place. It would take five minutes to explain it and ten seconds to sign the autograph.

'When we started not doing encores, we ended up having fights and riots at some of the shows. After a riot in Rotterdam the promoter had to put a sign up outside telling people we didn't do them. We had another one in Boston. People were outside throwing stones at us. The next morning I got a call from Mo Ostin, the President of Warner Brothers, who we'd just signed to, asking me what the fuck was going on. So we started doing encores, but the concession was "Blue Monday". As all this technology was becoming available, we thought it would be possible to write a song, and then just go on, press a button and walk off, and the machines will play the song. That was the idea. But then of course my vocals and Hooky's bass got in the way. So actually it probably would have gone down worse than not doing an encore. It was a terrible idea. Interesting, but terrible. The gear would have either got trashed or stolen. Very conceptual.'

Joy Division were something of a concept themselves. Bernard Sumner and Peter Hook formed the band after seeing a Sex Pistols concert at Manchester's Lesser Free Trade Hall on 4 June 1976. 'I walked out of that gig as a musician,' says Hook. 'I came home with a guitar and told my dad, "I'm a punk musician now," and my father said, "You won't last a week." Ever since a young age I've been an avid reader of the music papers and my escape during work was reading them. I was reading about all these heavy metal bands, Led Zeppelin and Deep Purple, but I never felt inspired by it - it seemed so untouchable. I kept reading snippets about this group called Sex Pistols and all they seemed to do was fight at their gigs. I saw the advert in the *Manchester Evening News* and said to Barney [Sumner], "We've got to go and see this band, they do nothing but fight." There was a lot of football violence then, [and] it felt like the working-class world I was used to as a lad from Ordsall and Salford.'

The group they formed - along with Morris and vocalist Ian Curtis - they called Warsaw, a reference to David Bowie's song 'Warszawa' (from his album *Low*). While their first recordings were heavily influenced by early punk, they soon developed a sound and style that made them one of the pioneers of the post-punk movement. To avoid confusion with the London punk band Warsaw Pakt, the band renamed themselves Joy Division in early 1978, borrowing the name from the sexual slavery wing of a Nazi concentration camp mentioned in the 1955 novel *House of Dolls* by Yehiel De-Nur, writing under the pen name Ka-tzetnik 135633.

With their clipped, industrial noise, and their sombre, icono-clastic image - grey, dour and unsmiling, and soon to be photo-graphed, somewhat iconically, by Anton Corbijn - they became darlings of the critics, and after a while could do no wrong. Their first album, *Unknown Pleasures*, was proclaimed a masterpiece by any music critic who valued their reputation (or their job).

Unbeknown to most people, Curtis's health was starting to be a concern. He suffered from epilepsy, and had started to experience bouts of depression. In May 1980, Joy Division were scheduled to start their first North American tour, although Curtis was worried about how American audiences would react to his illness. The evening before the band were due to depart for the US, Curtis returned to his Macclesfield home to talk to his wife. The couple had been experiencing marital problems, and that night he asked her to drop an impending divorce suit. Later, he asked her to leave him alone in the house until he caught a train to Manchester the following morning. Having spent the night watching the Werner Herzog film *Stroszek*, Curtis hanged himself in his kitchen.

The tour was cancelled, the band went into freefall, and as Sumner recalls, the remaining members were on the verge of splitting up.

'Obviously we were all pretty upset and, it has to be said, depressed after Ian passed away, and we could have done with a helping hand,' says Sumner. 'But we didn't get a helping hand, we got slagged off. For some reason the press started hating us. These were desperate times for us. We'd all given our jobs up, and after Ian died the future looked really bleak. We were just on the cusp of success when Ian died, and we had to start all over again. Year zero. And Rob [Gretton] insisted we play no Joy Division songs. Ethically we thought that was a very good standpoint. He said we shouldn't become successful on the back of Joy Division, you've got to make it yourselves and write new material. So, ethically, good, but possibly commercial suicide. We could have done with a bit of support from the press but we didn't get any. We didn't feel like we had a cat in hell's chance. So it made me angry, and I reacted to that.'

So Sumner stopped reading the press completely. The band's press agent sent him a batch of press cuttings once, and when he started reading them, he thought, 'My God, they really hate us, and if I read any more of this, I'm going to give up.' So he stopped reading anything about the band.

'I stopped reading any interviews that I did. And just sort of got on with it. Instead of using the press as a mirror, we used the audience as a mirror. The press might have been slagging us off, but the audiences were loving us. So you're going to listen to the people who love you, aren't you, rather than the people who hate you, otherwise you might as well give up. It turns out the press were wrong and the audience was right. So it was a sweet victory when "Blue Monday" became so successful.'

None of the band exactly warmed to the press. Around the time 'Blue Monday' was released, they were interviewed by Dave Rimmer for *Smash Hits*, then the biggest pop magazine in the world, although not one inclined to take New Order particularly seriously, and the band knew it. When Rimmer turned up to interview them in a Manchester bar, he said afterwards that he'd had to endure endless in-jokes, interruptions, a lot of time wasting and a general reluctance to take even the simplest of questions seriously.

'Try this ...' wrote Rimmer. 'What was Australia like [the band toured there in November]?'

'Warm.'

'Is the material on the new album similar to "Blue Monday"?'

'Listen to it and find out.'

After Curtis's death, Joy Division were on the verge of breaking up, but it was Gretton as well as pride that made them persevere. After Curtis died, Sumner was listening to stuff like *Berlin* by Lou Reed and the soundtrack to *A Clockwork Orange*, Eno's *Music for Airports*, 'moody music'. He was in no mood to start again, until he was persuaded to revive the band's US tour, this time as New Order (a name chosen by their manager after reading a story in the *Sunday Times* about a Cambodian rebel group, and not, as many believe, another Nazi reference). Sumner was also concerned about the band's ability to soldier on, as a lot of what they recorded after Curtis's death just 'sounded like Joy Division without the singer. It seemed pointless to ape Joy Division because we'd never be Joy Division again.'

There were obviously many conversations about whether or not they should continue at all.

'In September 1980, we were due to do a small tour of the Eastern Seaboard and record "Ceremony" and "In A Lonely Place", two songs we'd written just before Ian died,' says Sumner. 'We thought that by writing new material we could cheer him up and get him back, but I don't think "In A Lonely Place" was the kind of thing to play to someone who was suicidal in the first place. But we were in New York with [producer] Martin Hannett and Rob Gretton, and there were just the three of us - me, Steve and Peter Hook [Gilbert had yet to join], and of course the road crew. But after we'd finished in the studio, all of our equipment was stolen, so then we had to go out and hire lots of gear for the tour.'

While they were waiting for their new equipment to arrive, they went out. Every night. Their tour promoter Ruth Polsky would take them out to the likes of the Peppermint Lounge, Danceteria, Paradise Garage and the Mudd Club. Sumner can vividly recall the feeling he had on that trip, standing in all these clubs and thinking, 'Wouldn't it be great if they were all dancing to us?'

Fundamentally the band were being exposed to the kind of dance music they'd never heard at home, including specially prepared mixes of dance tracks. 'DJs would play an eclectic mix of music, including a lot of British music mixed in with rap and soul. The DJ would play something for everyone. You could also get into these clubs wearing trainers – you couldn't back in Manchester. The crowd was younger, cooler, easier going. Not posy cool, nice cool.'

It was a Damascene moment for all of them, and on their return to Manchester, they started experimenting like fury with electronics. They first used a drum machine on the song 'Truth' on the *Movement* album, recorded in the spring of 1981 with a Boss Dr-55 Doctor Rhythm. They then recorded 'Everything's Gone Green', using pulsed synthesisers for the first time.

'The first practice run was "Everything's Gone Green",' says Sumner. 'We'd been hearing this electronic sequencer music and I was a bit of a techno head. We were in the studio with Martin Hannett once in London, doing a bit of writing, and Steve plugged a little Doctor Rhythm into this Oberheim synthesiser, triggering a synthesiser through a drum machine set to a disco beat. The sound is actually a hi-hat. And that's when we fell out with Martin.'

Both Sumner and Hook say they learnt a lot about producing simply by watching Hannett, and when they started to find him too difficult, they just took over themselves. 'With the pig-headedness of youth we just said to Rob Gretton, "Me and Barney will do it, don't worry about it,"' said Hook. 'And so we did.'

'He [Hannett] would sit at the mixing desk and ignore us, basically,' says Sumner. 'He'd tell us we didn't know what we were fucking talking about. Then he'd turn the air-conditioning up to try and force us out of the control room. Lots of tricks like that. We wanted a more aggressive sound, and the sound he was delivering was too wispy and ethereal. We wanted something that would hit you between the legs. We badgered him so much that in the end he said, "OK, you two do it," and he went to bed. Which was perfect. The engineer told us we didn't know what we were doing, but sometimes some of the best ideas come about when you don't know what you are doing.'

Having their equipment stolen meant they had inadvertently cut all ties with their past, and they were able to replace it with machines and computers that were going to take them deep into the future. Sumner and Morris had started building their own equipment, as the kind of machines they wanted to use were just too expensive to buy.

'The sound was in our heads,' says Morris, 'but the machines were barely capable of doing it. The future was happening, but often it sounded a bit shit.'

'Me and Steve started making machines,' says Sumner. 'We had three synthesisers, one of which I'd built from an electronics kit, back in the days of Joy Division. We also had a little music sequencer that I'd made. I was aware that there was this new music out there, but to make it you really had to have a lot of money. A decent synthesiser could cost you twenty-five grand. A Roland micro composer was completely out of our reach. We couldn't afford to buy them so we built our own. We also wanted to play this kind of music live, which no one was doing.'

When they started to use their new equipment live, none of it was connected. Sumner would say to their technicians, 'We've got this drum machine, we've got this synthesiser and we've got this sequencer, but they're all ignoring each other.' All they needed, they said, was something to make them all communicate with each other.

Their tech team eventually found a solution to the problem, although the wiring was so precarious that one of them had to accompany the band on tour to make sure every plug went in the right socket.

'That made a man of him,' said Peter Hook. 'As soon as he went off to look at trams it would all go fucking wrong. The best was with the Emulator. We were constantly phoning up asking if they'd found the precise spot you had to hit the bastard with a hammer to get the fucking disc to load. Then our roadie came up with the idea of, if you took it off the stand, dropped it on the floor, picked it up and put it back on the stand – it would work. That was our fucking technological language! Basically, the great thing was with us, it was like they do with cars – you were the road tester.'

The next step was making 'Temptation', with its rippling sequencer riff, and in Sumner's case, an introduction to LSD.

'There was a band on Factory [Records] called Section 25, and I used to go and hang out with them at weekends,' he says. 'One weekend was particularly heavy, because someone had brought some LSD to the party. I knew I had to be back on Monday for rehearsals for the song, so even though I was in a bit of state on Monday, I made it. I remember driving down the motorway and all the cars on the other side of the road turned into bananas as they went around a bend. Anyway, I managed to hold it together, and then wrote the kernel of the song. I apologised for being late, but I made up for it by having an idea.'

This period is what Sumner later started calling New Order's 'pounds, shillings and pence year'.

'The vocals were written later in London, at Advision Studio near the Post Office Tower,' he says. 'I didn't have any words so I just made them up as I went, two lines at a time. It was in the middle of winter, and it had just started snowing outside. If you listen to the original 12-inch of the song, you can hear halfway through a lot of laughing and yelling, and that's when Rob went outside to get a snowball, and then came back and shoved it down my back while I was singing.'

With its haunting 'green eyes', 'blue eyes' and 'grey eyes' refrain, the song was often used in the dressing room after a show as a seduction tool. In the days when it was still an instrumental, when they played it live, lyrics would be ad-libbed. Hook says that Sumner would sing things like 'I've got a cock like the M1.'

Throughout this period, the band continued experimenting with electronics. Sumner was also fuelled by radio and club tapes sent from friends in Berlin and New York.

'When we used to record, we would meet and just talk about what we were watching on TV, what films we were watching, what music we were listening to, what books we were reading,' says Sumner. 'We would all talk, and when we eventually got bored, we started recording. And because you were bored, it came out of the air. Joy Division was like that too. It wasn't contrived. You just had to wait for the moment and you could tell when the moment was right. We just waited for something to fall out of the air.'

Their next record didn't so much fall from the sky as assemble itself in the studio with them. As the band kept making it up as they went along, they sometimes felt like chemists, using found elements in an attempt to create something completely new. And sometimes the machines did it themselves, completely by accident.

'Blue Monday' bridged the gap between rock and dance culture, not just because of what it sounded like, but also because it was only issued as a 12-inch, meaning it was designed specifically for the dancefloor. Many post-punk groups had tried to be 'funky' by using choppy guitars and changes in drums tempos, but they were just nibbling around the edges of the culture. New Order were actually changing it into something completely new. This was dance music for rock people, a cultural reset.

There were few bands who had changed so radically in such a short period of time. When they released 'Ceremony' in 1981 they still sounded like Joy Division, and yet barely eighteen months later they were already on their way to being considered genuine dancefloor mavericks. They even looked different. In Joy Division they had all looked like submarine commanders, distinctively austere. In New Order they wore shorts on stage and even occasionally smiled. This was a deliberate attempt to move even further away from the cold, cold image they had cultivated as Joy Division.

In their early classic photographs their demeanour is stoic, sullen almost, their look inspired in part by Kraftwerk.* But New Order were different.

'Blue Monday' was written (more like created) in the band's dingy rehearsal room in Cheetham Hill, in Manchester, which had a graveyard piled up in the back of it. Sumner always remembers the tea tasting pretty odd because of the water in the kettle. 'I said to Steve one day, "I'm sure something from those graves is leaking through into the water pipes ..."'

In essence, 'Blue Monday' was the pinnacle of Sumner's electronic learning process, a journey that for him as a consumer had started with Giorgio Moroder records back in the late seventies, and as a composer and musician had started with 'Truth'. The whole band were on the same journey, and yet it often felt as though Sumner was steering, leading the way. Having built all these homemade machines, and having accumulated all this equipment and all this knowledge, he knew he ought to be putting it to good use. Although none of the band expected this latest experiment to be quite so successful.

By drawing all their influences together they embarked on an epic recording process that would result in a song that was more like surrealist sculpture than a conventional recording. There were influences from records old and new, from those tapes sent by friends in New York and Berlin, the hi-energy sounds they'd heard in London's Heaven nightclub, on some of their reconnaissance trips to the capital, plus of course from the band's own field research in the clubs of Manhattan.

All they had to do now was use their own experience to fuse these disparate elements together, or rather to wrap them around the noise they were going to make themselves. No longer were they inching away from Joy Division's sonic gloom – they were running. At speed.

---

* Kraftwerk rarely smiled in their pictures, and compounded their anti-rock image by wearing suits. They were encouraged to do so by founder member Florian Schneider after seeing Gilbert & George in 1970.

'Blue Monday' is actually something of a jigsaw puzzle, put together from a wide variety of different sources, and wildly different influences. There is no need to complexify its construction, as it was genuinely eclectic. The drilling bass drum sound was an attempt to emulate Giorgio Moroder's computerised pulsations on Donna Summer's 'Our Love', while the electronic bass line was inspired by Sylvester's 'You Make Me Feel (Mighty Real)'. Then there is the haunting choral wash that runs through much of Kraftwerk's 'Uranium', Peter Hook's appropriation of *For a Few Dollars More* for his live bass, and the overall sound which was based on the dance remix of Klein & MBO's 'Dirty Talk' and 'E=MC²' by Giorgio Moroder.

It starts, of course, with the rapid gunfire drums, followed by the curling synth melody, monastic chanting, an angry guitar, synth strings and more, with every element building and building to a far from inevitable conclusion. The song begins with the kick drum intro, programmed on the Oberheim DMX drum machine linked to a little Powertran 1024 Composer sequencer Sumner had built. Morris programmed the beat, adding some frills along the way. The song's throbbing synth bassline was played on a Moog Source, followed by some strings courtesy of an Emulator sampler.

As they started recording, there were a couple of happy accidents that affected the recording, but which the band decided to keep. The first day's work was then erased by a faulty cassette, meaning they had to record it all again. Peter Hook's bass lead was one of the last things to be recorded, along with Sumner's vocals, using some hastily written lyrics. Soup to nuts, the recording took forty-eight hours.

'When the Oberheim turned up, that was the first time we'd had a proper programmable drum machine, which was exciting in itself,' says Sumner. 'I'd had this idea for the beat, this bub-a-bub-a-bub-a-bub-a-bub-a-bub-a-bub ... At that time I was a bit of a human sponge, and in various clubs my ears were always open. I'd been to see a band and there was a delay on the drums, which I knew we could use. I thought, "That's interesting." Then

129

I heard the Donna Summer record ["Our Love"] and I thought, "I'll have that."

'So I got the drum machine, and showed it to Steve, who programmed the basic beat in. I wanted it to be like this engine that drove the whole track. I wanted the drum machine to be the engine, and the other instruments attached to it would be the gears. Everything was interlocked. Apart from the strings. Then we did the vocals, and then Hooky came along and played his bass. It was like a machine to dance to, really. Which was very interesting because I didn't dance.'

'Blue Monday' was made by post-industrial progressive-rock musicians from an alternative label bringing together what no one had really thought of before: thinking beats. They were fusing heads and hearts.

'It's not really a song, as such, the way I see it,' says Sumner. 'It's more of a machine that sounds good on club systems, a huge machine that's bigger than any record. It was more like a bag of sounds than a song. I'd also been working with a group called 52nd Street, who were on Factory, who were like a punk outfit, and I'd been doing some synthesiser stuff for them, helping them out production-wise. And I played a couple of gigs with them. I started hanging out with them, and gong to clubs, funk clubs I suppose. In one club, Legends, it was the first time I'd ever heard sub-bass, bass that you could feel rather than hear. It was a whole new frequency, and it was a whole new type of dance music. So when I say a bag of sounds, you had the sub-bass, then you've got the DMX bass drum, which is very clicky, and not very bassy. Then there was my new synth, a Moog Source. My previous synth, a Pro-1, you had to reprogram after every song on stage, and it was a real hassle. Resetting all the knobs for a different sound. The Moog Source had memory buttons on it, so you could program sixteen different sounds with sixteen different buttons. It turns out it was probably the best bass synth you can buy on the planet. It was accidental really, as I hadn't bought it for that reason. I had to keep my finger on the sequencer at one point, in order to get the sound I wanted, but I made a mistake and it was out of time. But it sounded funky so I left it in. "Blue Monday" is full of happy accidents that helped us on the way.'

There were so many sequences in the song that Gilbert created a huge colouring-in chart, just in case the sequencer broke and they needed to reprogram it all. 'She spent hours colouring it in,' said Hook, 'like being at a really long meal in Pizza Hut with the kids.'

'The synthesiser melody is slightly out of sync with the rhythm,' says Gilbert. 'This was an accident. It was my job to program the entire song from beginning to end, which had to be done manually, by inputting every note. I had the sequence all written down on loads of A4 paper Sellotaped together the length of the recording studio, like a huge knitting pattern. But I accidentally left a note out, which skewed the melody. We'd bought ourselves an Emulator 1, an early sampler, and used it to add snatches of choir-like voices from Kraftwerk's album *Radioactivity*, as well as recordings of thunder. Bernard and Stephen [Morris] had worked out how to use it by spending hours recording farts.'

'There's a staple sound that you got on a disc with the Emulator, which is very Kraftwerk-like,' said Hook. 'In those days, it was very difficult to use a sampler. On the Emulator you didn't have to [sample the sound] as it came with it, otherwise we'd have had to do a tape loop, which is what you did in those days to sample.'

'It sounds corny now, but imagine looking forward at "Blue Monday" rather than looking back at it,' says Sumner. 'I remember being really impressed with it. I wanted to make music like Giorgio Moroder but with less commercial vocals. Something with a bit more intelligence. And then take it out and play it live, then we could be doing something really avant-garde.'

Sumner's voice was hesitant, diffident and strained, almost as if he's singing a guide vocal, a roadmap to be improved later. Juxtaposed with Hook's bass melody, and the synthetic pulses of the machines, Sumner sounds positively out of sorts. He was 'a small-voiced singer trudging across great expanses of bass and drums' according to one critic, although Hook says the struggle in Sumner's voice was a major part of the band's appeal.

'There was definitely an awkwardness about "Blue Monday",' says Sumner, 'but that's what made it so strong.'

Hook was disappointed with Sumner's lyrics, thinking aloud how better they might have been had Ian Curtis written them.

'People think that the lyrics are about journalists continually asking us questions about Ian's death, but that's not actually true,' says Sumner. 'The lyrics aren't about journalists, they're about a mood, they're describing my mood. It was a feeling of anger. Anger is an energy. In those days the music press constantly had their knives out for everyone. It wasn't just us. It was hip to slag people off. So we were all in a very dark place, and very hurt from Ian passing away. We were also struggling with Martin, who was getting into harder and harder drugs. And things seemed hopeless. We were fighting for air. But we did it.'

As for the title, it was Morris who came up with it. He had seen it the year before, when reading Kurt Vonnegut's 1973 novel *Breakfast of Champions*. ('It said, "Goodbye, Blue Monday",' said Gilbert. 'It was a reference to the invention of the washing machine, which improved housewives' lives.')

When did they know it was finished?

'We didn't,' says Sumner. 'It was an experiment.'

The finished track was seven and a half minutes long, which is the reason it was initially only available as a 12-inch. While there would eventually be a five-minute 7-inch version, the 'ultimate gadget odyssey' only ever worked at its full length. It was like an aural movie, and unlike most extended 12-inch remixes – which tended to simply take chunks of the original track and repeat them, often in a dub version – 'Blue Monday' twisted and turned like an electric eel, deliberately complex and constantly surprising.

If the length of the song was extravagant, it had nothing on its packaging. The original sleeve was one of the most expensive ever produced. It had three holes punched in it, designed by Mancunian creative director Peter Saville to look like a floppy disk, as the Emulator used floppy disks, which is where he got the idea from. Saville wanted to celebrate the fact that the record had been constructed using computerised equipment. However, the die-cut process of punching the holes meant that the band actually lost money on every copy they sold. And as the initial 12-inch sold around 500,000 copies, this cost the band over £50,000. 'Steve Morris was always really tickled by the fact that the thing that cost the money was the thing you didn't get – the bits of paper that were taken out,' said Peter Hook. 'Tony [Wilson] celebrated by giving us all a big brass plaque.'

Writing in the third person, in *24 Hour Party People*, the book adapted from the screenplay of Michael Winterbottom's film about Factory Records and the Haçienda (the Manchester nightclub Wilson and New Order co-owned),* Wilson said, 'Peter picked up his first floppy and fell in love. Of course. Wilson knew he had his single sleeve now. And he fell in love with Peter all over again, 'cause this record company stuff was just so much fun.'

'The first time I realised it was becoming successful, was when I was working in a recording studio in Manchester producing another band,' says Sumner. 'Tony Wilson came along. You always took whatever Tony said with a pinch of salt. He had a big grin on his face and he said, "So I've got some news about 'Blue Monday'." He said, "Do you want the good news or the bad news?" I said, "Well, I'll have the good news first." He said, "Well, the good news is it's flying off the shelves, selling like hot cakes, and exceeding all our expectations." Then he said, "The bad news is ..." and then he started laughing, uncontrollably. Then he

---

* The Haçienda opened in 1982 in Whitworth Street West and, despite considerable and persistent financial troubles, survived until 1997. The club was mainly supported by record sales from New Order. The name comes from a slogan of the radical group Situationist International: The Hacienda Must Be Built, from *Formulary for a New Urbanism* by Ivan Chtcheglov. The comedian Bernard Manning opened the club on 21 May. 'I've played some shit-holes during my time,' he told the crowd, 'but this is really something.'

said, "We're losing money on every copy we sell." I went fucking mad, and started screaming at him: "We do our bit, and then you cock it all up!" And then when I asked him what was costing us all the money he said it was the holes in the sleeve. So basically nothing was costing us the money.'

Saville himself has been rather defensive about the sleeve, blaming logistics and circumstance. 'I'd been to see the band in the studio and Stephen gave me a floppy disk to take home,' he told the *Guardian*. 'I thought it was a beautiful object. At the time, computers were in offices, not art studios. The floppy disk informs the design and the colour coding was from my interest in aesthetics determined by machines. It reflected the hieroglyphic visual language of the machine world. For example, the numbers in your cheque book aren't really for you, they're for a machine to read. I don't know if the story about the label losing money on the cost of the sleeve is true. I sent the cover straight to the printers because everyone was in a hurry. I doubt the printers even gave a quote for Factory to respond to. The band had handicapped themselves as no one was likely to play it on the radio because it was seven minutes long. Ironically it sold a lot, and with an expensive sleeve.'

The reaction among critics wasn't as fulsome as one might have imagined, however, as many of them were still smarting from the fact that New Order weren't Joy Division Mark II. Some of the press behaved in a similar way to the audiences in the mid-sixties when Bob Dylan went electric.

Musicians understood it though. The record seriously upset Neil Tennant, as it pre-empted the various ideas he and Chris Lowe were developing for the Pet Shop Boys. 'We thought, "No one else is doing gay disco, no one is doing New York hip-hop with white vocals." When "Blue Monday" came out, I more or less burst into tears.' Another story involves the Eurythmics' Annie Lennox and Dave Stewart being in a cab on the way from the studio having just completed their new album. Apparently, when 'Blue Monday' came on the radio, Stewart put his head in his hands and ordered the driver to take them back to the studio. 'We're going to have to start it all again,' he said. Kraftwerk - who were the standard by which every amateur British electronic band measured themselves - were so fascinated by 'Blue Monday' that they spent months deconstructing it, even visiting the studio where it had been recorded. 'They couldn't believe we had made it with such cheap equipment,' says Sumner.

'Blue Monday' actually charted twice, the second time because that summer it had been a massive hit with holidaymakers, who when they went into record shops on their return often asked for 'New Order' by Blue Monday.

'It was a bit like the Coronavirus, really,' says Sumner. 'It came along and made a big impression, and then there were rebounds. Every year when people went on holiday, to Spain, or wherever, people would come back and buy it. There was a resurgence of it every year.'

Radio 1 wanted them to cut it to three minutes, while *Top of the Pops* put a lot of pressure on Gretton to release a 7-inch version so the band could appear on the show - but predictably they refused. Their compromise was playing live, which turned out to be something of a disaster. After they appeared on *Top of the Pops*, the record actually went down ten chart places, which was unheard of. 'We were delighted, as we were punks,' said Hook. 'That's what it was all about: giving it to the man, you know?' That might have been the objective, but Hook's mother also gave it to the man when she saw him a few days after the broadcast. 'How could you?' she asked, rhetorically, as she cuffed him around the head. 'Chewing on *Top of the Pops*. I've never been so ashamed!'

Later in the year, the producer Bobby Orlando paid the band the ultimate compliment by using the track as the blueprint for his production of Divine's 'Love Reaction'. To their credit, New Order themselves acknowledged this when they started to cover Orlando's song live.

The record had a long afterlife. It was remixed by Quincy Jones in 1988 ('Which was very flattering to say the least,' said Hook), and was a hit all over again. The same year, Sunkist offered the band a figure north of £100,000 to record a special version of 'Blue Monday' for a TV commercial. The ad campaign proposed ridiculous new lyrics ('When you're drinking in the sunshine, Sunkist is the one ...'), and when they finally decided to record it, whenever Sumner was on the verge of laughing, someone from Sunkist would hold up a large piece of card with the sum of money written on it. They finished the session, but hated the result so much they shelved it. Considering how much money they lost on the Haçienda during the eighties, it's extraordinary to think that they turned things like this down. But punk principles are punk principles. They were once offered a £150,000+ sponsorship deal by Swatch, but couldn't cope with the idea of having a fifteen-foot watch on the side of the stage. They were so unrelentingly uncommercial, they even refused to sell T-shirts and merchandise at gigs, instead allowing other people to do it.

Then, at the height of the craze for mash-ups, Kylie Minogue mixed 'Blue Monday' into her performance of 'Can't Get You Out of My Head' at the 2002 Brit Awards, later releasing it on the B-side of a single: 'Can't Get Blue Monday Out of My Head' (which New Order then sampled themselves onstage at Coachella in 2005).

The song just wouldn't go away, nor will it ever.

'"Blue Monday" was the moment when everything clicked,' says the *Guardian*'s Alexis Petridis. 'A song without a chorus, on which the closest thing to a recognisable hook was the juddering drum machine pattern, which proved commercially unstoppable.'

The record remains the biggest-selling 12-inch of all time, and was recently voted the best party single by a thousand DJs in *Mixmag*. 'For three tossers from Salford to have pulled that off and still have an impact today is amazing,' said Peter Hook.

'I think its slightly dated, from my point of view,' says Sumner. 'It still gets people on the dancefloor, though. I was in a club in Berlin recently, and everyone was standing around, chatting, having drinks, and then the DJ put "Blue Monday" on, and absolutely everyone moved to the dance floor. Everyone. I still love playing it live because people respond to it so strongly. When we play it at gigs the atmosphere changes, it's like at a football game when a striker scores.

'It was anathema to many people when we did "Blue Monday", as they said it didn't sound like New Order. What the fuck's this? You know. But you've got to be brave, and have an open mind. This wasn't a record for the narrow-minded. It wasn't even something we were going to repeat. When we were in New York writing "Confusion", the next record after "Blue Monday", we wanted it to sound very different. "Blue Monday" was always a European sound, and "Confusion" was far more of a New York sound. We were spending a lot of time in Puerto Rican clubs in New York, and so the record we ended up making sounded very different to "Blue Monday".'

It is also not the kind of thing New Order can ever leave out of a set list, at least not by design. According to a Peruvian journalist who interviewed Sumner a few years ago, if the band were ever going to return to Lima, and didn't play 'Blue Monday', they would be lynched. The journalist wasn't smiling when he said it, either.

'We did Glastonbury once and forgot to put it on the set list,' says Sumner. 'We left the hotel in Shepton Mallet, and as everyone was hungry we decided to go to a fish and chip shop on the way to Glastonbury. There was a huge queue, so by the time we got to the festival we were late, there was only five minutes before we were due to go on stage, and everyone was panicking. And someone did a set list, we went on, did the gig - it was all right, not great - and then about half an hour later in the dressing room, I said, "Did we play 'Blue Monday'?" And then we realised we didn't. Imagine playing Glastonbury and forgetting to play "Blue Monday"! That's brilliant!'

Throughout the noughties, the war of attrition between Hook and Sumner started to escalate, and after a while Hook eventually left. There remains great enmity between them, but the things they share will never fade. 'Blue Monday' is one of the most important examples, one of the greatest and genuinely most influential records ever made.

'I do feel affection for the song, as it gave us life,' says Sumner. 'It turbo-boosted our career. Or at least my vocation. It's almost impossible to reinvent. If we have songs now that don't work, we remix them and make them sound more contemporary, but you don't need to do that with "Blue Monday". It is what it is, and you can't really change it. In that respect it's a bit like Glen Campbell's "Wichita Lineman".'

'I thought the songs we wrote around it were better,' Hook told the *NME*. 'I thought "Temptation" was a better song, especially live. I thought "Everything's Gone Green" was better. And I thought "Thieves Like Us" was far, far superior. But "Blue Monday" has a sonic impact that very, very few records have. It really was a gift, and it was quite ironic - and quite sad, really - that we stole it off a Donna Summer B-side. It is a weird song. It's become one of Manchester's greatest records. We were very lucky to write "Love Will Tear Us Apart" as Joy Division, which was a staple Manchester record, and then "Blue Monday" with New Order. We got one with each band, fantastic!'

'I think "Love Will Tear Us Apart" connects with people because of the emotional content within the song, and I think "Blue Monday" connects with people because of the startling lack of emotional content within the song,' says Sumner. 'It's kind of contradictory, really. I think the way that everything in it is synchronised, so it's like all these different gear cogs meshing together, and each synthesiser part is like a different gear - it all comes together like clockwork. If I could properly explain it, I'd write another one! But that's the beauty of music, there's no method to it.'

'When you're younger you can say it's a bloody albatross around your neck, but that's what people know you for,' says Morris. 'Don't knock it. I think it's great.'

'"Blue Monday" is, a lot of the time, my favourite piece of pop music by my favourite group,' says Paul Morley.

Can you hear it now? As those familiar opening drumbeats start thumping, drilling in a vacuum, and as the rest of the record gallops to keep up, so the clouds begin to part, the Haçienda hoves into view, and we're suddenly back in Manchester in the bosom of 1983.

Seriously, how does it feel?*

---

* With age comes ubiquity: One Sunday morning, as I was finishing this chapter, I asked my 21-year-old daughter if she liked 'Blue Monday'. She said she hadn't heard of it, so I played it for her. 'Oh yes, I know this. It's in every film ever made, ever.'

1984

The Postmodern Virgin

'Like a Virgin' by Madonna

This year, the Bowie reinvention blueprint got a novel twist in the form of a mediocre bar dancer who couldn't sing and couldn't write songs. But she was called Madonna and she wanted to be famous. And the eighties was the decade which embraced people who wanted to become famous, regardless of whether they deserved it or not. Madonna deserved it, obsessed with the idea of being remembered for her music, rather than as a human tornado. 'Like a Virgin' made her famous, but by no means defined her.

'I always thought of losing my virginity as a career move.'
– Madonna

New York in October 1984 was as intoxicating as it had ever been. Given the way in which the city was developing, with a surge in skyscraper construction and electronic billboards springing up in the least expected places, Manhattan was starting to look like a 3D animated version of itself. An MTV version of itself, with music pouring out of every flat surface, out of every car, every store, every ghetto blaster you passed on the street.

There were two records in heavy rotation that month: the club monster 'Loveride' by Nuance (which could be heard whenever you visited the likes of Danceteria, Area or Limelight, the three hot clubs of the moment), and Madonna's 'Like a Virgin', which was two weeks away from release, but was literally everywhere, bruising the downtown sidewalks, the midtown department stores and the walls of nightclubs from the Bronx to the Battery.

The New York streets seemed to be bristling with energy, flooded with electricity. Bristling with people, too: the increasingly deified graffiti artist Jean-Michel Basquiat, hot club entrepreneur Haoui Montaug, trendy filmmaker Jim Jarmusch, and the legendary Andy Warhol everywhere you looked. Every night there was the opening of a new nightclub, a book launch, a private view somewhere scary downtown. Even the hip hit movie of the day was a New York movie, Jarmusch's decidedly skewed *Stranger Than Paradise*. Creativity seemed to be pouring out of every disused tenement in the city, every pop-up supper club and cocktail squat.

While parts of Manhattan were still dangerous and in disarray – visitors were strongly advised to avoid no-go zones such as (pre-gentrification) Alphabet City, Hell's Kitchen and even parts of the West Village – New York suggested it had reacquainted itself with its mojo. The city had built its reputation on the fact that it never slept, proud that it was a twenty-four-hour town. At any point in the day or night, you could eat, drink, hail a cab, check into a hotel, order sex, hire a car, or go dancing. It was the kind of city that prided itself on being able to offer breakfast and blow jobs at any time of the day or night. And never more so than in 1984.

New York in the eighties was the perfect city for Madonna. Loud, ambitious, constantly changing, but built to last. Mischief seeks its own level, which must go some way to explaining her success at the time. During her career, Madonna would make a virtue of encompassing every female contradiction from suburban sex kitten to lap-dancing virgin, conjuring career options like a hydra-headed hyphenate. Her life, when it started to become successful – both on stage and off – resembled a multi-media freak show, part pop performance and part Broadway extravaganza.

In 1984, gossip swirled around Madonna like dry ice. All of a sudden she was the biggest show in town, and everything she had ever done was suddenly a story.

She was born Madonna Louise Ciccone to Catholic parents Madonna Louise and Silvio Anthony 'Tony' Ciccone in Bay City ('a smelly little town', she called it), Michigan, in 1958. 'How could I be anything else but what I am having been named Madonna?' she asked, rhetorically. 'I would either have ended up a nun or this.' After her mother died when Madonna was five, and unhappy with her father's new wife, she spent as much time rebelling as she did on her dance classes (as a girl she copied dance moves from Shirley Temple on TV). When she hit puberty, her rebellious side naturally came to the fore. Like many an entitled teenager, eventually she grew tired of her obscurity, and started acting as though she had suddenly found herself in a race against time. In the end the inertia of her tiny, Midwest world was all she needed to break free ... and move to New York. All she thought to herself was, 'Why did I wait so long?'

She left Michigan in 1978, moving to Manhattan, to the junction of Fourth Street and Avenue B, to try and make it as a dancer - she was a very good dancer, everyone knew that - already burning up with impatience and frustration. When she finally arrived in New York, she starred as a dominatrix with three slaves in a dodgy 'art house' film called *A Certain Sacrifice*, and posed for some 'erotic' photos. She got a job at Dunkin' Donuts and a scholarship at the Alvin Ailey dance school until she got fed up with what she called 'all those little, horrible, ballerinas'.

She had a fixity of purpose: she wanted to be really famous. (By 1965, Bob Dylan had become so famous that he naturally worried about being found out. Madonna had no such fears.) And after a few false starts, that's what happened. She hustled, danced a bit, sang a bit, hustled some more, and tried desperately to break into worlds that for a while just didn't want to know. She went out every night, hoping to be noticed by the right people, often wearing her BOY TOY logo belt. In her head she was the next Debbie Harry, the next New Wave Bad Girl.

Consequently, her life became one big publicity stunt. Of course, you could say that there is nothing more conventional than youthful non-conformism, but Madonna turned it into an industry. She knew she wasn't a great singer, but she also knew that this didn't really matter. In lesser hands, Madonna would have simply felt unfinished, but she knew she could fix whatever she wasn't so great at; all she needed was a break. After performing as a

drummer in the Breakfast Club, as a guitarist, and finally as a vocalist in a band called Emmy, she eventually signed to Sire Records,
a subsidiary of Warner Bros. Records, in 1982, who released her
debut album a year later.

And even her signing soon became a thing of legend.

In the summer of 1982, forty-year-old Sire Records founder
Seymour Stein was sequestered in the Lenox Hill Hospital on New
York's Upper East Side the first time he heard Madonna. The man
who had famously signed both the Ramones and Talking Heads had
a variety of wires and tubes pouring out of his body because of a
heart scare (he had been diagnosed with subacute endocarditis, and
had a massive hole between his ventricles). He was also plugged
into a Walkman, listening to demo tapes to while away the time,
which is when he first heard Madonna singing a rough version of
what would eventually become her first single, 'Everybody'.

'I liked the hook, I liked Madonna's voice, I liked the feel, and
I liked the name Madonna,' he said.

Stein called the DJ who had given him the tape – Mark Kamins,
who worked at the soon-to-be-legendary club Danceteria, as well as
being Madonna's boyfriend – to ask if he could meet the singer. Just
a few hours later, she was sitting by Stein's hospital bed, hoping
he would last long enough to offer her a contract.

'The thing to do now,' she said, ignoring the drip in Stein's arm,
'is sign me to a record deal.'

It seemed Stein had no choice, not that he was going to let her
slip away.

It would turn out to be one of the most important deals in
Warner Bros. Records' history. Over the next eighteen months,
Madonna would become the biggest star of the decade.

Madonna was the ultimate rebel, but a girl instead of a boy,
the cool wisecracking, gum-snapping girl with the sullen eyes,
ripped tights, dime-store wristbands, and go-to-bed-maybe-just-
been-to-bed hair. In the early days, she was the downtown Holly
Golightly we all saw in *Desperately Seeking Susan*, the film she
started making in 1984: the free-spirited downtown party girl in

her black fishnets, the girl described by the legendary film critic Pauline Kael in the *New Yorker* as 'an indolent, trampy goddess'. We shouldn't forget that the first time we see Madonna in the film, she's lying on the floor of an Atlantic City hotel room, taking Polaroids of herself.

'She doesn't want to live off camera,' Warren Beatty said of her, when they were dating later in the decade. 'Why would you want to say something if it's off camera?'

Not only did she become famous, she became notorious. If Marilyn Monroe – one of the American icons who was referenced whenever Madonna was mentioned by the press – had a reckless innocence, Madonna had a kind of brazen connivance. Madonna took Monroe's hair, style and clothes, but subtracted her vulnerability. There was nothing innocent about her, and she also had no interest in pretending otherwise. She knew she was the sum of her parts, even if those parts weren't especially exceptional. She even made her tummy a star, giving the American midriff the kind of exposure it hadn't had since the fifties, when two-piece bikinis became a sexual placebo ('I have the most perfect belly button,' she said). A nation of teenage girls copied her, baring their bellies in the name of cool. Her body parts were just as important to her success as any talent she may have had.

'My favourite button is my belly button,' she said to the man at *Penthouse*. 'An inny, and there's no fluff in it. I never wore a jewel in my belly, but if I did it would be a ruby or an emerald, not a diamond. When I stick my fingers in my belly button, I feel a nerve in the centre of my body shoot up my spine. If a hundred belly buttons were lined up against a wall, I could definitely pick out which one is mine.'

Elvis Presley learned to market his hips because he was made aware he had an ability to. It was the same with Mick Jagger's lips. Madonna didn't really have anything to speak of, so she made it all up. Her belly button, underwear as outwear, sex, *whatever*.

She said she wouldn't be happy until she was as famous as God, and although it was easy to treat the veracity of the quote with suspicion, because Madonna was meant to have said it, you kind of assumed it was true.

And because she went around saying things like 'Manipulating people, that's what I'm good at,' we took her at her word, perhaps distrusting her motivations in the process.

Like many sex symbols before her – her influences included everyone from Clara Bow to Debbie Harry, via Rita Hayworth and Joan Crawford – she positioned herself at the vanguard of contemporary erotic taste, being both alluring and formidable at the same time. Not only was this a combination that was hard to ignore, but also one that photographed well. Madonna reclaimed crotch-grabbing for women, taking it away from Mick Jagger, Robert Plant, David Lee Roth, even Michael Jackson, and giving it back to the girls. Hers was a celebration of women taking ownership of their sexuality, a proper empowerment. She made no secret that there was a difference between her ideal man and the men she was sexually attracted to. Men for her were either sex objects or conduits to power. And not much else. (She certainly didn't entertain weakness: a former publicist once explained, 'She smells fear like a dog.')

The remarkable thing was that the music industry allowed itself to be shocked by her. The public, too. Just what was it about her? After all, her appeal was really no different to the appeal of Frank Sinatra, Mick Jagger or Debbie Harry or Marilyn herself: half the population who expressed an opinion wanted to look like her, and half wanted to sleep with her. And a minority obviously wanted to do both.

The difference with Madonna was that she had total self-possession. She wasn't anyone's adjunct, she wasn't a plus one. She was all about Madonna. Yes, she had the ability to conform to what the media expected of her, but she was simultaneously pulling away from it. Hers was an unapologetic sexuality, an assertive sexuality, a sexuality that was all about power and fulfilment. Her fulfilment. She was never the co-star in a relationship. She *was* the relationship.

Not that she wasn't generous. As a *New York Times* writer once said, because Madonna treated the genders and other people's identities as fashion, she made those identities seem fashionable.

Identity was a game that no one played better than her, and she made a point of exploiting the media's fascination with same-sex relationships time and time again; yet she was happy to shine a light in the dark recesses of the culture, which in the eighties still marginalised sex, race and transgression.

The eighties allowed Madonna to be the greatest advocate for herself, but when she had a mind to, she became an advocate for so much more, namely a woman's right to act in any damn way she wanted to. Which, in 1984, was something which was still considered a radical notion.

'A woman fearlessly expressing herself and saying, "I'm encouraging all of you to be independent, to speak your mind, to express your sexuality freely without shame, to not allow men to objectify you, to objectify yourself,"' she said. 'I don't know, all of those things seemed like the natural way of where we should be going. And strangely, a lot of feminists criticised me for it, and I got no support from that group. They thought, well, you can't use your sexuality to empower yourself as a female, which I think is rubbish, because that's part of who I am and part of me as a female and a human being, my sexuality.'

She refused to be trapped by her own image, or by the media's apparent ownership of it. She was here to liberate herself, to liberate women in general. Soon she would become ring-fenced by her financial security and economic power, which in turn supercharged her cultural dogma. Still, she was vilified for being too uppity, too strident, too female. She refused to be defined by the criticism or by her own failures. Consequently, she has never been portrayed as a tragic figure: given her failed marriages, her dodgy films and her imperious nature, it would have been easy to frame her as a fallen star, but her image wouldn't wear it.

For a while she was criticised relentlessly for being a generic star, where in fact there had been nothing and no one like her before. She invented the blueprint for how successful women in the entertainment industry could conduct themselves: by seeking power and by keeping it. She became a moral agent, espousing gay rights, publicly seething over inequality, speaking out against racism, celebrating female physicality, being an advocate for tolerance, a pioneer of girl power. The common perception of Madonna is someone who moulded herself to suit society, whereas in reality she did precisely the opposite, changing society to suit herself.

People often call David Bowie influential, and yet he was really anything but. A band like Free or Led Zeppelin were far more influential, because they were responsible for thousands of four-piece bands wearing flared jeans and tie-dye T-shirts playing loud, masculine rock. Bowie was unique, and his influence was one of emancipation, not style or form. Madonna was genuinely influential as she created a role for herself that had never existed before, at least not in the music industry. If Debbie Harry was an ironic Monroe play, Patti Smith deliberately occupied the margins, ditto Siouxsie Sioux. Joni Mitchell and Kate Bush were extraordinarily gifted writers, while the likes of Barbra Streisand, Cher and Diana Ross were copper-bottomed entertainers.

Madonna was something else completely, being the first female pop star to not only project an image of control, drive and independence, but the first female pop star to truly own them too. Without her, there is no Spice Girls, no Beyoncé, no Lady Gaga, no Lana Del Ray, no Rihanna, no Lizzo.

Madonna didn't look like a prom queen, a *Playboy* model or a TV news anchor. She appropriated tough-boy style, throwing in a bit of cheese and a lot of attitude. She was baby-doll grunge before there was baby-doll grunge. She was a flower-child vamp, a student dominatrix, the carnal tomboy. In the beginning she pretty much defined the Valley Girl look, which was odd, as she had nothing to do with San Fernando: with her torn leotards, net tops worn over black T-shirts, clumsy shoes, clunk bracelets, hairspray, heavy make-up, and – of course – an exposed stomach, she could have been mistaken for a mall rat.

Then she switched it all up, and switched it all up again. She pretended to masturbate with a crucifix, told anyone who would listen she wanted fame and money. She popularised brassieres, bustiers, corsets, garters, and a whole bottom drawer of lacy dainties. The widely held view that Madonna made up for a lack of vocal ability with an avalanche of self-promotion is one she has never contested. Good taste has rarely been her companion, but she never gave a stuff for good taste anyway, being far more interested in street-style experimentation. She's also never been fallible, never had any kind of breakdown, always come out on top (even when the records have been so-so).

And in 1984, with 'Like a Virgin', she became Her Madgesty.

. . .

Her debut album, *Madonna*, had confounded the industry, as there was no apparent reason for its success, other than the sheer popularity of its hits. The critics, who in 1984 still thought they had the power to make someone successful, were perplexed. But it was the desecration disco of 'Like a Virgin' that first made her a star. After having three big hits with 'Holiday', 'Borderline' and 'Lucky Star', it was the first song from her second album that made all the difference. 'Like a Virgin' was the song that gave her a real global platform. It wasn't written by Madonna, wasn't even chosen by Madonna, in spite of it being the one song that most people still associate with her. It was written by the songwriting duo Tom Kelly and Billy Steinberg, who would also go on to write 'True Colours' for Cyndi Lauper, 'Eternal Flame' for the Bangles, 'I'll Stand By You' for the Pretenders and 'I Touch Myself' for the Divinyls.

Kelly and Steinberg had taken the song to Michael (son of Mo) Ostin at Warner Bros., in the hope he might want it for one of his artists. At the time, the industry's money was on Cyndi Lauper being the decade's breakout star, so there was a lot of pressure on Warners to deliver a killer second album for Madonna. Stein loved the song, as did Madonna, when it was suggested she record it.

Musically, Madonna did what the decade was allowing her to do, using mechanical dance affiliations to sell straight pop, exploiting the dance floor for her own purposes, making it up as she went along; she knew that as long as she stayed current, as long as her records sounded like the kind of bright, shiny pop that people were expecting, she was fine. And 'Like a Virgin' was bright, shiny pop.

While she might not have chosen the song, she chose everything else about it. She knew she wanted her new album to be produced by Nile Rodgers – not least because he had just reinvigorated David Bowie with the monumentally successful *Let's Dance* – wanting to blend his street smarts with her own. Initially Rodgers didn't think the song had a sufficient hook, but changed his mind when he realised he couldn't stop humming it.

His singer, meanwhile, knew what was good for her. Asked by *Rolling Stone* about her first impressions of 'Virgin', and her other big hit from the album, 'Material Girl', she said, 'I liked them both because they were ironic and provocative at the same time, but also unlike me. I am not a materialistic person, and I certainly wasn't a virgin, and, by the way, how can you be *like a virgin*? I liked the play on words; I thought they were clever. They're so geeky, they're cool.'

She knew a good thing when she heard it. 'When Madonna recorded it, even as our demo faded out, on the fade you could hear Tom saying, "When your heart beats, and you hold me, and you love me",' said Steinberg. 'That was the last thing you heard as our demo faded. Madonna must have listened to it very, very carefully because her record ends with the exact same little ad-libs that our demo did. That rarely happens that someone studies your demo so carefully that they use all that stuff. We were sort of flattered how carefully she followed our demo on that.'*

'Like a Virgin' bounces along, almost in perpetual motion, the beat stretching out in front of itself almost like one of those

---

* In 1989, Steinberg and Kelly both received invitations to attend the fiftieth birthday party of Freddy DeMann, the co-founder of Maverick Records, and at the time Madonna's manager. Previous to this, the pair had never met Madonna, even though they'd written her breakthrough global hit. At the party, Stephen Bray, who had also collaborated with Madonna on some of her early songs, introduced them as the writers of 'Like a Virgin'. Steinberg smiled and said, 'I've wanted to meet you for so long.' Madonna gave him the dead eye, and apparently said, 'Well, now you did,' and walked off with Warren Beatty.

long-legged geeks in old Hanna-Barbera cartoons, walking like a giant while cats and dogs run under his feet. The sound of the record is the sound of Chic. Apart from Rob Sabino, who played the various synthesisers on the song, the only other musicians are Bernard Edwards (bass), Tony Thompson (drums) and Rodgers himself playing guitar, all doing exactly what they used to in Chic. The featured instrument on the record is Thompson's drum kit, as Rodgers' engineer, Jason Corsaro, had found a way during the recording to amplify the drums without using a gated reverb. The trick was using an urban groove with a rock sound. 'That's one of the things that made the song so special,' said Corsaro. 'Because there was nothing but guitar and bass, the drums had so much space to fill. You could hear what Tony was doing so clearly.' Which was making a white sound with a black groove. 'It became the first dance-pop record to have a real rock sound.'

'Whether it's early Elvis, the Beatles, Tom Jones, Roy Orbison, or even Al Jolson, white people doing black music has always been a tried-and-true formula,' said Nile Rodgers. 'Especially when white listeners have no idea they're really listening to black music.'

'I was surprised how people took to "Like a Virgin",' Madonna once said, somewhat disingenuously, 'because to me I was singing about how something made me feel a certain way - brand new and fresh. Everyone else interpreted it as, I don't want to be a virgin any more. Fuck my brains out!'

'I was never remotely moved by her singing - such a flat and emotionless voice,' said Mark Ellen, who became the editor of *Smash Hits* in 1983, just as Madonna was taking off. 'But that's an old-fashioned value that doesn't really matter in the world in which she's always operated: musical theatre.'

Ellen says she was perfectly positioned to surf the MTV/video boom, but his first observation is the more pertinent. By allowing anyone to walk into the marketplace, the eighties encouraged anyone with an interest in success. This was no longer a success predicated on talent, but rather ambition. As pop diversified, atomised, as it fractured and splintered, so opportunities seemed to multiply every day. What this meant was simple: if there was someone making a noise like Madonna then there was probably room for them. Warhol had said it, and Madonna believed it, or at least as it applied to her. Maybe not everyone could be famous for fifteen minutes, but she could.

She was born in the disco – in Detroit's as well as New York's; it's where she drew her inspiration from, where she first had success, and where she developed her enormous gay following. And New York in the early eighties was desperately trying to reinvent the disco, as it was an idea that suited the city so much. And even though she would eventually try and renounce the dancefloor, and climb to what she considered more exalted levels, aspiring to emulate a host of role models, from Barbra Striesand to Frida Kahlo, she would always come back. The disco was where she felt safe, where she had control, and where she had an amazing instinct about what would come next.

Breezy and assertive, Madonna's pop was aural foreplay, reeling you in with sheer exuberance. So even though she was very much part of the new decade's inter-media agglomerate, she knew what it took to get everyone excited. She would soon become known for reviving David Bowie's ritual pop star metamorphosis, although the music didn't seem to change much, being a succession of slinky, digital grooves. She did her sex thing, too, causing outrage everywhere she went. The explosion of female sexuality that was at the heart of her appeal prompted calls for her to be banned on a regular basis – banned from TV, from the radio, from magazines, live concerts ... banned from everything!

Which obviously made her think that whatever she was doing was working.

Calculated in her provocations, and acutely aware of her limited creative bandwidth, she was shrewd in the way she marketed herself. It's not about what I can do, she seemed to be saying, it's about what I am: Madonna! Her goals were obvious from the off, although the most important goal was one it might have been easy to overlook in the early days of her career: never cede control.

And anyway, it wasn't really Bowie she was influenced by, if it was anyone it was the New York artist Cindy Sherman. She felt she was doing some kind of parallel work, based principally around self-invention. She could relate to her – becoming other people but still being herself, with a sense of irony, making social commentary as well as declarative pop anthems in the process. Madonna turned confidence and style into stardom.

She loved all the video stuff, too. Why wouldn't she? She knew that people worshipped their televisions. *Rolling Stone* asked her how she managed to put across such seething sexuality in her promos where so many others had tried and failed. 'I think that has to do with them not being in touch with that aspect of their personality,' she replied. 'They say, "Well, I have to do a video now, and a pop star has to come on sexually, so how do I do that?" Instead of being in touch with that part of their self to begin with. I've been in touch with that aspect of my personality since I was five.'

And there was no one who was going to disagree with her. When she was asked to appear at the first MTV Video Music Awards – held at New York's Radio City Music Hall on 14 September 1984 – Madonna, then a relatively unknown twenty-six-year-old, writhed around in a giant wedding dress, pantomimed masturbating and sang, 'It feels so good inside.' Originally, she had wanted to bring a fully grown Bengal tiger on stage with her, until MTV executives nixed that idea. Instead, she opted to descend a seventeen-foot-tall wedding cake, lasciviously interpreting the song as though she were playing charades.

Chip Rachlin was the head of acquisitions at MTV at the time. 'You'd think that at this stage of her career she'd have been head over heels to be part of [the show], but that wasn't the case,' he said. 'She was a bit difficult from the word go. She didn't want to perform one of her hits. She wanted to sing a new song, "Like a Virgin".'

Halfway through the performance, as she stepped off the cake, one of her white stilettos came loose. 'So I thought, "Well, I'll just pretend I meant to do this," and I dove on the floor and I rolled around. And, as I reached for the shoe, the dress went up. And the underpants were showing.' She continued performing like it was all choreographed, ending the performance flat on her back, with her dress way above her head.

She stole the show, making the other performers that night seem fuddy-duddy in the extreme (including David Bowie, ZZ Top, Tina Turner and Ray Parker Jr., whose 'Ghostbusters' had been the breakthrough song of the summer).

The B-52's' Fred Schneider was there that night. 'I went to the awards when Madonna did "Like a Virgin", and Cher was there. I was so excited to meet Cher. And Madonna comes up and says, "Do you think that was too shocking?" It didn't seem shocking to me. Having lived in Athens, Georgia, you see a lot of crazier stuff. But some punk comes up to Cher, and says, "Hey, Cher, where's Sonny [her ex-partner]?" And without missing a beat, Cher goes, "He's home, fucking your mother." That's the sort of story you remember.' It was also the kind of attitude that Madonna was developing.

During the eighties, traditional religion faced both external and internal affronts, not least from Madonna, who made a virtue of desecrating Roman Catholic iconography, scampering around on MTV, stroking her crotch and lasciviously taking ownership of her name, while crosses burned in the background. In the arena of the pop promo, all iconography was fair game, and everything was up for grabs. Sex, race, religion, class, any brand of conformity – it was all ripe for abstraction, ready to be lampooned. In the video for 'Like a Virgin', even the church appeared to occupy a supporting role, as only Madonna was allowed to be the star ('crucifixes are sexy because there's a naked man on them' she said). Everything that wasn't Madonna was in aid of Madonna. If you weren't Madonna then you were part of her ever-expanding Greek Chorus.

Suddenly, she had power. Someone called Andy Curry was hired to be a VJ on MTV, and in an interview arranged to announce his appointment, he was asked what he thought of Madonna. 'And I go, "Well, she's kind of a bitch." Everyone at MTV shit themselves: "You can't say that about Madonna!" They were not happy with me.'

Madonna's long-term publicist Liz Rosenberg always said that her client seemed to be amused and entertained whenever a big fuss was unfurling in the media. 'She was never defensive about anything she was accused of, never felt like she had to explain. I'd never seen an artist besides Johnny Rotten who was able to let people throw sticks and stones and not back down.'

The sound of 'Like a Virgin' was the sound of white trash vindication, the sound of a bratty little girl using her street smarts to get what she wants. The weird thing is, she made great pop singles almost in spite of herself, as she never looked as though she actually cared what her music sounded like; what she really cared about was its ability to be successful.

Naturally, this success legitimised her behaviour, and she started to get a reputation for being a bit of a diva. Which, to her, was a marvel, as it meant other people - the great unwashed, those who didn't know her, who couldn't know her - were now doing her marketing for her. Gossip. Tabloid innuendo. Trash headlines. Anecdotal facts. It was all content. Gossip would one day become the DNA of social media, but in the eighties it was media catnip. Madonna couldn't control the gossip about her, but she could help steer it.

In this new world, the scripture was simple: it was no longer a question of whether something was the 'right' thing to do, it was whether it was the right thing to do for Madonna. When a journalist accused her of having a reputation for being impolite, and not caring what people thought of her, she smiled, and replied, 'C'est vrai.' (In 1987, she reportedly declined an invitation for an audience with Pope John Paul II, saying, 'If his Holiness wants to see me, he can come to my show.')

The writer David Hepworth was also involved with *Smash Hits* in the early eighties. 'Publicity was not a by-product of what Madonna did, it was the product itself,' he says. 'Her profile owed as much to her ability to generate yards of press coverage as it did to the quality of her records. It was impossible to know whether this was by accident or design, just as it was impossible to know whether there was any distinction between her private and public lives.'

Hepworth discovered quite quickly that she seemed to delight in being the centre of attention, not much caring whether the attention was admiring or not.

The difference between Madonna and most of her peers in the industry was that her music, while being inventive, slick, and always 'of the moment', was merely a pivot to fame. Her knowledge of and understanding of the dancefloor was seemingly innate, and yet that knowledge would always be secondary when set against her thirst for popularity. Commodifying herself came easy. She was a material girl and she didn't care who knew it. In fact, it was easier if people *did* know it: at least then she didn't have to pretend to be anyone else. This kind of ambition would have been frowned upon in the seventies, as it would have been completely at odds with the notion of creative endeavour. In the eighties, ambition was a genre all of its own.

In their *Encyclopedia of Pop Culture*, Jane and Michael Stern spent three pages reflecting on Madonna's appeal. 'Since Elvis, it has been traditional for pop music idols to be - or at least to seem - somewhat innocent and rather bemused about their devastating effect,' they wrote. 'Not Madonna. She wallows in her power to arouse adulation, outrage, curiosity, and pseudo-sexual desire. It is that particular talent as a provocateur that is the secret of her success, far more than her singing voice, which is seldom the issue when critics or fans debate her talents.' The Sterns reminded us that while there were millions of people around the planet who couldn't name a single Madonna song, who couldn't tell you anything she had accomplished, they could easily describe the way she looks or acts and offer an opinion about whether or not it was proper or scandalous.

Politically, Madonna was seen as a prime example of someone who used the routes to market as a way to feather her own nest, almost as though she had been the lucky recipient of a lot of free money. But she wasn't building her future on an accumulation of debt, she was simply exploiting a global fascination for success. Because she was such a committed professional, her work was largely A-grade, and her ascent just happened to coincide with a shift in the culture that had started to celebrate ambition for its own sake. Her success was an American success, one that instantly communicated many of the values of US culture. On the one hand she espoused traditional American aspirations, and on the other she appropriated the aspirations of the outliers. She always called herself a feminist, and if you look at the effect she has had on pop culture since her arrival on the global stage in 1984, it would be hard to disagree with her. Criticised by women's groups who thought she'd set back the movement by thirty years, vilified by neo-conservatives for her deliberately shrill transgressions, and ridiculed by snooty white male rock critics for doing disco, at least the punters understood.

Towards the end of the decade she reflected on all this, in an interview about her friend, the famous downtown graffiti artist, Keith Haring. 'Another thing we have in common – and this happened quite early – was the envy and hostility coming from a lot of people who wanted us to stay small,' she said. 'Because we both became very commercial and started making a lot of money, people eliminated us from the realm of being artists. They said, "OK, if you're going to be a mass-consumption commodity and a lot of people are going to buy your work – or buy into what you are – then you're no good." I know people thought that about Keith, and they obviously felt that about me too. Well, the revenge was that, yes, there's this small, elite group of artists who think we're selling out. Meanwhile, the rest of the world is loving us! Of course, it's what *they* want too! It's so transparent! They're just filled with jealousy and envy. And it certainly didn't stop us ...'

It also didn't stop her from turning into a control freak, the kind of woman who would scream at her musicians if they had the temerity to go for a comfort break during a recording session. 'Time is money, and the money is mine,' she would yell, time and time again. When this happened during the recording of 'Like a

Virgin', Nile Rodgers called her on it, telling her she had no right to talk to people that way, even if they were working for her. When challenged, she had a tendency to fight back, twice as hard, and then, out of the blue, suddenly turn coquettish.

Rodgers is fond of telling the story about Madonna asking him if he found her sexy.

'Madonna, is that a serious question?'

'Yes.'

'You have to be one of the sexiest people I've ever known.'

'Then why don't you want to fuck me?'

Even when he told her that it was professional etiquette that kept them apart – 'I'm your producer!' – the exchange put him on edge for the duration of their sessions together. Which was no doubt the point of the exercise.

But by 1984 she had learned to fully trade off her sexuality, bringing it front and centre, fighting against the double standards that allowed a man to express his desires but encouraged a woman to suppress hers.

Regardless, the more famous she became, the more people tried to exploit her. Not long after the release of *Like a Virgin* there were various cash-in books, one of which, *Holiday with Madonna*, included this childhood reminiscence: 'I played with my Barbie dolls all the time. I lived out my fantasies with them. They were sexy. Barbie was mean. Barbie would say to Ken, "I'm not going to stay home and do the dishes. You stay home! I'm going out tonight. I'm going bowling, OK, so forget it!" You know? She was going to be sexy, but she was going to be tough.'

The book also offered these delights: 1) Madonna once made a movie of an egg being fried on her stomach. 2) She was a baton twirler and cheerleader in high school. 3) Madonna had a burning desire to succeed. 4) She was a girl on the go who had lived an amazingly full life. 5) Her wildest ambition: 'To be a memorable figure in the history of entertainment in some sexual comic-tragic way.'

Her family were the least surprised people of all when it came to her success. In the early years she would always say her ambition derived from the competitive environment in which she was raised. Coming from a big Italian family of eight brothers and sisters and going to a Catholic school primed her for an assault on the American Dream. 'Like all of America [it] gives an incentive to win, to aim for the top of the ladder.'

. . .

The *GQ* Men Of The Year Awards traditionally happened every September, towards the start of the month when everyone was just back from holiday. We hosted the event at places like Tate Modern and the Natural History Museum, but in 2007 we held it at the Royal Opera House in Covent Garden. The Awards tended to celebrate around twenty people who had made an outstanding contribution to the year just gone, and a lot of time and energy went into securing appropriate guest presenters. This year we were celebrating the designer David Collins, and we had asked Madonna to present it. After some very brief wrangling, she agreed, and so we set about making her appearance as painless as possible (for all of us).

It was protocol that every major star be given a minder, and on this occasion our features editor, Alex Bilmes (who would go on to edit *Esquire*), volunteered to look after her. We gave her the option of arriving after the red carpet photo call, and slipping in the back way, via the kitchen - just like *Goodfellas* - which is exactly what she decided to do. 'All I had to do was get her and her entourage from the stage door to the dressing room, and five minutes later from the dressing room to the stage, and then off and back out,' said Bilmes. 'Half an hour door to door, tops.'

But it didn't work out that way. The Awards were running late (they always did), Madonna arrived early, and so suddenly there was a major international mega-celebrity crisis careering over the mountain. Or at least into the Opera House, as Bilmes recalls:

'As soon as I opened the car door and introduced myself she seemed to decide to have a bit of fun, not exactly at my expense but certainly in my vicinity,' said Bilmes. 'It wasn't cruel or bullying. It wasn't flirtatious, either. It was just a kind of arch, almost camp role-play. Her: "What do you do?" Me: "I'm the features editor." Her (as if honoured to be in the presence of such an important figure): "Oh, you're the FEATURES editor." Me (weakly): "Yes." Her: "And are you a NICE features editor?" Etc. etc.

'When we got to the dressing room everyone realised there was no phone signal so they immediately left, and it was just me and her in the room. I poured us both a glass of champagne. What I noticed: she was extraordinarily still, composed, neat, compact. She didn't move unless necessary, and then she moved swiftly, and with purpose. She appeared completely calm and perhaps wryly amused by the situation.'

From Bilmes's point of view, they were getting along famously, like old pals. Then, apropos of nothing, she just said, sweetly but firmly, 'I'm ready now.'

'I scuttled outside to check and was told it would be another five to ten minutes. I went back in and lied. "Two minutes," I said.

'"I'm ready now," she said, "Let's go." No anger, no concern, just matter of fact: this is what's going to happen.'

When she'd done the presenting and the hugging and the photos, Bilmes walked back with her and her people to the car. Before she got in she turned and shook his hand, very businesslike, and smiled and leaned forward and spoke into his ear: 'Next time I'll keep you waiting.'

· · ·

So many people have their own Madonna tale. The songwriter Joe Henry went to the same school as her, and ended up marrying her sister. He remembers what she said the day Elvis Presley died, in 1977, on the day she turned nineteen, 16 August: 'She felt his spirit had passed out of his body and through her own in exodus,' he said. 'I laughed at her then for such outrageous self-possession, at the arrogance that I assumed must allow her to declare such publicly ... Today, when there is laughter, it is the laugh of recognition I hear – and it begins somewhere high above me, where things that once seemed implausible play with wild abandon and in broad daylight.'

There is a photograph of Elvis, signing an autograph for a twelve-year-old girl who looks suspiciously like Madonna, in Detroit on 11 September 1970, outside the Hilton hotel, where he was staying in advance of his show at the Olympia that night. The look on her face is probably the look you'd see on the face of any twelve-year-old girl at the time who was getting an autograph from Elvis: a combination of exhilaration, disbelief and wonder. The fascinating thing about the photograph is that Madonna is looking at the signature rather than at Elvis. The autograph made it real.

That twelve-year-old girl went on to achieve global domination, something she maintained for longer than almost any other perfumer in pop. In fact, there's nothing 'almost' about it. Her relentless drive and ambition have not only made her the pre-eminent act of the last forty years (mathematically at least, although certainly not critically), but her obsession with reinvention, and latterly with the idea of perpetual youth (we must assume that she is already an expert in cryogenics), has meant her career is now seen as a masterclass in longevity, almost a blueprint for survival. She remains the quintessential brittle disco maven, albeit one whose inability to cheat death may be her undoing.*

I can still remember what New York felt like in the autumn of 1984. Because the city seemed so alive, so the night was everything, the night was all. If you were in the city for any amount of time,

---

* I was a member of the *Observer* team that sent Martin Amis to New York in 1992 to interview Madonna about her coffee-table porno book, *Sex*, although Amis ended up interviewing the book rather than her, as he was deemed by her people to be too famous. Which we all obviously found hilarious. As did he – he dined out on the story for years. 'In the old, benighted, pre-modern days,' wrote Amis, 'a new book was normally sent to the reviewer, encased in a jiffy-bag, or, under exceptionally glamorous circumstances, a Federal Express wallet. But Madonna is perhaps the most postmodern personage on the planet, so in this case the reviewer was sent to the book, by supersonic aeroplane.' *Sex* was so popular that quite a number of people bought two copies, one to 'read', the other to file away for the inevitable day it was worth an awful lot of money.

you wanted to be out, every minute, sucking it all up and soaking it all in. By 1984, Madonna had almost replaced Warhol as the person you most wanted to bump into in the VIP bar of Limelight, or coming out of the wrong lavatory in Danceteria. Was Madonna going to be there? Well, of course we want to go then!

And the thrill of seeing her was only bested by the sight of her dancing to her own record, dancing to 'Like a Virgin', lost in her own music, daring anyone not to enjoy it as much as she was.

1985

The Special Relationship

'Born in the U.S.A.' by Bruce Springsteen

As MTV became the conduit through which the nascent stars of global pop in the eighties established themselves, one seventies renegade used it to become even bigger than before, and for a while at least, bigger than almost anyone. As Bruce Springsteen's 'Born in the U.S.A.' became his defining moment, it also created a political maelstrom.

> 'America's future rests in a thousand dreams inside your hearts. It rests in the message of hope in the songs of a man so many young Americans admire – New Jersey's own, Bruce Springsteen.'
>
> – Ronald Reagan

By the summer of 1985, a year in which Ronald Reagan, the recently nicknamed Teflon President, was sworn in for a second term in office, Bruce Springsteen had become so woven into American cultural mythology that he had temporarily eclipsed the fame of his idol, Bob Dylan. By the time Springsteen had finished playing his three concerts at Wembley Stadium in July (the most memorable of which was obviously the one on Independence Day), in the eyes of the British media he had become so synonymous with his country, he had a profile of Mount Rushmore proportions.

In a seemingly unprecedented cultural space, a confluence of fame, style and a media landscape that was now being driven by satellite and cable television, had positioned Springsteen as one of the biggest global stars of the decade. He was also still the greatest live attraction in the business.

The Fourth of July show was a masterclass in showmanship, a set containing thirty songs, and an evening of greatest hits culminating in a mix of *Born in the U.S.A.* crowd-pleasers and old rock'n'roll classics: when Springsteen came out for the encore (having already played for over two and a half hours) he first delivered a quivering version of Elvis Presley's 'Can't Help Falling in Love', before finishing off with 'Twist and Shout' and then a cover of the Contours' 'Do You Love Me'.

All of which were a very long way away from what 1985 looked like to most other people.

As he stood there, in his sleeveless shirt – all the better for showing off his newly acquired Popeye biceps; in anticipation of the tour he had been bodybuilding for two years, often running six miles a day – his blue jeans and his motorcycle boots (one cab driver who delivered a punter to his Slane Castle gig a month earlier said, 'He doesn't wear his money on his back'), Bruce Springsteen looked like pretty much any US blue-collar archetype: he could have stepped out of a James Dean movie, or Kerouac's *On the Road*. Hell, with a squint he could even have stepped out of *The Grapes of Wrath*. As he stood there, in front of a capacity 72,000 crowd, he turned from his audience to face the photographers behind him, soaking up the SLR attention like a solar panel. He had been gunning for this moment for fifteen years, and here – right now, in London, all over Europe, all over the world! – he was going to enjoy it. Part spiritual revival, part nationalist rally, and part rock'n'roll fashion parade, with two runways which usually flanked the stage acting like giant exclamation marks, Springsteen's *Born in the U.S.A.* show was a campaign event in itself, although the performer wasn't looking to be elected, he was looking to be loved. *Born in the U.S.A.* had taken him to the world, and he wanted to bask in its glory.

CBS Records had really gone to town for the London concerts, and in the corporate entertaining suites at Wembley they had built a replica of a fifties roadside diner and hired two dozen waitresses to serve 800 VIPs a day a menu of hot dogs ('Mainstreet Dogs'),

'Bruceburgers' and 'Clarence Fishburgers', French fries, popcorn and 'E Street Cheesecake', washed down with full-fat Coca-Cola, Budweiser and Colt 45s.

This was Springsteen Americana writ large.

His was a story of perspiration, inspiration and a peerless streak of single-mindedness, and it was finally coming good. Not only was *Born in the U.S.A.* the first CD to be manufactured in the US, it was the record that finally turned Springsteen into a superstar (whose popularity was rivalled only by the likes of Michael Jackson, Prince and Madonna). During a two-year period, he was on the cover of *Rolling Stone* no fewer than four times. The accompanying tour – his first to include a substantial number of stadiums – lasted eighteen months, over 150 gigs, and grossed nearly $100 million. It was so popular that by the end of the tour, every show had been bootlegged. And everyone turned out to see it: David Bowie, Pete Townshend, George Michael, Sean Connery, Mick Jagger, Elizabeth Taylor, John McEnroe, Princess Stephanie and Prince Albert of Monaco, and Jack Nicholson with Meryl Streep on his arm.

As the tour reached its conclusion, the *LA Times* interviewed a bunch of more-than-satisfied concertgoers. One, a nineteen-year-old waitress, Denise, said, 'He represents a healthy reaction to all the flash and glitter that rock seems to be all about these days. He's not just a pop phenomenon – a temporary thing. He really delivers … straight-ahead, no nonsense rock'n'roll … The life he sings about isn't always pretty, and he's not really - blindly - patriotic 'cause he sees what kind of promises America's made and hasn't kept. He's exactly what rock needs: a conscience.'

As the tour got longer, so did the length of the sets. As the months rolled on, a formula set in, with the band playing 90 per cent of the same songs each night, although occasionally there was a break with protocol. At one of the last shows on the tour, Springsteen had finished the final encore when someone in the crowd threw an artificial leg onstage. A whole male leg. Springsteen picked it up, and said into the mic, 'We've got to play one more for this guy.' He briefly conferred with his bandmates, wondering what they could play. Then he lifted up his head and said, 'Fellas, "Stand On It".'

. . .

Springsteen had first breached our borders in 1975, when he famously played two dates at the Hammersmith Odeon that November. The concerts were part of Columbia Records' push to promote Springsteen in the UK following the success of his third album, *Born to Run*, which had already generated a ridiculous level of hype, with the singer appearing on the covers of both *Time* and *Newsweek* the month before. The vast amount of publicity accompanying his appearance in London caused an embarrassed Springsteen to pull down a promotional poster in the venue's lobby proclaiming that 'Finally London is ready for Bruce Springsteen and The E Street Band.'

The shows were spectacular, although the accusations of hype made critics cautious, worried they were somehow being hoodwinked.

'After the Hammersmith shows, the cry went up: over-hyped, over-long and over here, as they'd said of Yanks before him,' wrote the journalist Michael Watts. 'The Singing Hamburger!' mocked John Walters, the radio producer, with just enough truth in the joke to give it force. Fast food plus fast cars equals Chuck Berry re-tread. Not the future at all, but the nostalgic past.

Nevertheless, in the intervening years, Springsteen's fame had become almost presidential, and by the time he visited Britain in 1985, he had assumed so much status, for many he had become the very idea of America itself. By the time of *Born in the U.S.A.*, the industrial-strength muscle-bound MTV hero – 'Ah-one-two-*thray!*' – was revelling in sweat-stained bandanas and air-punching aerobics (here was a man who could reasonably be held responsible for Bono, Jon Bon Jovi and Bryan Adams), and the UK had fallen under his spell. Here was a rock star who, instead of showing off his world, brought his audience into it.

After each encore, every night for nearly a year and a half, Springsteen called the band into a brief huddle backstage. 'We had a saying,' said his saxman Clarence Clemons. '"Are they still on their feet? Yeah, let's go back and get 'em. Can they still raise their hands? If they can, we haven't done our job." When we finally saw the guys in the front row falling down, lying over each other, then we said, "OK, they've had enough. Let's go home."'

One long night in Japan, Springsteen brought a young girl up onstage, as he did everywhere, to dance with him on 'Dancing in the Dark', one of the stand-out tracks on *Born in the U.S.A.* 'She was good, too,' Clemons recalled, 'but as soon as she got offstage, she collapsed. She fell right over.'

'I don't really think I could live with myself if I did it any other way,' Springsteen told *Rolling Stone* early in the tour, describing his faith in the power of his performances. 'A lot of what I do up there I do for myself, because you go out there and your pride is on the line, your sense of self-respect, and you feel like "Hey, there's something important happening here." You have a chance to do something. And you wanna make the best of it.'

Trying to capture the nature of Everyman is a daunting task, but ever since he first appeared, in the early seventies, Springsteen had endeavoured to do it time and time again. He seemed obsessed with imbuing the aspirations of small-town blue-collar America with a mystic glow. With a much-lampooned repertoire of songs extolling the virtues of pink Cadillacs, Jersey girls and gimcrack homesteads, Springsteen affected the American psyche in a way that Woody Guthrie could only dream of. Take *Born to Run*, that glorious statement of intent from 1975: it's *West Side Story* on wheels, a ruthless pursuit of sensation that sounds like Bob Dylan produced by Phil Spector, only much, much better. You only had to hear it once to know that no one believed in the redemptive power of rock music quite as much as blue-collar Brucey. Robert Hilburn, of the *LA Times*, saw him defining 'the struggle in life between disillusionment and dreams' (someone once said that the characters in Springsteen songs have a seemingly bottomless

173

capacity for taking slaps in the face without their faith in the dream being too severely shaken), while Dave Marsh, of *Rolling Stone*, suggested that Springsteen's approach was 'a refutation of the idea that rock was anarchic rebellion. If anything his shows were a masterwork of crowd control, an adventure in pure co-operation, a challenge to chaos.'

In the grand old tradition of folk singers, Springsteen put himself into the situations and crises befalling his characters, as he himself dragged them into his songs. By upholding the retrograde folk tradition he was legitimising his purpose: to sing from the streets, to articulate the challenges faced by those unable to express themselves.

Automobile imagery was crucial to those early romantic notions of sex and freedom, and the heroes of his mini-parables were poets-cum-car mechanics – dreamers and schemers who linger aimlessly on the low-rise industrial park fringes of society, down in 'Jungleland', 'Thunder Road', Greasy Lake of 'Spirit in the Night' or the infamous 'rattlesnake speedway in the Utah desert'. Most of the time, though, was spent on the Jersey Shore, drinking warm beer beneath rotary fans in dilapidated diners as their fuel-injected suicide machines sat patiently outside, gently humming after a 200-mile journey across a dozen county lines. Jesus, it must have been hard work trying to be this disenfranchised.

The presence of his African-American saxophonist on stage was particularly significant. Clemons symbolised Springsteen's musical roots, his debt to rhythm and blues, giving the E Street Band even more cultural equity.

Springsteen famously referenced Clemons when he broke off during his sets to tell one of his stories, hokey little fables that came across as fireside chats, even though he might have been standing in front of 100,000 people. Listening to them these days, they sound like the kind of thing Jack Black might have summoned up in *School of Rock*, and yet Springsteen delivers them with such sincerity that it's hard to take him to task.

At the time, Springsteen claimed he'd never had an image, though it would have been hard to find another rock star so easily objectified, and it was as easy to distil the Springsteen myth from the way he looked as it was from listening to his music. In the early days – the long days and dark nights of *Greetings From Asbury Park, N.J.* and *The Wild, the Innocent and the E Street Shuffle* – Bruce's beard and pimp cap gave him the air of any self-important East Coast troubadour; but by the mid-seventies he was starting to look even more generic: lumberjack shirt, faded blue jeans, leather jacket and motorcycle boots. He perhaps looked his best towards the end of the decade – the time of *Darkness on the Edge of Town*, which probably remains his defining statement – along with four-fifths of *The River* it's his best album – with his drawn, gaunt face, V-neck T-shirt and windcheater making him seem more like Jimmy Dean than Bobby Zimmerman.

Five years later it was Annie Leibovitz's iconic cover of 1984's *Born in the U.S.A.* which rubber-stamped his image: a white capped-sleeve T-shirt, a studded cowboy belt, and a pair of Levi's 501s with a red baseball cap hanging out of his right back pocket.* With Springsteen, it was always about the whole package, attempting to build a brand through the creation of what Wagner referred to as *Gesamkuntswerk* – the 'total work'. For him, his dress code, his album covers and even his interviews were supporting Brand Bruce.

Born in the U.S.A. had a rather circuitous beginning. In 1980 he had picked up a copy of Vietnam veteran Ron Kovic's autobiography, *Born on the Fourth of July*, and after a chance meeting with the author, the singer started a fundraising relationship with the Vietnam Veterans of America. Inspired by the possibilities of community involvement, he started making personal donations to a variety of local causes when he was touring. These new commitments started to affect his songwriting, too, making him focus on the universal rather than the personal, and causing him to examine the underbelly of the American Dream in more detail.

---

* Springsteen's manager Jon Landau had originally thought of using one of Jasper Johns' flag paintings on the cover, as they had 'just the right combination of distance and respect to undercut the superficial patriotism of Bruce's title'.

On 3 January 1982, at his rented home in Holmdel, New Jersey, he recorded more than a dozen demos on an old 4-track cassette player. Finding himself unable to build them into songs the E Street Band could handle, he decided to release them as they were. The result was the incredibly bleak *Nebraska*. One of the songs that didn't make the cut was his first attempt at 'Born in the USA' (the song's eventual title having been grabbed from the title page of a Paul Schrader screenplay he'd been sent), which at the time had a completely different melody. And so when Springsteen started preparing what would be the next E Street record he decided to build it around the song that had been inspired by Kovic's book. 'There's someone returning home and trying to find where they belong, if they belong,' said Springsteen. 'The music was martial and powerful, expressing a survivor instinct: I have been through this, I am out the other side, and I am alive.'

The album was so important to him, he wrote and recorded over seventy songs for it. 'I was interested in just what I could do,' he said. 'I didn't have any idea that particular record would end up being as popular as it was, but I knew when we cut that song that it was going to capture people's imagination, probably in a way that possibly I hadn't seen since *Born to Run*. You could just tell when you heard it in the studio that it was something. And then you just take the ride, you say, "Well, let me see what happens, and let me see where it goes."'

Jon Landau, Springsteen's manager and co-producer, says that it was one of the lesser songs on the *Nebraska* tape, but it was transformed in the hands of the E Street Band. 'We just kinda did it off the cuff,' Springsteen said. 'I never taught it to the band. I went in and said, "Roy [Bittan, the band's piano player], get this riff." And he just pulled out that sound, played the riff on the synthesiser. We played it two times, and our second take is on the record. That's why the guys are really on the edge ... To me, [drummer Max Weinberg] was right up there with the best of them on that song. There was no arrangement. I said, "When I stop, keep the drums going." That thing in the end with all the drums, that just kinda happened.'

Some have said that the *Born in the U.S.A.* album is Springsteen's *Let's Dance*, and in a certain sense they're right, and yet *Born in the U.S.A.* has Springsteen's DNA all the way through it, whereas *Let's Dance* always feels as though Bowie has seconded himself to appear on it.

Even though in 'Born in the U.S.A.' they had a guaranteed barnstormer, Landau felt that Springsteen and his band needed a more commercial song to release as the album's first single. After all, this was a record that they both wanted to be successful. His charge wasn't immediately impressed with the suggestion. 'Look,' he snarled, 'I've written seventy songs. You want another one, you write it.' Nevertheless, that night, tired, frustrated and despondent, Bruce headed back to his hotel room, alone, to craft one more song. What he came up with was 'Dancing in the Dark', ironically a song about his inability to write a hit single, and what Springsteen described in his autobiography as 'my song about my own alienation, fatigue and desire to get out from inside the studio, my room, my record, my head and ... live.' The production is euphoric, with a crisp backbeat designed to appeal to DJs, accessorised by Bittan's super deluxe synth line. 'It was just like my heart spoke straight through my mouth without even having to pass through my brain,' says Springsteen, a sentiment which could just as easily be applied to the album as a whole.

In a bid to gain dancefloor credibility, and to make the song more MTV-friendly, it was then given to Arthur Baker to create a 12-inch remix. This was so successful it became the best-selling 12-inch of the year in the US. In another sop to commerce, Landau commissioned a pop promo from director Brian De Palma, a straight performance video where Springsteen misguidedly attempts to 'rock dance' his way through the song (q.v. Kevin Bacon in *Flashdance*). Towards the end of the video, Springsteen reaches down into the crowd to pluck a lucky girl to rock dance with him, a girl who turns out to be Courtney Cox, later to find fame as Monica in *Friends*.

Not long after the album's release, he was ever-so-fleetingly co-opted by the right, when, with a swift sleight of partisan opportunism, Ronald Reagan's speech writers erroneously claimed that 'Born in the U.S.A.' was in fact an all-American patriotic anthem rather than a post-Vietnam rant; the President's team not only misinterpreted the beleaguered irony of *Born in the U.S.A.* itself, but thought that Springsteen's onstage persona was comparable to Sylvester Stallone's jingoistic stooges, Rocky and Rambo. On the campaign trail in Hammonton, New Jersey, on 19 September 1984, Reagan attempted to reach out for the youth vote, rasping, 'America's future rests in a thousand dreams inside your hearts; it rests in the message of hope in songs so many young people admire: New Jersey's Bruce Springsteen. And helping you make those dreams come true is what this job of mine is all about.' As the *Christian Science Monitor* later commented, Springsteen thus became 'the first popular singer to be recruited by a President of the United States as a character reference'.

The singer soon disavowed Reagan of this notion, although he was savvy enough not to make an all-out attack on him, knowing that he was the most popular President since Franklin Roosevelt. A couple of nights later, on stage in Pittsburgh, Springsteen (described by one critic at the time as 'an instinctively left-leaning, if conservative, working-class political ingenue') issued a barbed rebuttal, pondering aloud about the President's favourite Springsteen album: 'I don't think it was *Nebraska* ...'

The future had further repercussions when Democratic Party candidate Walter Mondale also tried to co-opt the song, claiming Springsteen's political support before having to apologise.

In fairness, if you weren't listening, it would have been an easy mistake to make. The record is a military behemoth, a fire 'n' brimstone holler that sounds as though it was made purely to be played before American football games and pro-wrestling events. With its nuclear snare drum, its almost trumpet voluntary synthesiser, its army of Fairlights, and the distraught and overly passionate vocal, you could have been forgiven for believing that the ridiculously large audiences on the *Born in the U.S.A.* tour all thought it was the new National Anthem. Heartfully, if not impartially, Jon

Landau declared it 'the most exciting thing that ever happened in a recording studio.'

Plus, as Springsteen had been working overtime in the gym, pumping up his body to beefcake proportions, he looked like a rock'n'roll model for GI Joe or Action Man. Morphing from the skinny 'greaser-poet' of his earlier tours into a well-sculpted gym bunny, he had turned into a superhero version of himself, a 3D cartoon with jackhammer arms and a shit-eating grin. Big venues required big gestures delivered by big muscles; partially clothed in denim and leather, he was literally ripped and torn.

This period of exploiting his physicality was only temporary, though, and although his classic songs tended to celebrate the male experience, he had spent equal amounts of time pondering his own masculinity. Springsteen had never been an especially libidinous performer, and you'd never exactly call him a sexy star, not compared to, say, Mick Jagger, Steven Tyler or David Lee Roth. His fan base at the time was predominantly male. He had a tendency to appeal to boys who desperately wanted to be older, as well as men who wished they were younger. Like the boys in Albert Camus' *The Outsider* (another male adolescent passion) who leave the cinema with affected gaits after watching cowboy films, songs like 'Thunder Road' made men in Golf GTis think they were driving souped-up Thunderbirds, made men working in photocopy shops dream of cruising down Route 66. And no album encapsulated this more than *Born in the U.S.A.*

The strangest thing about *Born in the U.S.A.* is the way in which it somehow celebrates an alternative reality, because while on the one hand Springsteen was full of distain for Reagan's euphoric and pumped-up escalation of fifties 'Morning in America' boosterism, on the other the music is so celebratory it feels as though it's celebrating the USA itself (which is obviously one of the reasons Reagan's campaign team chose to use its title track in the re-election offensive). The optics here were almost exquisitely contradictory, as Springsteen tries to redefine himself by becoming a national symbol.

The thing is, he had always been aware that pop - like fashion - was an industry built on almost legislative obsolescence, and so dedicated himself to elevating his art, trying to fuse his Dylan-esque tendencies with a type of rock'n'roll that was unequivocally authentic - while at the same time celebrating genuine pop classics by the likes of Roy Orbison, the Byrds, James Brown, Mitch Ryder and Phil Spector. Fundamentally he was driven by a belief that rock had an ability to enfranchise and empower, obsessed with the notion that it had a genuine redemptive force.

In the eighties, this was writ large.

With *Born in the U.S.A.*, the more forthright nature of his music came to the fore, as most of the album sounded like its very own jukebox. As *Rolling Stone* said in their review at the time, 'Though the characters [in the songs] are dying for longing for some sort of payoff from the American Dream, Springsteen's exuberant voice and the swell of the music clues you that they haven't given up.'

• • •

The American Dream was always very much Springsteen's wheel-house, so it was perhaps no surprise he became so associated with it, even when he was calling it into question.

Springsteen was also slipping seamlessly into the MTV rotation cycle, and throughout 1984 and 1985 he became as ubiquitous as Van Halen, Madonna or Don Henley's 'The Boys of Summer'. Here, in colour, on television, being pumped into millions of suburban living rooms, he could espouse his never-ending highway of rock'n'roll glory. He was even more inclusive than he thought, and suddenly he became a gay icon. This had nothing to do with the rather homo-erotic cover of *Born in the U.S.A.* - according to gay semiotics, a red bandana worn in the right back pocket of your jeans indicated that the wearer takes the passive role; looking back on his look of the time, Springsteen called it 'simply ... gay' - but more to do with his sense of self. To many this appeal lay in his ability to describe his hard-earned, rough-hewn version of love, which was immediately recognisable to those for whom desire had often meant sacrifice.

The US press were largely devotional. They were keen to anoint someone who so very obviously embodied modern American liberal values, although there were obviously a few dissenting voices from those who thought they could detect a whiff of sanctimony. In 1985, *Vanity Fair*'s James Woolcott criticised Springsteen's 'cornball' sincerity: 'Piety had begun to collect around Springsteen's curly head like mist around a mountaintop,' he wrote. 'The mountain can't be blamed for the mist, but still - the reverence is getting awfully thick.'

Ever keen to knock someone down just for having the audacity to stand up, the British music press were temporarily suspicious about Springsteen's new persona. As they watched him parade around the stage, dwarfed by a huge Stars and Stripes, they started to wonder if Bruce had become beholden to the imperialist machine, and examined his fist-pumping salutes a little more closely. Was their beloved Rock God turning into a cliché? Was he some kind of cultural attaché, a Trojan Horse for the 'special relationship'? Was he now little more than a jingoistic stooge? While the 'special relationship' between the UK and the US dates back to a 1946 speech by Winston Churchill, the term didn't become part of the vernacular until the eighties, when the political, diplomatic, cultural, economic and military aspirations shared by Margaret Thatcher and Ronald Reagan started to capture the media's imagination. On the incredibly popular satirical puppet show, ITV's *Spitting Image*, Thatcher was portrayed as wild-eyed and demented, while Reagan appeared in sketches invariably called 'The President's Brain is Missing'. The popular impression that Thatcher was the President's poodle belied their heated private arguments, not least over abolishing nuclear weapons (she was far more strident). And although Thatcher privately opposed the US invasion of Grenada, and Reagan unsuccessfully pressured her not to engage in conflict with Argentina over the Falklands (after the war the US continued to sell arms to Argentina), they obviously shared similar views on the Soviet Union and economics (even if the UK Treasury had a far more Victorian attitude towards taxation).

Thatcher also became the European leader the Kremlin took most seriously, when, in March 1985, Mikhail Gorbachev became General Secretary of the CPSU. Remarkably he was the only Soviet politician she had previously formed a close relationship with, thus giving her even more leverage with the White House. It certainly gave her more authority. In spite of Thatcher and Reagan's differing approaches to politics, they formed a close bond that allowed them to strengthen the Anglo-American alliance at a time when the international order was undergoing profound change, and would soon have to contend with the dissolution of the Soviet Union and the reunification of Germany. Reagan's folksy charm actually disguised a fierce ideology, and both hawks and doves alike were astonished at the speed with which he managed to corral Gorbachev into discussions regarding nuclear disarmament. The pair would have their first face-to-face negotiations in Geneva in November 1985.

In spite of making a fuss when Reagan started using 'Born in the U.S.A.' at his rallies, Springsteen was usually quite guarded about his politics. But when he was in Britain in 1985, he openly supported the Labour Party and the striking miners who had downed tools the year before in a bid to prevent the Conservative Government from closing the pits which were the lifeblood of communities across the country. When the *Born in the U.S.A.* tour rolled into Newcastle's St James' Park in June, three months after the strike had been called off, he made a generous donation to help feed families in County Durham and Northumberland who had spent the year struggling through the dispute. Alan Cummings was a thirty-year-old miners' lodge secretary in County Durham when Springsteen wrote the cheque, and he says his own family benefited from the food it paid for. 'That £20,000 came at a time that we were really struggling. It went to the North East area support group, for Durham and Northumberland. That money was shared equally, to buy food for the kitchens. We were getting a lot of help at the time from people, but that was a huge amount of money to put into the system. It was a marvellous gesture to do that.'

The multi-million-dollar troubadour would become more outspoken the older he got, speaking up for local food banks and trade unionists, rallying against the maltreatment of Vietnam veterans and migrant workers. Quietly, and then a little more vociferously, his attitude instinctively seemed to be inspired by Roosevelt's New Deal, acknowledging his country's need for relief, reform and recovery. Later still he would publicly champion Barack Obama, and plant himself even further on the left. In 2018 he called President Donald Trump 'deeply damaged' and 'dangerous', accusing him of stoking the politics of fear and calling up the ugliest and most divisive ghosts of America's past. '[Trump] has no interest in uniting the country, really, and actually has an interest in doing the opposite and dividing us, which he does on an almost daily basis. So that's simply a crime against humanity, as far as I'm concerned. It's an awful, awful message to send out into the world if you're in that job and in that position. It's just an ugly, awful message. It's a scary moment for any conscientious American, I think.'

. . .

I didn't get Springsteen for years. Wasn't interested. Having been brought up on a diet of glam rock, honest-to-goodness Reading Festival-type hard rock, punk and then dance music, Springsteen's overblown pomp seemed silly. Unnecessary. How could a Home Counties schoolboy identify with a lovelorn steelworker, a hot-rod jockey or a Vietnam vet? Springsteen sang about 'highways jammed with broken heroes on a last-chance power ride', while all I was doing was driving to the off-licence. But then I went to America and it all made perfect sense. The space. The sky. The open roads that disappeared infinitely into the distance. A big country demands big music, and that's exactly the sort of music Bruce Springsteen made. Epic. Cinematic. Unashamedly unironic. It wasn't the music of New York or Los Angeles (previously the only places in the US I had substantial knowledge of), it was the music of everywhere in between. The industrialised East Coast, the Blue Ridge Mountains, the Ozarks, Texas, Iowa – pretty much everywhere else. Never an inadequate or a narcissist, Springsteen was a man whose internal workings were all on the outside. Whereas punk celebrated the mundanity of urban, lower middle-class life, Bruce eventually helped me escape it.

In 1987, Springsteen made an effort to escape his own environment and deflate the myth he had taken so long to build by releasing the decidedly low-key *Tunnel of Love*, managing to distance himself from his enormous fan base in the process (if Bob Dylan could dismantle his image then surely Springsteen could too). Intensely intimate, it's his most personal memoir, a divorce record about his failed marriage to Julianne Phillips. The cover shot compounded the effect, Bruce's sombre black suit and faintly ridiculous bootlace tie making him appear more like the manager of some upwardly mobile cocktail and enchilada joint in the Midwest than an out-and-out Rock God (he looked like he'd walked out of *Paris, Texas* straight into *Miami Vice*). Literally and metaphorically, the shirtsleeves were back, the revisionism taking him from superstar Everyman to self-doubting thirtysomething.

These days a lot of rock stars seem to use up the bulk of their inspiration by the time of their second album, but with Springsteen it took twenty years, when he moved to the West Coast after a lifetime based in New Jersey. He famously benched the E Street Band, got married again, had a bunch of kids and started writing songs about watching television ('57 Channels (and Nothin' On)'). He swapped the gauche pink Cadillac for a $14m Beverly Hills mansion, parked the battered '69 Chevy in his double-fronted garage, hung up his cowboy boots and settled down for a night with his second wife and a couple of bottles of Californian Chardonnay. He indulged in self-parody, too: cavorting about the stage looking like a Rodeo Drive vagabond in neatly pressed jeans, gypsy blouse and dagger-pointed boots; a rich man in a poor man's shirt. The idea of 'Bruce Springsteen' became a bit naff, and for men over a certain age he became a guilty pleasure, like jumping up and down at a Sex Pistols reunion gig.

Inevitably, for a time he found his persona difficult to manage, difficult to protect, something his wife and E Street stalwart Patti Scialfa knows oh so well. 'When you are that serious and that creative, and non-trusting on an intimate level, and your art has given you so much, your ability to create becomes your medicine,' she says. 'It's the only thing that's given you that stability, that joy, that self-esteem. And so you are like, "This part of me no one is going to touch." When you're young, that works, because it gets you from A to B. When you get older, when you are trying to have a family and children, it doesn't work. I think that some artists can be prone to protecting the well that they fetched their inspiration from so well that they are actually protecting malignant parts of themselves, too. You begin to see that something is broken. It's not just a matter of being the mythological lone wolf; something is broken.'

Throughout the nineties, he made the long walk back from the wilderness. First came 'Streets of Philadelphia' (which bagged him an Oscar), then in 1995 the difficult but critically well-received album *The Ghost of Tom Joad*. A dour acoustic record full of Steinbeck and Guthrie titbits, devoid of artificial colouring, it sold around 120,000 in the UK, roughly a tenth of *Born in the U.S.A.* But it was a record that mattered.

Middle age brought a fully fledged reunion tour with the E Street Band four years later, along with the release of *Tracks*, a celebratory four-CD boxed set of mostly rejected material, followed by the release of *18 Tracks*, an edited version including a reworking of 'The Promise', a song he wrote and recorded for the album that became *Darkness on the Edge of Town*, but which lay around for twenty years while he decided what to do with it. It's considered by some to be the best song he's ever written, and its mournful romanticism – 'two-bit bars', 'broken spirits' and 'broken cars' (any more clichés up your chambray shirtsleeve,

185

Springsteen?) – was a reminder that what he did best was syn-
thesise the pulp American experience. (It may be heresy, but I
maintain the best Springsteen song was actually written by Tom
Waits, 'Jersey Girl', to be found on *Live/1975-85*; not forgetting of
course that Waits was also responsible for the best Eagles song,
'Ol' 55', from *On the Border*.)

In 2016, he published a wildly successful and candid autobiography, *Born to Run*, that shed light on a long-standing battle with
depression and his drive to perform that seemingly reunited him
with a lot of people who hadn't been so engaged with him since
the glory years of 1984 and 1985. Then a year later, in October 2017,
he even took to the boards, in *Springsteen on Broadway*, performing
five nights a week at the 960-seat Walter Kerr theatre on 78th Street
in Manhattan, just a saloon bar spit from Times Square, playing
guitar and piano and recasting episodes from his autobiography.
Officially the run was originally scheduled to finish two weeks later,
but due to the high demand for tickets and problems with touts,
additional dates were added to take it through to the following
June. In all honesty it was unlikely that Springsteen would have
bothered preparing a show if he was only going to perform it for
a few weeks, and the initial short run was probably advertised to
see what the commercial response was, and also of course to gauge
whether or not the Boss actually enjoyed doing it. As it was, the
show was extended a second time in March 2018, taking the run
right through to 15 December.

Springsteen's original idea was a simple one. Prosaic, even:
break from his tradition of playing long band shows in front
of tens of thousands of people. He wanted to downsize for a
while. 'My vision of these shows is to make them as personal and
intimate as possible,' he said. 'I chose Broadway for this project
because it has the beautiful old theatres which seemed like the
right setting for what I have in mind. In fact, with one or two
exceptions, the 960 seats of the Walter Kerr Theatre [make it]
probably the smallest venue I've played in the last forty years.
My show is just me, the guitar, the piano and the words and

music. Some of the show is spoken, some of it is sung, all of it together is in pursuit of my constant goal – to communicate something of value.'

There were two sections of the show that were more revealing than any others. The first grabbed you almost before you'd sat down, as Springsteen spent the opening five minutes of the show self-deprecatingly demolishing any rights he may have had to represent the working man (it was lacerating, completely surprising and because of that, brought a collective smile to the house); the second, conveniently just before the last section, was where he talked about the two motivations that seem to propel all performers – namely the desire to leave home and explore, and then inevitably the unnecessarily torturous search for a way back.

These moments, in fact the whole show, spoke volumes about just how much Springsteen is woven into modern American mythology, although there could have been no greater contrast to seeing him perform at Wembley Stadium thirty-two years earlier. Back then he was the hard-rocking blue-collar imperialist, bringing his hard-earned brand of liberalism to all corners of the globe. By 2017 he was an elder statesman, almost fit for office.

. . .

Back in 1985, a week or so after Springsteen's final Wembley show, Bob Geldof and promotor Harvey Goldsmith celebrated pop's newfound ability to assuage Western guilt by putting on Live Aid – the dual-venue benefit concert held on Saturday 13 July, at Wembley Stadium as well as the JFK Stadium in Philadelphia, to raise funds for relief of the ongoing Ethiopian famine. Billed as the 'global jukebox', it was the most important pop event of the decade, maybe of all time. But it went ahead without Bruce Springsteen.

Bob Geldof had been circling him for months, and not securing him was his biggest disappointment regarding the event. Springsteen said he was too tired to play, later saying he 'simply did not realise how big the whole thing was going to be'. He later said he regretted turning down Geldof's invitation to appear, and that he could have played a couple of acoustic songs had there been no slot available for a full band performance.

However, at the time it was a big fat no.

Harvey Goldsmith says it was never going to happen. 'It wasn't a disappointment to me because it was a reality,' he says. 'I was working with Springsteen, and I knew exactly what was going on. He was just too tired from the tour. I told Bob that and he just wouldn't have it. Bob kept saying, "He has to go back." He couldn't stay that week and that was the end of it. Then Bob moved the dates.'

The concert was originally scheduled for 6 July, but in order to try and accommodate Springsteen, Geldof moved the date to the 13th.

'He moved the date because he thought Springsteen would do it, and still he wouldn't,' says Goldsmith. 'I kept telling Bob he wasn't going to do it, but he wouldn't listen. He just wasn't going to do it. Springsteen has never done any of those events; the only thing he ever did was the Amnesty shows. I think Bruce Springsteen only wants to do shows he can control. No one is going to tell him what he should and shouldn't do and that's the end of it. He's never done any of these since. I kept telling Bob that, but he refused to take no for an answer. In that respect Bruce Springsteen is the only person ever to get one over on Bob Geldof. Springsteen left his stage behind at Wembley so we could use it, which was kind of him, but he was never going to perform on it.'

Yet in a way Springsteen had already contributed to Live Aid's success. Apart from helping raise millions of pounds in much needed aid, he had made the stadium experience acceptable again, by turning it into an event, not just an experience. This was exacerbated by the success of Live Aid. After that, simply everyone wanted to play stadiums. In the second half of the eighties, no self-respecting global superstar wanted to be seen in an arena, demanding that their managers book them an outside summer tour. Prince wanted to play stadiums, as did R.E.M., Madonna, Michael Jackson and U2, and play stadiums they did. But apart from U2 -

who would go on to define the stadium experience for decades to come - Springsteen played stadiums better - bigger - than anyone, managing to wrap his arms around tens of thousands of people each night, talking to them as though he were still playing the Stone Pony in his Asbury Park, New Jersey, home.

For Bruce Springsteen, and for everyone else in the stadium business, this was quite simply the revenge of the gatefold sleeve.

1986

The
State of
Independence

'Bigmouth Strikes Again' by the Smiths

To his contemporaries, Steven Morrissey was 'the village idiot'; to his acolytes, Johnny Marr was a feminised guitar hero. Between them they created one of the most memorable songwriting partnerships of the decade, formed perhaps the greatest British band of the decade, and pretty much invented 'indie' in the process. Nineteen-eighty-six would prove to be the Smiths' apotheosis, with their album *The Queen is Dead*, and possibly their greatest single, 'Bigmouth Strikes Again', a wilful terrace singalong, complete with self-referential lyrics and a great big wink.

> *'I was never young. This idea of fun: cars, girls, Saturday night, bottle of wine … to me, these things are morbid. I was always attracted to people with the same problems as me. It doesn't help when most of them are dead.'*
>
> *– Morrissey*

I've only ever interviewed three people who insisted on recording the interview themselves, just to make sure there weren't any 'mistakes' in the transcription: the *Deathwish* director Michael Winner, the Conservative politician Oliver Letwin … and Morrissey. I went to interview the singer not long after the release of *The Queen is Dead*, when he was as famous as he was ever going to be, and although his outspoken nature had helped him become probably the biggest indie rock star in Britain at the time, there were things which had been said in print that Morrissey had taken exception to; certain journalists had taken 'liberties' with his own version of his narrative.

Even before I had a chance to mention them, he'd started taking pot-shots at the press. 'There is simply no point [in speaking to mainstream media],' he said. 'They don't print what you say, and they print what you didn't say. There's hardly any point in me being there! The function of reporting has disappeared. Now, all journalists are megastars and the only aim of their interview is to express and establish *their own* personal views, and to hell with whatever the interviewee says.'

But then Morrissey himself was his very own creation, so he couldn't really object to other people trying to embellish the legend a little. Ever since the Smiths first became successful - back in 1983, a year when the charts were owned by the likes of Culture Club, Wham!, the Thompson Twins and Howard Jones - critics had been taking their own pot-shots at Morrissey, taking him to task for being a miserabilist, a 'celibatarian aesthete', and for wallowing in his own shambolic melancholy. They had yet to start calling him a dangerously naïve or 'ironic' racist, but there were already rumblings in the foothills. And he bounced it all back, safe in the knowledge that his legion of fans were happy to endorse a man who made public his disillusionment with the rampant permissiveness and superficiality of pop.

The thing is, when someone is recording you, and so immediately introducing an element of distrust into the relationship, it encourages you to confront the reasons for this, and perhaps to ask slightly more barbed or at least more direct questions. When Morrissey and I met, I felt emboldened by the fact he was using his own Walkman to record me, and I asked him about starting to be accused of racism, and whether he thought he was being accused simply of disliking dance music. The original accusations had obviously upset him ...

'I don't think my opinions were particularly wayward,' he said. 'After that a lot of people rang me up and wrote to me, saying, "At last someone is saying this - we're tired of all this stuff ..." But the journalist made me sound demonstrative, and it's certainly not a crusade by any means. But I've never completely embraced dance music. I never ever went to clubs, I never danced, or anything like that. I went to concerts, I went to see groups in gig situations. But I do possess records by people who just happen to be black. It has happened!'

'Most of the people who don't like you, they dislike you because they think it's all one big act, a coy role for yourself,' I said to him. 'I must admit I'm sceptical.'

'I know. I can't really blame you, but there's very little I can actually do about it, apart from visiting everybody individually in their homes and spending a weekend with them. I can't think of any remedy.'

'When did you lose your virginity?' I asked, almost surprised I had done so.

'I've never been asked this,' he said. 'Actually, it was in my early teens, twelve or thirteen. But it was an isolated incident, an accident. After that it was downhill. I've got no pleasant memories from it whatsoever.'

The Smiths themselves were almost the perfect pop band – a tight-knit group who made a splendid guitar-heavy noise, fuelled by a songwriting team who very quickly became as loved by their fraternity as Jagger and Richards once were by theirs, as loved as Laurel and Hardy, or indeed cheese and pickle. Steven Patrick Morrissey and Johnny Marr – Morrissey playing the librarian, and Marr the rock'n'roll groupie, a guitar hero for people who didn't like guitar heroes. Was there a grander statement of intent than 'Hand in Glove', their debut single from 1983? Was there a more beguiling record in 1985 than 'How Soon Is Now', an hypnotic and solemn whirligig that made Joy Division seem like Billy Ocean? Was there ever a more defining statement than 'Heaven Knows I'm Miserable Now', with a lyric that immediately put Morrissey right up there with Randy Newman, Noel Coward or Ray Davies?

Before the descent into familial warfare, and the growing concerns about Morrissey's nationalism, he and Marr were considered to be genuine alternative heroes. They had, after all, invented indie. They didn't invent the independent record label (they were signed to Rough Trade but could have just as easily been signed to CBS or a division of EMI), they weren't the first 'independent' group, and it would be easy to look at a band like Orange Juice, say, as a prime example of an eighties group setting sardonic, camp lyrics to jangly guitar pop. But the Smiths were the first band to take indie to another level, the first band to make indie guitar rock properly commercial. No one else at the time sounded anything like them in terms of their music, their lyrics, production, style or intimacy.

'We invented indie as we still know it,' said Johnny Marr. 'We were of that generation that came after punk and post-punk. We're grateful for the revolution, but there was a bit of homophobia there, and sexism. There wasn't in indie. People don't talk about it now, but it was non-macho. If you were an alternative musician, you were political, because of the times [Thatcherism and the Falklands War]; it was taken for granted that the bands you shared a stage with had the same politics.'

You could also say that Morrissey's amplified persona helped rubberstamp the idea of what an indie figurehead could be, and the way in which he embellished his character, his personality, his style and the sensibility he presented in interviews became indelible. He was funny, too. So, on the one hand you had an extravagant introvert who was more than happy to be adored; and on the other you had a shy extrovert who just happened to be the most gifted guitarist of his generation.

To wit: indie.

'The term "indie" started cropping up in our reviews, to describe us as opposed to New Order and Depeche Mode, who had an electronic aspect, and the Bunnymen and the Cure who were on major labels,' said Marr. 'Indie seemed to be applied to us in terms of the guitar approach and the fact we were on an independent label, but being sold in Woolworths. I think the Smiths were indie through and through.'

The Smiths were so important that when the *NME* finally got a new editor in 1985, after the resignation of the long-serving Neil Spencer (who was moving on to the *Observer*), the incoming Ian

Pye told anyone who would listen that the future of music right now 'basically belonged to black music and a few mavericks like Morrissey. In fact, just Morrissey and Morrissey alone.'

He may have had the unfortunate manner of a dotty old aunt, and he may have been full of camp conceits, but Morrissey had the wit and wisdom of a true British vaudevillian. Like Pete Shelley in his Buzzcocks days, Morrissey had the sense to inject a large dose of irony into much of what he wrote. For instance, the only other media personality who professed to practise and enjoy the same sexual habits as Morrissey (total abstinence) at the time was the *Carry On* comedian, Kenneth Williams. And he was nothing if not self-aware. Years later, when the Smiths had collapsed, and he was launching his solo career with EMI, 'I was presented with a choice of defunct labels ... things like Decca. I didn't want to be on EMI, and Parlophone seemed like the obvious mod suggestion, which I didn't really want either. His Master's Voice, I thought, had a certain perverted grandiosity and thus spoke to me directly ...'

There was his voice, too. In very particular ways, Morrissey's closest compadre was Steely Dan's Donald Fagen, another vocalist who couldn't really sing, and who dealt with difficult subjects in a cartoon voice, who came across as someone who, in his more lucid moments, probably thought the idea of being in a 'rock'n'roll' group was somewhat beneath him, and who had to always put some distance between himself and the performance in order to lend the exercise some dignity. Both Fagen and Morrissey contextualised their subject matter, thus creating a very real but invisible cord between mid-seventies Californian ennui and mid-eighties Northern camp.

But the cult of the Smiths was always more powerful than the cult of Morrissey, because even in the early days of their career, he was seen as not a necessary evil as such, but definitely a component that had to be endured rather than always enjoyed. He wrote hysterical lyrics, was a domineering frontman and gave good interview (actually great interview), but it was the wistful chord changes emanating from Johnny Marr's guitars that had us all in thrall. Morrissey was certainly a larger than life personality, a cartoon prima donna who dropped all the right references and did a merry dance around whatever maypole was thrown at him, but it was his guitarist who we all found fascinating, a man who could wring genuine tragedy from Morrissey's Mancunian tenement operas, a man who could conjure up everything from maudlin ballads and relentless modern thrash to psychedelic music hall and sparse, simple pop.

Morrissey and Marr were thrown together by a mutual love of sixties girl groups and Brill Building virtuosity, by a fondness for old British pop icons such as Billy Fury and Sandie Shaw and a determination to write and perform classic guitar pop, the kind that didn't need overt marketing or expensive videos (in the early days the band refused to make promotional videos at all). There was a 'truth' in what the pair of them aspired to, an honesty that would shine through in the particular way they planned everything, from song titles to record sleeves (which were a mixture of Northern working-class heroes and gay icons) and interview topics. Under Morrissey and Marr's guidance, the Smiths were very, *very* particular, bringing back what a lot of fans and critics would call authenticity but what in practice was just simple care and attention.

'The Smiths aimed to tell a particular truth,' wrote Jon Savage in the *Guardian*, 'about lives ignored by the mainstream media and about a grim, north-western landscape that helped to create a bleak, vengeful emotional state. Morrissey wrote about poverty in "Jeane", the Smiths' most affecting (and underrated) song from this period. This was the world of Shelagh Delaney's *A Taste of Honey*: the kitchen-sink desperation of the early sixties revisited twenty years on. The implication: very little has changed.'

The Smiths were anti-matter: anti-'rock', anti-'pop', and obviously anti-'dance', instead wanting to champion the exhilaration of ordinariness, with Morrissey's reflective lyrics focusing on the isolation of adolescence, the iniquities of romantic relationships, and the glory of inadequacy. In effect the Smiths were anti-eighties, which meant they immediately created their own genre: indie, then, or at least the kind of thing students liked. In the US, they were regarded as college rock, whereas in the UK they were considered to be harbingers of a genuine movement – a marshalling of young, committed outsiders.

The Smiths opened a gateway through which you could leap in order to escape the decade that bore them. They were the antithesis of the decade, which meant they became forever associated with it. In the atomisation of pop, the Smiths were their very own atom, and a great one at that. The Smiths happened when the rest of the world wasn't looking, when it was fawning over the arrival of the likes of Howard Jones and Nik Kershaw, and when the idea of a truly innovative, transgressive young rock group was starting to seem terribly old-fashioned. By 1983, music had become folded into the mainstream entertainment complex to such an extent that for many observers it seemed as though it was going to be this way for ever. By 1983, outsiders didn't appear to have a platform, didn't appear to need one. Because weren't Howard Jones and Nik Kershaw thought to be outsiders themselves? It was sad, but true, and we were certainly encouraged to think so.

On the face of it the Smiths wanted to ditch everything that people superficially thought of as rock'n'roll – leather trousers and long hair and drugs and ecstatic gurning – but the most important aspect, the gang mentality, became their forte. The Smiths were a gang and so were their fans. Morrissey had a rockabilly quiff but also wore NHS glasses and a comedy hearing aid; he wore jeans but had a bunch of gladioli shoved into one of the back pockets. Most of what they did was at odds with what was expected from Northern guitar bands. They were so successful at their image that they became easy to lampoon. Because of Morrissey's obsession with British kitchen sink dramas, romanticising the gay, working-class criminal world, coupled with Marr's spidery guitar lines and dark glasses, the Smiths became fair game. I remember Nick Logan, the editor of *The Face*, wandering around the magazine's HQ in Marylebone, affecting his finest Morrissey whine, the day after closing an issue: 'I've got nothing in the fridge, oh what am I gonna do ...'*

In 1984 I'd interviewed both drummer Mike Joyce and bass player Andy Rourke, during a time when just being in the Smiths was enough to grant your immortality, before we all knew that it was basically all about Morrissey and Marr and no one else. When I asked Joyce why he thought the Smiths had acquired such a loyal following, he said: 'Because what we say is quite basic,' he said. 'It is truthfulness and it's deeper than just the music. It's four minutes of feeling and conviction. We are a very modern band. People write to us and say that they have to listen to the Smiths every morning before they can do anything - that is marvellous. We want to get that feeling across to as many people as possible. Communication has got to be the most beautiful thing in the world.'

He was right, of course, because the one thing that certified the Smiths' appeal was their ability to connect. You only had to look at them on television - fleetingly - to not only understand precisely what they were about, but to like it, too. The Smiths were immediately appealing because they were so anti-eighties, and yet the eighties is the only decade in which they could have existed.

It was Rourke's first ever time with a journalist, although he handled himself well, toeing the party line and admitting that Morrissey spoke for all of the band when he gave interviews. 'Morrissey can get on with anybody. He's so good at getting our views across that we don't need or want the exposure.'

People would soon start disagreeing with Rourke over his assessment of Morrissey's ability to charm. In the space of a little over eighteen months he went from being the shy, fey librarian rock

---

* When I asked him how he relaxed at home, Morrissey raised an eyebrow and gave me a knowing smile: 'Well ... TV certainly helps me relax; not mentally, I mean I don't watch *Terry and June*, but it takes the edge off me. I do have a vast collection of video tapes though. Anything pre-1970, generally fifties and sixties English films. I like *Carry On* films, early British comedy, things like *Hobson's Choice*, *Far from the Madding Crowd*, *The Family Way* ... *The Leather Boys*.'

star, to an arrogant, disobliging smart-arse whose only ambition appeared to be the burnishing of his own ego. After all, he had become 'Morrissey', and he knew that there was no one else he knew who could have said that. People still loved him, mind, but we were presented with an alternative view for those who wanted to think slightly less of him.

But back in 1986, wallowing in the immediate success of *The Queen is Dead*, he was still the indie kingpin, the Neurotic Boy Outsider par excellence, the Lonely Planet Boy, the garlanded milksop.

He seemed to cast himself as the Alan Bennett of pop, a doleful spectator. The press tried to paint him as gay, he said he was an asexual celibate, and no one was any the wiser. He was a miserabilist and yet he had a brilliant Oscar Wilde-like wit, an ability to sketch away with a mordant flourish. He was a militant vegetarian, a hater of Tories and a complainer of note. His indifference to mainstream culture cast him - and then every one of his ever-expanding army of disciples - as an outsider. This was something Morrissey revelled in, as it made him seem more interesting than he actually was. He had a terrific sense of humour, but he wasn't considered to be the life and soul of the party; in fact, before he was famous, he was the kind of person to be avoided at parties.

Tony Wilson remembered Morrissey from the seventies, and he wasn't impressed. One of Manchester's cultural elite, a Cambridge graduate, journalist, Factory co-owner and television presenter, Wilson was one of the few who had seen the Sex Pistols play the city's Lesser Free Trade Hall in 1976 - along with future members of Joy Division, the Fall, A Certain Ratio, Ludus, Simply Red, Buzzcocks, Magazine, the producer Martin Hannett, the journalist Paul Morley and Morrissey himself.

'He was the speccy kid in the corner, the clever little swotty outsider boy, and very brilliant,' Wilson said. 'He wrote a fantastic short play about eating toast, and I think he gave it to me and I lost it. Then, at some point, whenever it was in 1980, he phoned me up and said, "Would you come and see me." I drove out to King's Road, Stretford, to his mum's house, went to his bedroom upstairs and sat on the edge of the bed while he sat on a chair, surrounded by James Dean posters, and he informed me that he had decided to become a pop star. I sort of went, "Well, Steven, that's very interesting," and inside I was thinking, "You must be fucking joking. You're off your fucking head, you're the least likely rock'n'roll star imaginable in the universe.'"

Which he was. And that's one of the reasons why the Smiths were so successful.

. . .

If much of the early eighties was about disguising sexuality, with many of the futuristic bands deliberately confusing their sexual identity for purposes of style - Boy George, David Sylvian, Annie Lennox, Phil Oakey, Marc Almond, Adam Ant and so on - by the middle of the decade, as AIDS became demonised by the right, much of the pop arena was becoming more militant (q.v. Bronski Beat and the Communards). And yet sexual ambiguity continued to be a well-worn, and often necessary, routine. A style, almost. In Morrissey's case, celibacy was the kink, a perversion that brought smiles as well as suspicion. 'I'm just simply inches away from a monastery,' he quipped once.

In a 1986 interview with *Rolling Stone*, Morrissey explained that the gender ambiguity in the subjects of his lyrics was intentional. 'It was very important for me to try and write for everybody,' he said. 'I find when people and things are entirely revealed in an obvious way, it freezes the imagination of the observer. There is nothing to probe for, nothing to dwell on or try and unravel. With the Smiths, nothing is ever open and shut.'

Back in 1985, I asked him if his attitude towards sex had changed. After all, 'You were very uptight about it at one point ...'

'Well, I've never really had any attitudes towards sex,' he replied. 'It's never been my strong point ... I've not really had much time to cultivate any attitudes. No, it's always been somewhat of a foregone conclusion. I never feel that I give completely satisfactory answers to journalists, which is why they're still asking me, but I'm still mystified by why they want to know. I never wanted to start a new movement, I never wanted to wave a banner for celibate people. I never wanted to go to the House of Commons and lobby, for instance. It's accidental that it [the celibate stance] actually came out in the first place, and now it's become a tatty banner. I've been consistently probed on it, and the statement I make is that I've got nothing to do with it. To be honest with you I don't think about it [sex] that often, so I don't see why I should become a spokesman for people who don't do it that often!'

'How many things have you done which you're ashamed of?'

'None ... nothing at all. I say that quite regretfully, because I suppose it's a measure of actually living a semi-exciting life that you've done things that will seriously make you cringe. But not me. Everything I've ever done has been totally legitimate.'

'When was the last time you felt real passionate love?'

'Practically never. No, I've never been in that situation.'

'Really?! Have you never wanted to? Your lyrics imply that you have.'

'Yes, I have. But in reality, it never happens. In order to think, isolation is a necessary evil. I have to be alone. I can't really stand people's company for too long. It's terrible – but I can't really share. Occasionally I feel the need for some physical commitment – which never, I might add, ever happens. Everything's so entangled now that I often wonder if it will ever happen. I don't think it will, to be honest with you. I mean, not many people reach twenty in my state.'

'Have you ever wished for a more stable, conventional life?'

'Yes, I have, but obviously as you can gather there are several great obstacles that I can't really seem to get past. I can't seem to advance beyond friendship with most people. And for the most part I don't even manage that. I only have one or two friends, whom I've known for ten years. Generally, I don't make friends with people – it's not something I plot, it's not something I insist upon ... it just naturally happens.'

If you had analysed Morrissey's statements, and his deliberate put-downs, you could have been forgiven for thinking he'd been created by committee, as his list of grievances against the modern world seemed like a litany of reactionary gripes. Here was a twentysomething icon of working-class youth who often sounded like someone who might already be collecting their pension. In a way, the sudden escalation of lifestyle opportunities - in media, design, architecture, sport, travel, food, and leisure in general - was the perfect background for a cantankerous poet. The modern world was Morrissey's foil, and he toyed with it mercilessly. You could easily imagine him being offered a cappuccino and rather pointedly asking if he might just have a coffee, 'If it's all right with you.' Ironically, Morrissey's distrust of and misgivings about the modern world - however arch and manufactured they may have been - appeared to chime with those expressed by his nemesis, the Prime Minister.

Of all the British pop stars who came to prominence in the eighties, none held Margaret Thatcher in less regard than Morrissey; or at least none were quite so public in their disdain. His hatred - and it did appear to be genuine hatred - didn't abate, either. When she died in 2013, at the age of eighty-seven, Morrissey sent an open letter to *The Daily Beast*:

Thatcher is remembered as The Iron Lady only because she possessed completely negative traits such as persistent stubbornness and a determined refusal to listen to others.

Every move she made was charged by negativity; she destroyed the British manufacturing industry, she hated the miners, she hated the arts, she hated the Irish Freedom Fighters and allowed them to die, she hated the English poor and did nothing at all to help them, she hated Greenpeace and environmental protectionists, she was the only European political leader who opposed a ban on the Ivory Trade, she had no wit and no warmth and even her own Cabinet booted her out. She gave the order to blow up The Belgrano even though it was outside of the Malvinas Exclusion Zone - and was sailing AWAY from the islands! When the young

Argentinean boys aboard The Belgrano had suffered a most appalling and unjust death, Thatcher gave the thumbs up sign for the British press.*

Iron? No. Barbaric? Yes. She hated feminists even though it was largely due to the progression of the women's movement that the British people allowed themselves to accept that a Prime Minister could actually be female. But because of Thatcher, there will never again be another woman in power in British politics, and rather than opening that particular door for other women, she closed it.

Thatcher will only be fondly remembered by sentimentalists who did not suffer under her leadership, but the majority of British working people have forgotten her already, and the people of Argentina will be celebrating her death. As a matter of recorded fact, Thatcher was a terror without an atom of humanity.

Nineteen-eight-six was a year punctuated by disaster. In January, the *Challenger* Space Shuttle broke apart seventy-three seconds into its flight, killing all seven crew members aboard. In April, an explosion at one of the reactors at Chernobyl created the worst nuclear disaster in history. Four months later, Aeroméxico Flight 498 was a victim of a mid-air collision, and crashed into the Los Angeles suburb of Cerritos, killing all sixty-seven on both aircraft and an additional fifteen on the ground. Technology advances helped the Soviet Union launch the Mir Space Station, Robert Palmer had us 'Addicted to Love' and Ferris Bueller took a day off. Nineteen-eighty-six also saw the birth of Lindsay Lohan and the Olsen twins and the deaths of Cary Grant and Thin Lizzy's Phil Lynott. Photographers were also busy documenting the lives of Spike Lee, Arnold Schwarzenegger, Joan Jett, Halle Berry, Mike Tyson and Oprah Winfrey, whose chat show debuted nationally

---

* Settling the controversy in 2003, the ship's captain Héctor Bonzo confirmed that the *General Belgrano* had actually been manoeuvring, not 'sailing away' from the exclusion zone, and had orders to sink 'any British ship he could find'.

in the US. And on Saturday 28 June, at Wembley Stadium, George Michael and Andrew Ridgeley bid farewell to 72,000 of their fans at Wham!'s last ever concert, The Final. Elton John made a special appearance, and, given this was 1986, you would have been disappointed had he not.

The list of best-selling albums in the UK this year is sobering, featuring only one record that is considered now to be in any way 'classic' – Paul Simon's much-maligned, but increasingly revered *Graceland*. Others might suggest Madonna's *True Blue* and Dire Straits' *Brothers in Arms* as being worthy of critical attention, although it's unlikely that many people would go to bat for A-ha's *Hunting High and Low*, Five Star's *Silk & Steel*, the Eurythmics' *Revenge*, Queen's *A Kind of Magic*, or even Whitney Houston's debut album (a slow-burn that had actually been released at the very beginning of 1985). The artists making up the rest of the Top Thirty weren't much to write home about, either, a list featuring the likes of Chris de Burgh, Simply Red, Genesis, Phil Collins, Simple Minds, Level 42 and a host of compilation albums. The only other albums to accumulate similar cultural resonance were the Pet Shop Boys' *Please*, Prince's *Parade* and Kate Bush's *Hounds of Love*.

The Queen is Dead was made during a time when it was still deemed important – nay, necessary – for gold standard rock groups to deliver important albums. And while the Smiths had already released three albums – *The Smiths*, *Hatful of Hollow* (a compilation) and *Meat is Murder* – they hadn't yet delivered their *Sgt. Pepper*, their *Ziggy Stardust*, their *London Calling*. *The Queen is Dead* was meant to be that record.

'I had a very, very strong intuition and feeling before we made *The Queen is Dead*,' said Marr. 'And I felt a lot of pressure. I knew we had to deliver something that was great. I felt we *were* great, and we'd been called great, but I didn't want to get away with just coasting. The other thing is, I wanted us to be as good as my heroes. From day one, I wanted us to be as important. Right from the off with the Smiths, in my head we were our own Rolling Stones. On top of that, we were being talked about in legendary

terms. So, you'd look at bands like the Who or the Small Faces -
that pantheon of British bands - and think, "Well, are we going to
do it or not?" Now's the time - it's the third album.'

Morrissey told me similar things.

'I like the idea of the Smiths being thought of as an entirely
British group, but it's quite a natural thing,' he said, when we first
met. 'It wasn't an added commodity, never has been. Also, that
statement tends to imply that you won't be successful anywhere
else in the world, which in our case isn't far from the truth. I do
like the idea, though, of being a uniquely British phenomenon. We
are *undeniably* British.'

Typically, he thought that British music was better than any
other kind. 'It certainly has been. I'm not really quite sure about
now but the history of British music is better than anyone else's
history. In the seventies America hardly existed in musical terms
- it was a total anathema. In the sixties it was passable, but that
was mainly due to Elvis Presley. There must be a reason why it's
still important for international recording artists to be successful
in Britain, and it's taste really - they know that British people
have more taste.'

The Queen is Dead was a fraught record to make as the band
were in the middle of a long-standing legal dispute with their
record company, they were arguing about management strategies,
and bassist Andy Rourke had recently been fired from the group
- due to his heroin addiction - and replaced by Craig Gannon,
but was back in the fold when they started recording. And yet
both Morrissey and Marr were going through a purple patch of
creativity. Throughout their short four-year career, they were both
incredibly prolific, although it's still fascinating to remember that
on one Friday afternoon at his Cheshire home in 1985, Marr wrote
the music for 'Cemetry Gates' (sic), 'I Know It's Over' and 'Frankly
Mr Shankly', three of the album's greatest tunes.

Morrissey also showed that far from being bored by the critics'
constant comments about the deliberately arch references in his
lyrics, he was still playing them at their own game: 'The Boy

With the Thorn in His Side', for instance, is one his most meta lyrics – 'How can they hear me say those words/ And still they don't believe me?'

The band were loved, though, as was this album.

'The whole of the first side is nothing less than perfection, commencing with a title track of epic worth,' wrote Nick Kent in the *NME*, who one might have thought had already dished out enough superlatives in his career. 'Driven by a vicious drum tattoo, bone-crunching bass and a snarling viper-like wah-wah guitar vamp, Morrissey unveils a lyric that mixes verbal slapstick with withering insight to document the hideous reality that currently exists as a sluttish excuse for dear old Blighty.'

'Morrissey is a true star,' wrote Simon Frith in the *Observer*, 'an obsessive for whom every doubt or slight becomes a production number – no nonsense about him being an ordinary Joe – and as I prefer his light to his heavy music, *The Queen is Dead* sounds just fine. It is, for the most part, a comic work: Northern Nostalgia meets Deadpan Despair, with swinging sixties guitar patterns, echoes of Lennon and McCartney, and a crooner's lilt in its voice.'

As for the title track, Morrissey's republican bleat, it semaphored not only his lyrical dexterity, but also his cultural bravado – he was more than happy to metaphorically spin around the room, with a beer bottle in one hand and a microphone in the other, clattering one sacred cow after another.

The Smiths' career mirrored my own tenure at *i-D*, and I remember feeling oh-so privileged that I had the opportunity to constantly espouse their brilliance in the pages of our magazine. Honestly, while I was sceptical about Morrissey's holier-than-thou personality (come on, we all were), I spent an undignified amount of time and ink banging on about a) how good they were, and b) how much I loved them. And even though my writing was gauche and inelegant, I wasn't wrong. They *were* great, and on this record, they proved it, Marr with his orchestration and melody, and Morrissey with his sardonic flourishes. As one critic said, 'Few people can switch between high- and low-brow, vulgar comedy and poignant self-doubt so convincingly and rapidly over thirty-six minutes.'

As for 'Bigmouth Strikes Again', Johnny Marr thought it was going to be their 'Jumping Jack Flash', a big, old bouncy bruiser of a song. 'I wanted something that was a rush all the way through, without a distinct middle eight as such,' he said. The song is obviously an attack on the media, with Morrissey describing being hounded by the press and comparing himself to Joan of Arc. 'With this song, you can see why he made journalists cream their pants,' said Mike Joyce.

The tone of the record is even more kitchen sink than usual, which was reflected in the album's cover. The gatefold sleeve contained one of the most iconic images of the Smiths, a photograph of the four of them taken outside the Salford Lads Club, a recreational club in the Ordsall area of Salford, on the corner of St Ignatius Walk and the original Coronation Street, and which soon became a pilgrimage site for the band's fans. The picture was taken by Stephen Wright. '*The Queen is Dead* shoot was in late November in Salford on a damp, dark day,' he said. 'It should really have been cancelled as the light was so poor for photography. We spent a bit of time at a couple of locations but the Salford Lads Club was the key one. You can even see Johnny shivering in some of the images. Somehow the casual poses and the grim weather give the photos a certain natural and gritty character, and I love the way Morrissey stands there, arms folded and smirking slightly like the Mona Lisa.'

The cover itself - designed in great detail by Morrissey - features Alain Delon from the 1964 film *L'Insoumis* (*The Unvanquished*), his image emerging from darkness, and so hinting at isolation and drama (the film's background is the Algerian War, with Delon playing a French Foreign Legion deserter). Delon wrote to Morrissey giving his approval, although it came with a caveat. Delon told him that his parents were upset that anyone would call an album *The Queen is Dead*. For Morrissey, the perpetual teenager (he was twenty-six at the time), this was glorious validation.

Towards the end of my interview with Morrissey, I asked him if he ever worried about becoming a cliché, a caricature of his gladioli-wielding self. Perhaps unsurprisingly he said he wasn't. 'Not really,' he smiled, indulgently. 'I feel that I'm not about to go off on any new dramatic tangents. I'm always going to be me, however sad that may be. I don't think I could ever deliberately change, even for fear of becoming quite repetitious. And if I don't change, and it all goes downhill, then so be it. I couldn't be a tailormade pop star, not really, not at all.'

What else could he realistically do?

'Nothing. I'm entirely talentless ... it was all a great big accident - I just came out of the wrong lift.'

And if it all came to an end tomorrow?

'I think I'd slide away to some Devonshire village, somewhere quite dark and green and quiet. The only burning ambition I have left is to write plays ... but that won't happen for a while. I will do it, but at the moment this thing is wrapped around me like a shroud.'

There was more (there always was with Morrissey).

'I have to be alone,' he said. 'Being in the Smiths and the whole experience has practically changed nothing. I genuinely don't mix. I live a very isolated life. I talk to journalists and I appear in magazines and I make the odd record, but otherwise I live a very unspectacular lifestyle. It's a very peculiar thing to juggle with. I'm an intensely private person, but yet it doesn't get seen that way in interviews because I speak so often and so personally. I think I should back off, disappear and become some kind of stagehand.

'I never go out publicly. I never go to clubs or things like that [slightly disingenuous here, methinks]. I hover around Sloane Square occasionally and I go shopping, but that's about it. I like the Kings Road because it has a lovely catwalk feel. I don't travel very far and wide, and I certainly don't hike to any trendy spots. But I do like watching people in the Kings Road, all the ones who have perfect symmetry ... the ones whose clothes all fit perfectly.

It makes me quite envious ... all those people who look so neat and so clean, they inspire me. I especially like footwear. Only occasionally do you see people who are so abstract that they look absurd.'

He also expressed a penchant for the quaint side of British life, the world of restraint and lace doilies, of tea cakes and dinner ladies, although in hindsight this was probably because he had yet to be exposed to the attractions of seven-star hotels, twenty-four-hour room service, limitless sunshine and global adulation.

'I quite like the rather dark side of Britain,' he told me. 'Rain and fog and the countryside, the theatre district of London. I don't like anything particularly advanced. Having a television and video is completely at odds with these feelings, but you can't have an old-fashioned video, now can you?

'I think I do [live in the past] to a certain degree, but no, it's really only a matter of taste. I just find that things buried in the past are so much more interesting than anything around today. I hate things like McDonald's - I prefer the world of tea rooms and mysterious little chip shops to the world of fast food. Unfortunately, it's difficult to find many interesting old tea rooms in London, but I have found the odd place where I can sit without feeling intimidated.

'I'm a desperately humble person - I don't have a yacht you know. I do have a car, a 1961 Consul - but I can't drive it. It's waiting in the garage for the magical day when I learn to drive ... which of course will never happen because I can't grapple with the Highway Code. I don't really go on holidays. I don't like going to other countries to be honest with you ... I do it very rarely. I have had a tan. I went to Los Angeles recently and got one there, but it didn't make it back to Britain. It got stopped by Customs - you're not actually allowed to come through customs with a tan.

'I go on trains every now and again, because I have to, but I haven't been on a bus for four years. I don't miss it. Initially I had those very typical views about the South, and I really viewed London as enemy territory. But once I'd stayed here for a long period of time all those things dispelled. I still have a healthy obsession with Manchester, but it's difficult to feel part of the daily life because I'm never there.'

But for many he was always there, as Morrissey became someone to project onto, someone we projected onto whenever we felt like it. We didn't just objectify him, we co-opted him, and turned him into the strident voice we all needed at some point (regardless of whether we were left- or right-of-centre). Morrissey was the legitimate excuse, the intellectual subsidy, the reason to go into battle (at least until the main course arrived). That's why Morrissey became a fundamental part of the decade: he was the brickbat for all of us, the one we used to throw whenever we needed to send a missile into an argument. He was the firecracker, the firebomb, the explosive device, the intransigent IED.*

. . .

The Smiths' last ever concert was at the Brixton Academy on Friday 12 December 1986. The show, which had originally been booked for November, needed to be pushed back a month after

---

* In the summer of 2011, I found myself backstage in the Pyramid stage at Glastonbury, waiting for U2 to make their Sunday night headline appearance. Having briefly wandered out into the throng, I had returned to the holding pen, chatting with promoters, agents, roadies, wardrobe assistants, photographers, stylists, publicists and fellow journalists. One of the support acts was Morrissey, who, from what I could tell from where I was standing – about fifty feet behind him – appeared to be doing as much talking as he was singing. As he went into a rant about the then Prime Minister David Cameron, I could see people around me start to eye-roll; not because they were staunch defenders of the Conservative and Unionist Party, but because, as I soon found out, every one of them appeared to have a problem with Morrissey. Everyone I spoke to backstage that day – and I spoke to a lot of people – was holding some kind of grudge against the singer because of some minor grievance or other. He had – allegedly – cancelled a show, cancelled an interview, missed a flight, reneged on an agreement, blanked them, shouted at them in public etc. I have no idea if any of the grievances were true – let's say for the sake of argument that they weren't – but I left Glastonbury that night convinced the former Smith had an extraordinary ability to engender intense dislike.

Marr was involved in a near-fatal car accident. Even so, by the time they walked onto the stage in Brixton, it wasn't just the band who looked as though they were ready to conquer. The typical Smiths fan was always assumed to be a withering adolescent trapped in his bedroom writing angst-ridden poetry ('Writing frightening verse to a bucktoothed girl in Luxembourg,' in the words of their leader), but towards the end of their career, their concerts seemed to be populated by gangs of beery lads. Brixton Academy certainly was. When I put this to Morrissey he said he quite enjoyed the idea that Smiths concerts were actually quite violent. 'We even have people breaking their legs and backs. They're very healthy people. They're not outpatients ... This image of a typical Smiths fanatic being a creased and semi-crippled youth is *slightly* over-stretched. If the audience was a collection of withering prunes those things wouldn't happen.'

The break-up of the Smiths the following year would coincide with the decline of the indie sector, as independent labels either found themselves going out of business or swallowed up by the majors. Johnny Marr would go on to have a successful if fairly peripatetic existence, as his ex-partner tried to relive past glories, occasionally writing a classic song - 'First of the Gang to Die', 'You're Gonna Need Someone on Your Side', 'Suedehead', 'Spent the Day in Bed', etc. - but usually just sounding like a lyricist without a musical genius. (Elvis Costello once referred to Morrissey post-Smiths as 'someone who comes up with the best song titles in the world, only somewhere along the line he seems to forget to write the song.')

I would have further run-ins with him. We were doing a big piece on Morrissey in *GQ* sometime in the noughties, and having done the interview we were meant to be photographing him in his (rather capacious) bungalow in the Beverly Hills Hotel (paid for by *GQ*, of course). Everything had been arranged for weeks, and our abundant team reflected the seriousness with which we were treating the job: a photographer, three assistants, a hairdresser, make-up-artist, videographer, the journalist, the magazine's creative director, our driver, a fashion editor and their two assistants. But then Morrissey suddenly turned. He slipped quietly into his bedroom, and got one of *his* assistants to call the record company in London, who then had to call the creative director back in Los Angeles to let him know that Morrissey had changed his mind. Wasn't feeling it. Wanted everyone to go, etc.

There was another time, too (would we ever learn?), when we attempted to celebrate him at our annual *GQ* Men of the Year Awards. The magazine had already been printed, containing a long and expansive interview, accompanied by a selection of wonderful and actually quite expensive photographs. Morrissey was in Spain touring, and so it had been arranged that we would send a private jet to pick him up from wherever he was outside Madrid, in order for him to be flown to London, where he would pick up his award on stage at the Royal Opera House in Covent Garden. But the plane just sat there on the tarmac, while we waited for Morrissey to not turn up. Which is exactly what he did: not turn up. He had changed his mind. Wasn't feeling it, etc. We had spent £35,000 on the plane (Lord knows where we found the money), so I figure he still owes us for our trouble.

But while he's obviously a fairly disappointing human being, some of Morrissey's records - and practically every record he ever made with the Smiths - remain inviolate, remnants from a period in British popular culture when poetry and band lore were still paramount, and when Johnny Marr and Steven Patrick Morrisey could do no wrong, no wrong at all.

Appropriately, the final word should go to Johnny Marr. Could the Smiths ever reform?

'I can't answer that question,' he says. 'Honestly, it's too taxing to grapple for an answer. It probably *is* a good thing that it won't happen, yes. If it were the right thing to do, and it was going to be a beautiful experience for the audience, the musicians and everyone, and there was bunting in the streets, then that would be a good thing, too. But for me, it's as abstract as saying wouldn't it be great if there was a multi-million-dollar blockbuster movie that was a cross between *ET* and *The Railway Children*. Yes, it would be NICE, but it's not going to happen, is it? It's idle fantasy.'

1987

The Colour Purple

'Sign O' the Times' by Prince

Making the kind of creative decisions that were inscrutable to those who didn't know him - and actually many who did - Prince nevertheless managed to define the eighties in his own inimitable fashion, both commercially and aesthetically. And while *Purple Rain* and 'Kiss' may have been his most mediated missions, his 1987 single 'Sign O' the Times' was definitely his greatest accomplishment. The album it spawned is also one of the decade's best.

> *'Prince is a bad motherfucker. I'm glad I'm working with you, but another dream I have is working with him too.'*
> *– Eddie Murphy to Michael Jackson*

> *'Yes, he's a natural genius. But I can beat him.'*
> *– Michael Jackson to Eddie Murphy*

You don't call yourself Joan as Police Woman, the Timbuk 3 or Einstürzende Neubauten if you want to become famous. If you want to become famous you call yourself Prince. He may have been gifted the name by his parents, but Prince was the one who decided to keep it, the one who understood - probably from the age of twelve and maybe even a bit earlier - that his parental nurturing and his moniker were actually warranted. Something of a child prodigy (he had mastered over twenty instruments by the time he recorded his first album), he wanted, almost from the start, to be a big pop deal, a 'super influencer'. Madonna may have been right when she said that he had, like her, 'a chip on his shoulder, he's competitive, he's from the Midwest, from a screwed-up home, and he has something to prove.' And because he was born at exactly the right time, in a media environment that actively encouraged ambition, he used everything in his power to make his dream manifest.

Prince became famous because he was talented and impatient and because he was lucky enough to grow up in the sixties.

By 1987, Prince Rogers Nelson was in what he no doubt would have called a transitional phase. He was twenty-eight years old, more famous than he could ever have imagined being, and yet still compelled to constantly experiment. He was a movie star (his 1984 film *Purple Rain* had taken a ton of money at the box office - $70 million, against a $7.2 million budget), a sexual pin-up, even - somewhat incongruously - a fashion plate. Crossing barriers of race, gender and genre to capture the mood of the times, Prince's potent blend of sex and spirituality almost justified his enormous ego. He was a bedroom balladeer, penitent Christian, whimsical storyteller, fastidious orchestrator and cartoon guitar hero, presenting an alchemised collage of modern R&B, funk and spiritual soul. He was also a workaholic. The year before, Miles Davis - of all people - had dubbed him 'the Duke Ellington of the eighties'. The same year, Prince actually wrote a letter to Davis: 'Dear Miles,' it read. 'You gotta hang out with me and Sheila E because a lot of people have to find out who you are.' He had signed the correspondence, with typical restraint, 'God'.

He was driven, and he wanted everyone to know it. 'The reason I don't use musicians a lot of the time had to do with the hours that I worked,' he said. 'I swear to God it's not out of boldness when I say this, but there's not a person around who can stay awake as long as I can. Music is what keeps me awake. There will be times when I've been working in the studio for twenty hours and I'll be falling asleep in the chair, but I'll still be able to tell the engineer what cut I want to make. I use engineers in shifts a lot of the time because when I start something, I like to go all the way through. There are very few musicians who will stay awake that long.'

Like a lot of very famous people (and those who start acting as if they're famous from a young age), Prince's self-awareness came in waves. 'I'm a little bull-headed in my ways,' he said, a little while later. 'Then sometimes everybody in the band comes over, and we have very long talks. They're few and far between, and I do a lot of the talking. Whenever we're done, one of them will come up to me and say, "Take care of yourself. You know I really love you." I think they love me so much, and I love them so much, that if they came over all the time I wouldn't be able to be to them what I am, and they wouldn't be able to do for me as what they do. I think we all need our individual spaces, and when we come together with what we've concocted in our heads, it's cool.'

It was the *Purple Rain* album that had really done it, a record that seemed both of its time and somehow in opposition to it, a package that contained a collection of extraordinary songs that appealed to those who could dance ('Computer Blue'), those who couldn't ('Let's Go Crazy'), those who used their music as a seduction tool ('Take Me With U'), those who liked to lie out in the summer grass and smoke themselves silly ('Purple Rain') and those who were just going to listen to it in the car on the way to the gym ('When Doves Cry'). Honestly, what more could you have wanted from an album? *1999* was a pretty well-rounded record, but *Purple Rain* almost had everything.

In a way it was the eighties equivalent of Fleetwood Mac's *Rumours*, an album as varied as it was surprising. *Rumours* might appear slick and generic now – it sounds to my ears like the greatest 'summer evening's drive' record ever – but it seemed almost motley when it was released. The electronic keyboards, rich harmonies and enveloping drum sound may have evoked a mythical California, but the record was enjoyed for its variety. And *Purple Rain* was similar in that respect; it almost sounded like the eighties itself, atomised and delivered piecemeal.

Prince knew the type of record he was making, as he originally asked Fleetwood Mac's Stevie Nicks to write the title track's lyrics. He wanted a power ballad, big and ballsy, and yet with a hint of regret, and a sliver of hope. Nicks was initially up for the fight, but then demurred. 'It was so overwhelming, that ten-minute track ... I listened to it and I just got scared,' she said. 'I called him back and said, "I can't do it. I wish I could. It's too much for me."'

This is actually something of a shame, because you just know that Nicks would have added some warmth and empathy, and would have made the song more human. Like so many acts who became big in the eighties, Prince would forever be accused of being too distant, too aloof. This is one of the things that critics of eighties pop mention time and time again, and often they're right: when you have acts who are deliberately acting out a role, and when those acts are producing records using machines instead of instruments, the end result can feel somewhat manufactured. Regardless of how good the material is.

'"Purple Rain" was one of the songs we were working on before we decided what the film was going to be,' Prince collaborator Lisa Coleman told the *Guardian*. 'At first he wasn't sure "Purple Rain" was actually a Prince song. It was kind of a country number and he gave it to Stevie Nicks, but she felt intimidated by it. So one day he decided to fool around with it at rehearsal. Wendy started hitting these big chords and that rejigged his idea of the song. He was excited to hear it voiced differently. It took it out of that country feeling. Then we all started playing it a bit harder and taking it more seriously. We played it for six hours straight and by the end of that day we had it mostly written and arranged.'

Prince toured *Purple Rain* relentlessly, promoting the record, the film, the very idea of Prince himself, and yet it brought him close to a nervous breakdown. '*Purple Rain* was 100 shows, and around the 75th, I went crazy,' he said, 'and here's why. They didn't want to see anything but the movie. If you didn't play every song, you were in trouble. After 75 you don't know where you are - somebody had to drag me to the stage. I'm not going! Yes you are! They were the longest shows because you knew what was going to happen.'

Purple Rain made over $70m in its opening run and helped consolidate the idea of Prince in people's eyes. It was the film of his life (sort of), and the film of his look. Neil Tennant, who had yet to leave *Smash Hits* to start the Pet Shop Boys, wrote about it on the film's release.

'Prince loves to pout,' he said. 'To press together his moist, full lips while throwing a sulky, sensuous stare with his big eyes. Even more, he loves to sit astride a powerful new motorbike, angrily kick-start it with a tiny, booted foot, and speed into the distance. And, of course, he loves to perform. With *Purple Rain*, he's constructed a feature film in which he can do all three, dominating the screen with those favourite poses. Judged as a feature film, *Purple Rain* is a bit amateurish, too long and slow. As a "Rock film", it is very ambitious and far superior to most with its frantic concert scenes. And for what it reveals about Prince, it is fascinating.

'"And you - what do you dream about?" Apollonia [his girlfriend] asks Prince early on in the film. He only pouts in reply but his answer is clear. Himself.'

Purple Rain was a calculatedly black new wave record, something to appeal to mall rats as well as clubbers, an album that - like Fleetwood Mac's *Rumours* - was going to sound very good on the radio, in clubs, and - very important this - in pick-up trucks. Using MTV's grudging acknowledgement of black music as a way of pushing himself forward, *Purple Rain* was like Michael Jackson's *Thriller*, only rockier; like the Rolling Stones' *Tattoo You*, only funkier; like Van Halen's *Jump*, only blacker.

During MTV's first few years on air, almost no black artists had their videos shown. The few who were selected included Donna Summer, Musical Youth, Herbie Hancock, Eddy Grant, Joan Armatrading and of course Michael Jackson and Prince. The channel's rationale for rejection was that the artists didn't fit their 'carefully selected album-oriented Rock format', thus excluding the likes of Rick James, whose 'Super Freak' was a massive hit in spite of the MTV ban.

MTV's original head of talent and acquisition, Carolyn B. Baker, who was black, had questioned why the definition of music had to be so narrow, as had a few others outside the network. 'The party line at MTV was that we weren't playing black music because of the "research",' she said, some years later. 'But the research was based on ignorance ... we were young, we were cutting edge. We didn't have to be on the cutting edge of racism.' However, it was Baker who had personally rejected James's video, 'because there were half-naked women in it, and it was a piece of crap. As a black woman, I did not want that representing my people as the first black video on MTV.' It was a vicious circle, because as MTV weren't playing videos by black artists, so record companies stopped paying for them, because they knew they would have difficulty persuading MTV to play them.

Even Michael Jackson had trouble getting on the channel initially. When CBS executives asked why his videos weren't being shown, they were told, 'His music's not rock.' CBS boss Walter Yetnikoff decided they weren't playing them because Jackson was black: 'I said to MTV, "I'm pulling everything we have off the air, all our product. I'm not going to give you any more videos. And I'm going to go public and fucking tell them about the fact you don't want to play music by a black guy."' MTV relented and played 'Billie Jean' in heavy rotation. Afterwards, the *Thriller* album went on to sell an additional ten million copies.

David Bowie did his bit to help, too, asking the MTV VJ Mark Goodman why the channel had such an aversion to black talent. While promoting *Let's Dance* in 1983, Bowie took the two-year-old network to task for playing virtually no videos by black artists. 'Having watched MTV over the past few months, it's a solid enterprise with a lot going for it,' Bowie said to Goodman. 'I'm just floored by the fact that there's so few black artists featured on it. Why is that?'

Having first nonsensically suggested that the channel was trying to play videos that fit 'into what we want to play on MTV', Goodman then went on to put his other foot in his mouth: 'We have to try and do what we think not only New York and Los Angeles will appreciate, but also Poughkeepsie or the Midwest, pick some town in the Midwest that would be scared to death by Prince, which we're playing, or a string of other black faces. We have to play the type of music the entire country would like.'

Goodman continued, saying that the likes of the Isley Brothers or Marvin Gaye wouldn't mean much to a teenager in the Midwest, and then Bowie countered with the rather more salient point that they probably would if they happened to be black.

Nevertheless, the success of *Purple Rain* gave Prince power, the power to experiment.

The Face's Nick Kent was one critic who thought Prince's refusal to ape the success of *Purple Rain* was one of the most genuinely audacious decisions of his career. 'That resolution impelled him to explore areas that allowed him to grow into a state of genuine progressive artistry,' he said.

The success of *Purple Rain* didn't escape Michael Jackson's attention, either, as Prince's album, movie and accompanying tour completely took the shine off the Jacksons' 1984 *Victory* reunion tour. Jackson was also worried that Prince was connecting more with the 'street', which is why Jackson's 1987 album *Bad* was such a blatant attempt to court the burgeoning urban market. There was even talk of him asking Prince to appear on the record, in a cameo role, like Paul McCartney on *Thriller*, but this obviously came to nothing (Prince wasn't interested and Jackson wasn't going to ask twice). Jackson also found it impossible to convincingly compete with Prince in terms of the libidinous nature of his material (he was once called 'the Joe Strummer of orgasms'); when Jackson started singing about sex, it simply sounded weird and forced (just how weird and how forced we would find out later). Prince's emotional landscape was broader, as was his ability to use it to inform his work.

. . .

The eighties was the first decade during which mediated entertainers first became genuine media icons, and Prince was one of the most mediated of all. His signature look was the ruffled shirt with the fingertip-dragging cuffs, high Beau Brummel collars, the purple jacket, toreador pants, a cane and a motorcycle. He wore impossibly shiny shoes, eyeliner, royal medallions, chiffon scarves, a precision-trimmed moustache and gold epaulettes (having moved on significantly from the first few years of his career, when he looked as though he spent most of his time wearing Iggy Pop's underwear). A fabulous dresser, masculine in his feminine clothes, he always looked regal. For a while during 1984 and 1985 it seemed as though he couldn't go anywhere without a rain of purple confetti and little smoke bombs going off around him. He was on television, in magazines, on the front pages of newspapers, and on radio twenty-four hours a day. Real-life sightings were rare, and interviews non-existent, so even the suggestion of Prince coming out of a hotel or walking into a restaurant were genuine news stories.

Until he started throwing his toys out of the purple pram, rowing with his record company, and embarking on a ludicrous strategy of flooding the market with too much product, Prince was The Man, and for much of the eighties he was The One To Watch. He embodied a parade of paradoxes: sexual chameleon, James Brown clone, enigmatic imp and (occasionally) a near-genius songwriter, Prince treated his acclaim seriously, continually using his own success as a benchmark, forcing himself to outdo himself with each subsequent album. And for a while it worked.

The poet Paul Muldoon once said that 'The great artist is not only on the front line but engaged in single combat. The opponent is a version of himself and, almost inevitably, it's a fight to the death.' During the eighties, Prince seemed to compete with himself every day. Some believe he was engaged in a cosmic war between good and evil, but his real fight was against mediocrity, or - heaven forfend - repetition.

He was feminine, petite, and as a friend once said, like a scale model of an adult. 'A doll, an Action Mannequin.' Possessed of a deep voice that would have suited a much bigger man, he could often sound like a DJ on a late-night smooth jazz station, carefully trying to seduce his listeners. He was also a man with a seemingly never-ending number of nicknames - Groinhead, the Purple Imp, His Royal Badness, the Prince of Funk, the Prince of Punk etc. - he was a sub-editor's dream. And while he was occasionally prone to elaborate self-indulgence, lyrical pomposity and obviously by-rote platitudinous calls to unity, he also gave a very good impression of being obsessed with sex, which, let's face it, never hurt anyone's celebrity ascendancy.*

The cliché at the time among journalists was that Prince was as insatiable with his appetite for musical experimentation as he was for sex.

Perhaps more importantly – after all, this was the eighties – he looked the part. It's impossible to over-emphasise the importance of Prince's style in the first half of the decade, a way of looking that was deliberately idiosyncratic as well as being carefully formulaic. At the beginning of his career, he tended to look rather generic in his photo shoots, almost as though he were channelling a James Brown/Mick Jagger cross-breed, with his Farrah Fawcett hair, pimpish moustache and almost always topless. He ruthlessly exploited the whole 'is he?/isn't he?' schtick, the ambiguity of his Trojan Horse style helping spin a web of mystery. Of course, the mystery started to look a lot less mysterious when he started wearing plastic corsets and thigh-high stockings (they certainly weren't appreciated by the Rolling Stones fans who booed him off stage when he opened for them on their 1981 tour).

Naturally, it was his *Purple Rain* look which became iconic: the frilly top that approximated Princess Di's pie-crust shirts, his stack-heeled boots and the military jackets that came complete with echoes of Jimi Hendrix, Pete Townshend and Sgt. Pepper himself. This look was mirrored by all the acts he brought with him, those he toured with, and those he helped sign to Warner Bros. – mirrored by Wendy & Lisa, Sheila E, the Family, the Revolution, everyone, a whole army of purple protégés in silk, lace and leather. Prince pushed the boundaries of what it was acceptable

---

* After his parents separated, his mother, who didn't know how to talk to her son about sex, left porn lying around the house by way of explanation. 'I was given *Playboy* magazine, and there was erotic literature laying around. It was very easily picked up. It was pretty heavy at the time. I think it really affected my sexuality a great deal.' You don't say …

to wear, even within the confines of a rock'n'roll fantasy world already inhabited by overtly heterosexual heavy metal brutes in Spandex and fishnets, the ones who often looked like Superheroes in a lingerie commercial.

Years later, Frank Ocean – who many would compare to Prince – would say, 'He [Prince] made me feel comfortable with how I identify sexually simply by his display of freedom from and irreverence for the archaic idea of gender conformity.'

'The camp of his work gave him an out,' wrote Sasha Geffen in *GQ* in 2020. 'He could sing about his femininity in a heightened reality of his own making, and its lurid artificiality gave him cover from heteronormative scrutiny.'

Squint, though, and you could see that Prince wasn't really doing anything different to what any other pop star had done, from Elvis and Jagger right through to Bowie and Marc Bolan – namely dress like a girl in order to get the girl. 'People say I'm wearing heels because I'm short,' he once said, with a smile. 'I wear heels because the women like 'em.'

After all, the legendary critic Robert Christgau ended a brief review of Prince's *Dirty Mind* in 1980 like this: 'Mick Jagger should fold up his penis and go home.'

When Chris Rock interviewed Prince for VH1 at the tail end of the nineties, he asked him about this.

'The androgynous thing,' Rock said to Prince. 'Was that an act, or were you searching for your sexual identity?'

'That's a good question,' Prince said. 'I don't suppose I was searching, really. I think I was just ... being who I was. Being the true Gemini that I am. And there's um, there's many sides in that as well. And there was a little acting going on, too.'

In 1981, Prince had begged an interviewer not to compare him to Michael Jackson, although at the time it seemed unlikely that any self-respecting journalist would have done such a thing. But by 1987, it was standard journalistic practice to compare him to just about every black crossover star of consequence, including Little Richard, James Brown, Jimi Hendrix and Sly Stone. By 1987,

Prince was a global star of such magnitude that Warner Bros. Records decided to place a worldwide embargo on his new album. This meant that advance copies were withheld from radio, TV and press until its worldwide release, with the record company telling anyone who wanted to know that tapes of the LP were safely stashed away in a safe, with a round-the-clock bodyguard standing by. At the time, this could have meant that the record was so offensively awful that they wanted to limit the amount of bad publicity it generated before going on sale, although in the case of *Sign O' the Times*, they were actually trying to generate as much hype as possible.

It was a different record from *Purple Rain*, in fact it was a very different record from the opulent, psychedelic *Around the World in a Day* (1985) and the minimalistic funk of *Parade* (1986), the two albums that preceded it. He'd disbanded the Revolution, the band that had backed him since *Purple Rain*, and he'd been developing a record based on an alter ego called Camille, whose tracks were recorded with his voice tweaked to sound even more womanly than his trademark falsetto – recording his vocals at a slower speed then speeding up the tape to feminise his voice (an old trick of both Stevie Wonder and George Clinton).

The album he eventually released on 31 March 1987 was a Prince solo record that, like his earlier albums, was essentially a one-man-band recording. Not content with mastering guitar, bass, keyboard and drums, Prince became a virtuoso on the Fairlight CMI sampler and the Linn LM-1 drum machine as well. If *Purple Rain*, with its new wave song structures, warm, inclusive and empowering Glitterfunk, boisterous percussion and arena-ready production, had made him a crossover star, with *Sign O' the Times* he went back to the strictly solo feel of his early albums. Only by 1987 he was obviously a much, much better songwriter. Of the sixteen songs on *Sign O' the Times*, only three have co-writers, and save for one track ('It's Going to Be a Beautiful Night'), outside musical accompaniment is almost non-existent. Prince's major musical collaborator at this point was probably his long-suffering engineer Susan Rogers, who recorded him at different studios in Minneapolis (at his new, 65,000-square-foot Paisley Park compound), Los Angeles, and even Paris. Prince would call her in the middle of the night and ask her to come in and record something he'd just thought of. When he did, he would regularly sing with his back to her, or ask her to leave the room, standing alone in the studio wearing only some track pants and his trademark platform flip-flops.

Sign O' the Times began as *Crystal Ball* in 1986, a triple album that Warner Bros. understandably refused to release. 'They told him no, which was something that hadn't really happened up until that point,' said Rogers. 'After all, they'd agreed to let him write and produce his own music from the beginning and to go off and make a movie when he was 23 and not really big yet; they pretty much let him do as he pleased but said no to the triple album idea.'

He had a couple of other still-born projects, too, one of which was the pseudonymous *Camille*. So in early 1987 he picked the best bits from all of them, and assembled a double album that took diversity to new margins, bubbling over with ideas and bouncing between sex and religion, between Joni Mitchell and Sly Stone, via searing funk, coy ballads, rap, prog and the obligatory drum machine. It was the perfect rock'n'soul interface, a record of vaulting ambition, whose music still encompassed an extraordinarily varied range of styles, including soul, psychedelia, electro, rockabilly and rock – yet again making a virtue of eclecticism. As ever he appeared to be wrestling with the twin pillars of carnality and spirituality that had defined his career, yet with a new kind of music – naked funk, skinny R&B. Some of the songs were so bare they didn't sound finished.

'I hate the word experiment,' he once said. 'It sounds like something you didn't finish.' But Prince was a repeat offender.

The record was nothing if not unconventional, a volte-face of the most expansive kind. The received wisdom nowadays is that Prince figured it was a pointed retort to the suffocating cocoon of expectations that fame had woven around him, although in reality it was probably more like the sensation you get when you've just climbed to the top of a very steep hill. Not only do you have to walk back down, but what's the point of climbing it again? And who needed another *Purple Rain* anyway? Ultimately Prince's masterpiece could be best described by Greil Marcus's review of Fleetwood Mac's unrepresentative *Tusk*, the record they struggled to make after the multi-million-dollar success of the super-slick *Rumours*: 'Fleetwood Mac is subverting the music from the inside out, very much like one of John Le Carré's moles – who, planted in the heart of the establishment, does not begin his secret campaign of sabotage until everyone has gotten used to him and takes him for granted.'

Ben Greenman, who has written hundreds of thousands of words about Prince for various publications, including the *New Yorker* and the *New York Times*, is articulate in explaining why *Sign O' the Times* has always been a critics' darling in Prince's catalogue. '*Sign O' the Times* is not the equal of *1999*, or even *Purple Rain*, but it is unsurpassed as a demonstration of acrobatic versatility,' he says. 'The album's musical style ranges across spooky political R&B, full-throated psychedelic pop, bone-rattling skeletal funk, and pocket soul so gentle and nuanced you could almost call it folk – and that's just in the first four songs.'

There is a consensus that the brittle nature of machine-driven drums and a reliance on electronic sounds made a lot of eighties music seem cold and thin, a sensation exacerbated by the way in which CDs appeared to condense everything. Critics of eighties music often say it is metallic and unemotional, containing sounds and feelings that have been flattened and dampened and commoditised. Prince was accused of this, too, and yet the polymathic diversity of *Sign O' the Times* redeemed him in many people's eyes.

The title track and lead-off single wasn't so much a protest song as a lament. The song is bleak, but epic, a demo, almost, but with apocalyptic lyrics and a great refrain – sweet and sour, big and small. The lyrics read like a newspaper, containing Prince's various Op-Eds on the issues of the day: gang violence, poverty, drug abuse, impending nuclear disaster, the Space Shuttle *Challenger* accident, and AIDS ('a big disease with a little name'). 'He is a pop Caravaggio fetishising the apocalypse, as he had before in "1999",' said the writer George Chesterton. A spartan electro-blues, when you first heard it on the radio - sandwiched between the likes of Jackie Wilson's 'Reet Petite', Ben E. King's 'Stand By Me' and Boy George's 'Everything I Own' (all three went to Number One in early 1987, two reissues and a cover) - it felt more than just casually significant. It wasn't angry so much as despondent, an acceptance of reality.

'I don't live in the past,' he had told *Rolling Stone* in 1985. And indeed he didn't.

. . .

You could use any year as a springboard for impending doom or geopolitical variance, and yet 1987 certainly had its moments. There was the *Herald of Free Enterprise* disaster, when a roll-on/roll-off ferry capsized moments after leaving the Belgian port of Zeebrugge, killing 193 passengers and crew; the Hungerford massacre, when an unemployed antiques dealer and handyman called Michael Ryan shot dead sixteen people, including a police officer and his own mother, before shooting himself; the Kings Cross fire; the Glanrhyd Bridge collapse, the Remembrance Day Bombing in Northern Ireland; and at the beginning of the year, the Archbishop of Canterbury's envoy Terry Waite being kidnapped in Lebanon, remaining a hostage until 1991. The major political event of this year in the UK was the re-election of Margaret Thatcher in June's general election, making her the longest continuously serving Prime Minister of the United Kingdom since Lord Liverpool in the early nineteenth century.

In the US the big news was the Iran-Contra affair, where senior government officials secretly facilitated the sale of arms to the Khomeini regime (the subject of an arms embargo), hoping to use the proceeds to fund the Contras in Nicaragua (after admitting he had approved the sale, then testifying that he hadn't, President Reagan eventually said, 'The simple truth is, I don't remember').

Ronald Reagan and Mikhail Gorbachev also continued their nuclear disarmament chess game, while Reagan used his visit to West Berlin in June to try and occupy the media high ground by encouraging his Soviet adversary to open the Berlin Wall: 'Mr. Gorbachev, tear down this wall!'

The stock market wasn't immune to global tensions, either, and the infamous Black Monday of 19 October reflected a slowdown in the US economy, falling oil prices and escalating tensions between Iran and the Americans. However, the crash was exacerbated by newfangled computerised trading. As one statistician said afterwards, 'There's no such thing as "it can't happen".'

This was also the year porn queen 'Cicciolina', born Ilona Staller (the future wife of Jeff Koons), bared her breasts in Rome's Piazza Navona having been elected to the Italian Parliament; the year Pope John Paul II welcomed Austrian President Kurt Waldheim, a former Nazi, to the Vatican; the year Michael Jackson reportedly proposed to Elizabeth Taylor. It's no wonder that this was the year that Prozac hit the market for the first time. Nevertheless, this was the year and 'Sign O' the Times' was its song.

Interestingly, one reviewer said it was the sound of the good times collapsing.

'Sign O' the Times' also makes a nod towards hip-hop, as Prince was keenly aware that hip-hop was rising up and shifting the sound of success. Not that he was too happy about hip-hop's onslaught, of course. Fundamentally he was threatened by it, worried his virtuosity and fame was being pushed to the margins because of the generational shift. Increasingly he would hunker down in his ever-expanding Paisley Park home, turning himself into even more of an Oz-type enigma. Who needed a maverick in the world of BPM? He regularly turned down requests for permission to sample his work, scared perhaps that the culture would then have the upper hand. 'Some of these acts I really dig but I don't want my music used that way,' he said in 1997.

Should we have been surprised? Perhaps not. After all, Prince was such an obsessive that if anyone was going to mess with

233

his work, it was going to be him. In essence he was the Todd Rundgren, the Frank Zappa, the Stevie Wonder of his day, a funky little polymath, quixotic to the core. A slave to the studio, his life was music. When you walked around Paisley Park, pearlescent plectrums littered the rooms like confetti, and there was always one within arm's reach, just in case. There were stashes of CDs everywhere, too, and always more than one copy of *A Decade of Steely Dan*, which had only just come out. He wasn't a perfectionist, though, more like a sorcerer. 'He used to say, "We don't sound like those other people,"' said Susan Rogers. '"We don't sound like Michael Jackson. We don't spend all that kind of money. We go fast. We make mistakes." He wouldn't have had that output if he'd been a perfectionist. He was a virtuoso player and a genius with melody, a genius with rhythm, a genius at writing songs. It just poured out of him - he couldn't wait on perfection. The important thing was to have the sound serve the idea, not the other way round.'

And it all came out on *Sign O' the Times*. The album features all the standard accoutrements of the decade - the aforementioned Linn drum and Fairlight - yet it has fared well, and the songs here are as varied as any he recorded - some as stark and as minimal as a seventies video game, others as extravagant as a Lacroix frock. It's all here, and so is he: Prince, the Cobb salad of the studio. He was not averse to marshalling the occasional happy accident, either. One of the first songs he recorded for the album was 'The Ballad of Dorothy Parker', whose unusual sound was caused by a power-failure due to a snowstorm. The blackout meant the tape machine ran at half speed, erasing the song's top end. Prince liked the result so much, he kept it.

Sign O' the Times is certainly austere, a panoramic picture, almost, of what Prince thought was happening around him, and of course what was happening in his own head. Which for him was obviously far more important. If he could mine sweep the cultural waterfront and involve it somehow in his work, then so be it; but for him, his whims were always going to take precedence.

'By today's standards, *Sign O' the Times* may seem a cold album,' says George Chesterton. 'But all things being cyclical, Prince and the plastic, superficial eighties followed the sincerity of folk-rock and the ideological purity of punk. In this context, Prince was the successor to David Bowie, in that the art and artifice were the point. Heart for heart's sake was not an issue. It was the ideas that mattered. Now we value emotional nakedness above all else, in a culture where workaday honesty is judged to be "real" while around us songs, radio, TV and films become reflections of Facebook status updates.'

Some tried to frame it as a concept album, but it was anything but. The only concept was Prince himself. It was fractured, undisciplined in a way, an almost perfect piece of postmodernism (although completely unlike the postmodernism that was affecting every other discipline in eighties culture, like architecture, design and food).

In the culture generally, the decade was rushing back into the past, as retromania became a genuine craze, like Cabbage Patch Dolls, Gremlins, or Ray-Bans (which were themselves a fifties throwback item). Nineteen-eighty-seven was actually a big year for nostalgia, as so much of the American entertainment industry was harking back to the recent past. If you went to the cinema, the past was presented as though it were an inviting blanket on a suburban lawn, or a cold, refreshing Coke at a Drive-In. In the space of a few months you could have watched *Dirty Dancing*, *Radio Days*, *Dragnet*, *Tin Men*, or *Chuck Berry: Hail! Hail! Rock'n'Roll*. The Beatles' back catalogue was finally released on CD, and newspapers were full of celebratory pieces on the twentieth anniversary of – deep breath – *Sgt. Pepper's Lonely Hearts Club Band*, Cream's *Disraeli Gears* or Love's *Forever Changes*, or the first albums by Jimi Hendrix, Pink Floyd, the Doors, even the Velvet Underground (who weren't even a thing in 1967, not outside of certain squalid parts of Manhattan, anyway).

There was such a celebration of boomer culture that it somehow felt as though there was a *Back to the Future* movie released every couple of months or so. And when *Rolling Stone* magazine chose to recognise their twentieth anniversary with a seemingly never-ending number of special editions, lionising the late sixties and everything contained therein, we were encouraged to think that nothing had been the same since. In the eighties, the sixties weren't remembered as a period of insurrection, free sex and drug psychosis, far from it, but rather as a way-station on the narrative arc of popular culture.

Set against all this, *Sign O' the Times* appeared to be ridiculously modern. Some of the old funk tropes were in evidence – sex, death, God and so on – but the bulk of it sounded like the kind of thing you could reasonably expect to hear if you were waiting to board the international space station, having been rocketed there from Earth.

The record was not just Prince's high-water mark, it also signalled his slow demise. The dark, dense *Black Album* was recorded then shelved immediately after *Sign O' the Times*, its fleeting reputation as a great lost album undermined once it was actually released (in 1994). Supposedly, Prince disowned it because he felt it was 'evil', opting instead to record and release the upbeat but underwhelming *Lovesexy*. Prince appeared naked on the cover of *Lovesexy*, generating industry gossip that his head had been reduced in size to make him look more 'normal'; it says a lot about the quality of the record that this was the most memorable thing about it. Everything Prince would release after that would succumb to the law of diminishing returns, and he was never the same again. Soon, the culture said it had had enough. An example of Prince's perceived trashiness appeared in an episode of *Friends*, when Ross and Chandler debated whether or not to visit the Hard Rock Café. Ross: 'I'm telling you I like the food!' Chandler: 'You like the *Purple Rain* display!'

He retreated to his Xanadu, a Prospero for the times, a Willy Wonka in mufti, content to acknowledge his own genius in secret.

Prince treasured the privacy Paisley Park afforded him. He enjoyed his fame but didn't feel the need to engage with his greater public, becoming a notorious recluse. He made a lot of records but didn't like talking about them too much. The paradox is that, for all his warts and insecurities, he was adored as much as the likes of Madonna, Bruce Springsteen and Michael Jackson- the other stadium giants of the eighties - who all had a far more urgent need to manipulate their audiences.

While he didn't like anyone addressing him by name, and would later rebrand himself first as a symbol, and then The Artist Formerly Known As Prince (or TAFKAP to use the diminutive), his crew and his staff all called him 'Boss'. Not because they asked him to, but because they liked him. Journalists would often sidle up to them in Paisley Park, or on tour, and whisper questions. Invariably they would be met with a smirk, and something like, 'He's just a regular cat like you and me,' even when he plainly wasn't.

He was ridiculously specific in his terms of agreement when he agreed to meet journalists, which was rare in itself. First, no tape recorders were to be used; secondly, no notepad or pens were allowed to be brought into the room; and thirdly, and most strangely, there were not to be any questions. Then, when you eventually sat down with him, he would act all coquettish and coy. He would feign stupidity or indifference or deliberately pretend not to understand your point, although his most effective mask was an expression of absolute vacancy. A blank. They say that living in mystery is a stage of stardom, a reaction to early fame, and yet this became Prince's default position. Not talking. Not granting access to Princeworld.

Of course, there were those close to him who thought that the less he spoke the better, and that it was wise for him to stay away from recording devices and television cameras. Former Warner Bros. publicity chief Bob Merlis once recounted an early story that may go some way towards explaining why Prince rarely granted interviews during his initial rise to fame: 'Prince did an interview with a woman at *Record World* [in 1978]. They talked about whatever, then he asked her, "Does your pubic hair go up to your navel?" At that moment, we thought maybe we shouldn't encourage him to do interviews.'

He was indulged, too. He could be demanding, petulant and would rarely listen to reason. He obviously manufactured many points of difference, but not all of them were as dignified as he might have hoped, especially his irritating penchant for what his fans came to call 'Princebonics', his childish way of writing, using '2' instead of 'to', 'U' for 'you' or an illustration of an eye for 'I' for instance, the kind of thing you might expect to find scrawled on the exercise book of a twelve-year-old. Carolyn Baker, once a vice president of artist development at Warner Bros., was quoted about her charge back in the day: 'His whole world is coloured differently from mine. People used to say, "Will you tell him to do something?" And I'd say, "No, you need to work around it." He has a vision. He has got to be able to do it his way ... It's kind of like being with an alien.'

Alternatively, the comedian 'Weird Al' Yankovic was once assigned to sit in the same row at an awards ceremony. Yankovic later remembered: 'I got a telegram – and I wasn't the only one – from Prince's management company saying that I was not to establish eye contact with him during the show. I just couldn't even believe it. So immediately I sent back a telegram saying that he shouldn't be establishing eye contact with me either.'

While he looked to the world like the complete narcissist, a showman for whom attention was all, Prince's best work is not the stuff that screams. Listening to the work from a distance, music that once seemed so explosive now sounds self-possessed, elegant and full of purpose, so assured as to need neither qualifiers nor explanations.

Regardless of whether or not you liked his music, Prince is important because he is a prime example of how the eighties made it possible for him to thrive, an autodidactic hyphenate who used media to amplify his talent, his ambition and ultimately his fame – a fame he quickly put in aspic by distancing himself from anyone wanting to get close to him. Once he had reached his citadel, that was it, he simply pulled up the drawbridge, like Michael Jackson and Madonna, the other eighties superstars who were now starting to act like old-fashioned Hollywood celebrities.

And by turning himself into a legend, so his death was treated as it would have been were he Valentino or Elvis.

The Hollywood death has always had a grim, global allure, the death that feels so much bigger than life. To die in Hollywood is not only to reinforce the understanding that the Faustian pact is sometimes too much of a burden, it also somehow reinforces just how famous you are. To die unnaturally in the 90210, 90068 or 90069 area codes is to have your death included in the pantheon of Hollywood Babylon, an example of the celebrity trade-off.

In the twenty-first century, one would think that social media would diminish this feeling, but in a very real sense it's actually done the opposite, by exacerbating the distance between the famous and those mediating that fame. When celebrities die today, the widespread use of social media suggests their passing is owned by everyone, that their fame was shared by all those who found them famous. But all it really does is make the owner of the app look like even more of a consumer. Of the 130 or so celebrities who have died of drug-related incidents since 2010, when Instagram was launched, probably the most famous are Amy Winehouse (who died in 2011), Whitney Houston (2012), Phillip Seymour Hoffman (2014), Scott Weiland (2015), Prince (2016), George Michael (2016) and Tom Petty (2017), and these tragedies haven't been salved by social media, they've simply been amplified by it.

An unplanned Hollywood death is still a big moment in Tinsel Town, particularly if you live there. And even though Prince didn't die in Hollywood, but instead at his home at Paisley Park – of an accidental overdose of the opioid fentanyl – his death was predictably seen as one. So consequently Prince became bigger in death than at any time since 1984, a monolithic presence in the culture, ripe for re-examination and undue flattery.

Was Prince sometimes too clever for his own good? Almost, unbelievably, some thought so. He was too cocky, too flamboyant, too imperious, too talented, too non-white perhaps? He certainly had an ability – some might say a desire – to wind people up.

Engagingly, he was not the kind of person who worried too much what people said about him.

Often he was disparaged for the same reason Salieri despised Mozart – because it all came too damn easy for him.

I saw him once, close-up, at an awards ceremony in one of the big museums in London, and actually he couldn't have been more perfect. Sitting on a large, circular table, he sat, facing away from his guests, facing the room, with what can only be described as the widest of shit-eating grins. He was surrounded by women – there were twelve places set for dinner and none of his eleven guests were men – and he was dressed like a dandy, in black, but with plenty of feathers and a stovepipe hat. He knew precisely the effect he was having on everyone else in the room, and he couldn't have cared less what anyone thought.

Because he was Prince, and he was funky. And pugnacious, too.

Was he just too much of a polymath, rather too good at too many things? Seventeen years after making probably the best album of the decade – shall I say that again? – Prince did something that appeared to soothe the clammy brows of those who sought to bring him down, who felt he was still an uppity arriviste.

On 15 March 2004, George Harrison was posthumously inducted into the Rock and Roll Hall of Fame. As part of the ceremony at the Waldorf Astoria in New York, an all-star band performed 'While My Guitar Gently Weeps', one of Harrison's best-known Beatles songs. The group featured Tom Petty (from the Heartbreakers, Traveling Wilburys), Jeff Lynne (ELO, Traveling Wilburys), Steve Winwood (Spencer Davis Group, Blind Faith, Traffic) and Dhani Harrison (George's son) as well as Prince himself. During the rehearsal, most of the guitar solos were played by Marc Mann, a white-man's-overbite guitarist in Lynn's band, including a note-for-note replica of Eric Clapton's remarkable solo on the *White Album* version. Prince, meanwhile, kept himself to himself, playing along with the rest of the band as though he were a journeyman session player.

Come the live show, it was all very different indeed. For the first three minutes or so, Prince seemed happy to stand in the shadows, but as the song reached its final furlongs, he moved centre-stage, his red Borsalino catching the light, as he used his guitar to burn the place to the ground. His three-minute guitar solo was one of the greatest moments in all of rock'n'roll, a moment that's been viewed over fifty million times on YouTube, and deservedly so. Prince's performance was as good as anything hewn by Jimi Hendrix, Eddie Van Halen, the Edge, or even Clapton himself. The incendiary way he managed to wring so much extraordinary noise out of his machine remains completely bewildering, almost as though he were using some kind of empowered, magical wand. For anyone who hasn't seen the clip, this is not hyperbole, trust me, as every time I play it, it mystifies me. As for the rest of the band, they simply looked on, shell-shocked almost, plodding their way to the song's inevitable conclusion, acutely aware that they had been royally shown up.

As Prince finished, signalling to the band that it was time to draw the proceedings to a close, he threw his guitar up in the air, up into the rafters, and proceeded to walk offstage.

Steve Ferrone, Tom Petty's drummer, was playing that night. 'I didn't even see who caught it. I just saw it go up, and I was astonished that it didn't come down again. Everybody wonders where that guitar went, and I gotta tell you, I was on that stage, and I wonder where it went, too.'

As some wag said afterwards, it was almost as if George Harrison had grabbed the guitar himself in mid-air to signal, 'That's enough of that.'

1988

The
Second
Summer
of Love

'Theme from S'Express' by S'Express

During the late summer of 1987, a gaggle of holidaying British DJs stumbled upon the synergy between house music and Ecstasy in the clubs of Ibiza. By the early summer of 1988, the UK was alive with the Balearic beat, as the trippy, futuristic sound of Chicago acid house swept through the land, democratising clubland and creating an equitable youth movement that did away with the need for any velvet ropes. And the accidental acid house record that galvanised the nation was S'Express's 'Theme from S'Express'.

'In early 1988, there were still people coming to the Haçienda in suits with shoulder pads, then all of a sudden they were in dungarees.' – Dave Haslam

Given that it was one of the most egalitarian of British youth cults – officially the only one to ever successfully turn football hooligans into hippies, albeit briefly – it was out of character for acid house to turn its nose up at any of its constituents, but then again acid teds weren't exactly the most delightful of creatures. They travelled in same-sex packs, abused any DJs who tried to add any nuance to the sound of 'Aciiiiiiiiiiiid', and were just as incurious as their namesakes, the ageing teddy boys who wandered the earth in the seventies hankering for the days of Elvis Presley and Johnny Burnette. The acid house fanzine *Boy's Own* even had a slogan for them: 'Better dead than acid ted.'

Still, they were an understandable by-product of probably the most unlikely youth movement since the teds themselves.

'There was an *aciderati* who always criticised the acid teds, saying you'll never catch us in a field waving our hands in the air,' says Mark Moore, the man behind one of the year's biggest records, and one of the UK's first house tracks, 'Theme From S'Express'. 'Well, I went to a lot of those fields, and they were great. Going to all those raves was terrific, as there were such a lot of people who were into it that you just wouldn't have expected, like Mick Jones from the Clash, for instance. There were all of these random people going from party to party, most of them out of their heads on Ecstasy, it was mad.'

S'Express were one of the beneficiaries of the second summer of love, a testament to the way in which youth culture in 1988 had changed so quickly.

If the eighties was a decade in which aggressively synthesised percussion revolutionised the music industry, acid house was another step change, a brand extension of the recently arrived house music that would soon galvanise the nation's youth.

Acid house originally came from Chicago (the term 'house music' refers to the Chicago club, the Warehouse), and was defined by the squelching bass sound of the Roland TB-303 synthesiser. Released in 1981 and originally intended as a bass guitar accompaniment for organists and guitarists, its only problem was that it sounded almost nothing like a real bass guitar. The synth was considered to be a commercial failure for Roland, and was discontinued in 1984, although some producers continued to experiment with it. The characteristics of the 303 that encouraged them to do this was the distortion you got when pushing the filters to the maximum, which produced a kind of liquid sound filled with squelching and squealing. The machine was idiosyncratic, and so appealed to boffins. In 1985, three such boffins calling themselves Phuture started messing around with their newly acquired 303, putting together twelve minutes of frenetic, hypnotic basslines, which they called 'Acid Tracks'. One night they gave a tape to Ron Hardy, a DJ who worked at Chicago's Music Box, who played it four times in quick succession. The first time it was met by incomprehension, the fourth by delight.

The record was eventually released in 1987, just in time for Paul Oakenfold's birthday. Oakenfold's twenty-fourth birthday has since become part of dance music's folklore. In August that year, four London DJs - Oakenfold, Danny Rampling, Nicky Holloway and Johnny Walker - went to Ibiza for a week-long celebration, hiring a villa near San Antonio, by the bay - which in essence must have been something of a busman's holiday. Here, amid the palms and the crickets, the mumbling winds and the kidney-shaped swimming pools, the boys kicked back, spending days in the sun, sipping cocktails under an opalescent sky.

Obviously they spent a lot of their time sampling the local nightlife, although it was open-air Amnesia that caused them to re-evaluate what they were doing back in the UK, a club that started at 3 a.m. and lasted until noon, and which encouraged a diverse social mix, unlike most of the other Ibizan clubs. The club's resident DJ, Alfredo Florito, was a master at weaving soul, funk and indie, and that particular week played João Gilberto, Prince, Carly Simon, Talking Heads, Cyndi Lauper, the Art of Noise and Bob Marley among more esoteric choices such as the Thrashing Doves' 'Jesus on the Payroll', Elkin and Nelson's 'Jibaro' and a smattering of Argentinian tango. This was what was known collectively as the Balearic beat, although Alfredo would tie it all together by the judicious use of new house records coming out of Chicago, in particular the 'Acid Tracks' mixes by Phuture.

Often born of necessity - stretching a limited but musically varied number of records to fill long summer days and nights - 'Balearic' records eventually formed a Mediterranean canon, a canon that became its very own genre. When the Ibizan club Pacha had opened in 1973, you might have heard James Brown mixed in with Crosby, Stills and Nash, or wondered why the DJ was fading from bubblegum pop like the Archies ('Sugar Sugar') into Jethro Tull or Bob Marley. The reason was that these were the only records that had made it to the island.

Jose Padilla was another famous Ibiza DJ: 'There was not much choice,' he said. 'It's not because in Ibiza we liked to play like that.' He says they were forced to play Talk Talk, or Belgian new beat, or rock or reggae, because they had so many hours on the dance floor to fill. Thus, everything became acceptable after a while.

Oakenfold's appreciation of Amnesia was helped by an introduction to a new drug, Ecstasy, or MDMA to give it its chemical name, a 'happy drug' that produced a euphoric state and encouraged a state of togetherness. 'We all tried Ecstasy for the first time together, and then the whole thing made sense,' said Nicky Holloway. 'Alfredo was playing [Chicago house label imprints] Trax and DJ International next to Kate Bush and Queen, all the white English acts we'd turn our noses up at. But on E, it all made sense. Half an hour or so after you necked a pill you would suddenly feel this euphoric wave go through you, like shooom! - hence the name of Danny's club - and you suddenly felt that everything in the world was all right.

'That first night, the last tune at sunrise was U2's "I Still Haven't Found What I'm Looking For". That night I found everything I had been looking for. All four of us changed that night. I can remember saying I think we may be on to something here.'

Ecstasy had arrived on the island in the early eighties, via a circuitous route, all the way from the American Midwest, where it had been developed as yet another drug to assist psychotherapy (it began life as a pharmaceutical aid for sexually insecure couples). The most popular explanation of its arrival in the Med involves a branch of the free-love-espousing religious Rajneesh movement, who moved to Ibiza from Oregon, where they had been able to buy the drug illegally in bars, because of a nearby governmental facility. The island's growing population of sun-drenched hippies obviously took to it with delight.

'Ecstasy was for the rich people that used to go to the private parties [on the island],' Afredo is quoted as saying. 'Everyone used to say, "You give it to a woman and she opens her legs." But the hippies, and the post-hippie people, they used to take the drugs more seriously. They wanted an experience that was going to open their minds, and Ecstasy wasn't that type of thing, it was a pleasure drug.'

A pleasure drug that by 1987 had already become something of a Balearic religion.

On their return to London, the holidaying DJs set about launching their own mini versions of Amnesia: Oakenfold with Spectrum, Holloway with the Trip and, most famously, Rampling with Shoom. Acid house had arrived, and with it, a new drug culture that soon had both the police and the tabloids in a spin. After a couple of 'Ecstasy deaths', the *Sun*'s 'medical correspondent', Vernon Coleman, issued this warning: 'You will hallucinate. For example, if you don't like spiders you'll start seeing giant ones. There's a good chance you'll end up in a mental hospital for life ... If you're young enough there's a good chance you'll be sexually assaulted while under the influence. You may not even know until a few days or weeks later.' It was the kind of hysterical scaremongering the papers had previously used with the Beats (marijuana), mods (amphetamines), hippies (LSD), punks (amphetamines again) and yuppies (cocaine), and the side-effects seemed remarkably similar (especially the stuff about spiders). The hysteria was relentless: 'The screaming teenager jerked like a demented doll as the LSD he swallowed earlier took its terrible toll ... The boy had been sucked into the hellish nightmare engulfing thousands as the acid house scourge sweeps Britain. Callous organisers simply looked on and LAUGHED.'

Ecstasy had actually arrived in London from the US in the summer of 1981, around the time of Prince Charles's wedding to Lady Diana Spencer, in July. It arrived in the form of MDA, which was far more psychedelic than its successor MDMA, and also tended to last longer (sometimes up to six hours). Ecstasy was a more social drug, being more empathogenic, and more likely to enhance sensual pleasures. MDA often as not made you feel as though you'd just taken some dodgy LSD. Ecstasy proper also made a brief appearance in 1985 at Taboo, the debauched, cross-dressing, and rather brilliant post-New Romantic nightclub run by the Australian performance artist Leigh Bowery. Here, people bought pills for £30 a pop, went and had sex in the loos, and then danced themselves dizzy to hilarious hi-energy, like the genre-defining 'After the Rainbow' by Joanne Daniels.

Ecstasy was not just a more empathetic experience, its arrival also coincided with Margaret Thatcher's third election victory, a pinch point in British politics and one that hinted that the mood of the nation was becoming less strident, and was perhaps ready for a change of some sort. 'When the drug reached Britain en masse,' wrote John Harris in *The Last Party*, his book about the rise of New Labour and the confines of Britpop, 'it wasn't difficult to discern a striking socio-economic subtext: the "loved-up" E high represented as clean a break with the individualistic mores of Thatcherism as could be imagined.'

But while it may have had its own drug, acid house didn't really have an ideology, didn't have a political message. Could renouncing the world, separating yourself from society, and buying big baggy T-shirts be considered a manifesto? Maybe it could. Little of the music contained a message, other than a sort of benign demand to have a good time, and apart from a general sense of being outside of conventional society, the main thrust of what the media would laughingly call a cult, was a communitarian spirit only experienced if you were actually on Ecstasy.

Mark Moore wasn't driven by Ecstasy, or spiders come to that, but for the last few years had been obsessed with what had recently been identified as house music. A prominent London DJ, former Blitz Kid and refugee from a boarding school for the dispossessed, he was about to become the figurehead for a micro-generation obsessed with dance music and drugs.

Moore's mother had moved to London from South Korea in the late fifties, after the Korean War, and then married a young lawyer called Stanley. Cultural differences eventually got the better of them, and they divorced when Mark was four, in 1969. Since moving to the UK, his mother had steadily built up a property empire, and between them his parents had created a safe, middle-class existence for Mark and his elder brother Joseph. There was a big house in Golders Green, there were riding lessons. But after the divorce, his mother had something of a breakdown, and in a decline that shocked everyone around her, she soon lost everything.

'She was trying to bring up two kids on her own and it got too much for her,' says Moore. 'She went bankrupt, and I remember having to hide behind the sofa when the debt collectors came round.' His father, meanwhile, quickly remarried, although his new bride apparently had no interest in either Mark or Joseph. The brothers were briefly put in a children's home in Potters Bar before being sent to a boarding school in Ipswich called Woolverstone Hall, once nicknamed the poor man's Eton. Almost a social experiment, the idea seemed to be to see what happens if you put a bunch of poor kids from London, from broken families, into a slick public school environment. And for a while, for Moore, it worked.

'It was a safe space for me,' says Moore, from a distance of fifty years. 'I had a bed, I had two drawers I could put things in, but by then I had no possessions left. I started collecting bus tickets; every bus I went on I would keep the ticket. That's what I put in my drawers. I've still got them.'

Moore hated the holidays, though, as his father, unwilling to have them at home, would put the two boys in a bed and breakfast in Belsize Park and gave them money he instructed them to spend in Kentucky Fried Chicken. Between the ages of eleven and fifteen, during every school holiday, the brothers were left to fend for themselves. Moore would spend his money going to the cinema in the West End, ignoring food, not eating properly, and rapidly developing a sense of injustice. One day, via his brother's Dansette record player, he discovered punk rock, and it was everything he had been looking for.

'I was so angry at the world, pissed off and hurt. Why was I in this situation? Why had I lost my mother? Why had I lost everything? I was really angry. So I started playing what I thought were these stupid punk records and my life changed.'

He played Patti Smith's 'Piss Factory' and thought she was talking to him, being in a dead-end job with no prospects, and no way out. It made him want to escape. And so he started working his way through his brother's record collection, through the Ramones, the Clash, the Buzzcocks, the Tubes ('I loved "White Punks on Dope"'), the Sex Pistols ... 'When Johnny Rotten sang about there being no future, I interpreted that as there's no future for you unless you get up off your arse and do something about it. I had shivers down my spine. I suppose punk made me come out of my shell.'

Records turned into gigs – the Damned at a youth club in Finchley, the Clash and Siouxsie and the Banshees at places like the Marquee and the Music Machine. Moore was still only fourteen, however, and so his brother used to make him arrive at gigs separately, leaving their B&B half an hour later, so he didn't cramp his style. Out of boredom, he and his friends would mooch along the Kings Road, staring at the overpriced punk clothes they couldn't afford to buy, occasionally knocking on the doors of John Lydon and Sid Vicious. Incredibly, Sid and his girlfriend Nancy Spungen once let them in, obviously disoriented by heroin. 'Sid was adorable, really docile. We thought they must have had a late night the night before; "Why are they so sleepy?" We were fourteen – we didn't have a clue.'

Then, stretching his social circle, he started squatting with friends in Kings Cross, taking a lot of blues, enjoying his new sexual freedom ('I think you always know deep down when you're gay') and promptly fell in with the early Blitz Kids.

'The first club I went to was Billy's, where Steve Strange and Rusty Egan were hosting their Bowie nights. I was taken there by a friend of mine called Teresa who looked exactly like David Bowie in *The Man Who Fell to Earth*, with that shock of red hair. I think she was on the game. She said this is where everyone is going, everyone dresses up, they play Bowie and Roxy Music all night and you're going to love it! I did. That's where I first met people like Boy George and Steve Strange. Then I went to Blitz, Hell and all the other clubs. My mother hated the fact that all I did was go to clubs and parties all the time, but I suppose if we had used the word networking back then it might have appeased her a bit.'

It was at Hell where Moore first became interested in DJing, and as the club wasn't always full, he'd quiz Rusty Egan about the records he was playing, many of which were electronic. The first club he was a regular at was Philip Sallon's first club, Planets, where the DJs were Boy George, Jeremy Healey and Richard Law. When Sallon opened The Mud Club, Moore used to help carry the records for the resident DJ there, Tasty Tim ('I used to carry them in these huge big baskets on the tube'), and eventually started filling in for him. In a few months he was working at Heaven, which for dance aficionados was not only the hippest gay club in Europe, but also the most important club in London.

His trick? Eclecticism.

'At the time you went somewhere and they'd play soul music all night, or reggae, or disco, but I played right across the board, from schoolboy disco and imported rap to hi-energy, underground electronic stuff, glam rock, and even show tunes, songs from *South Pacific* or *The Sound of Music*. It was anything goes. The theme from *Rupert the Bear*, *Stingray*, *Captain Scarlet*, anything. We were also sticking two fingers up to what was meant to be cool. We were anti-poseur, anti-cool. I used to do a lot of warehouses parties, where I could experiment.'

After a while, in early 1986, this eclecticism quickly turned into regular playlists predominantly made up of house records. If you went to Heaven at the time, all you heard was house. 'Weirdly, for ages house wasn't really given a name, they were just these records, a lot of which came from Chicago, which had the same beat. We used to mix them in with records that had the same tempo, like Bobby O, New Order, or Yello, anything electronic. We didn't really know what we were playing, as it didn't have a name for ages.

'A lot of DJs can claim they were playing house music in '86, and that's fine, but at Heaven we were the only people playing it all the time. The thing that a lot of people forget, and which gets written out of history, is that the gay community adopted house before anyone else did. London at the time was full of clubs where you had a lot of rare groove and hip-hop but not so much house, as a lot of people just thought it was gay music. I loved it, because it was basically what disco had morphed into. Disco died a death, was chased out of town, and was treated like the anti-christ during the Disco Sucks era, but it had not only mutated into house music, but it had fused with post-punk electronics like Depeche Mode, even Kraftwerk. House was basically the next generation of electronic disco. Then you had deep house, which was more soulful, and sometimes gospely, and then of course you had acid house. But for me, house was the new disco.'

The influence of gay subculture on dance music has become diminished over the years, as mainstream culture built its optics around a narrative that revolved around the Italian-hetero fiction of *Saturday Night Fever*. New York's Studio 54 may have been an alternative reality for disco, but it was essentially a fantasy, as so few 'real' people actually went there. As disco fell from favour in the early eighties, it was pushed back underground, back to gay clubs that had helped propagate it in the first place. Urban gay clubs continued to nurture disco in all its forms, sidestepping hip-hop and focusing on a form of music that had escapism built into its DNA. And as AIDS was decimating much of the gay club-going community, so disco became a salve, a form of communion for those who were being demonised by a heteronormative culture.

House certainly had its roots in the gay community, and its history starts with Frankie Knuckles, the disco DJ from New York, who played records with Larry Levan at the Continental Baths, a gay bathhouse in downtown Manhattan. In 1977, Levan was offered a job as the resident DJ of a new three-storey club that was opening in Chicago, The Warehouse. As Levan was already committed to his residency at Paradise Garage – at the time one of the biggest gay clubs in the world – he suggested Knuckles, who relocated to the Windy City, and The Warehouse, a gay club that catered primarily to black and Latino men. There, and at other clubs such as The Power Plant, house was born, a high-tempo and percussive development of disco, and one that informed much of the dance music that would define the second half of the eighties.

House connected to disco by prolonging it. 'It mutated the form,' says the critic Simon Reynolds, 'intensifying the very aspects of the music that most offended white rockers and black funkateers – the repetition, the synthetic and electronic textures, the rootlessness, the "depraved" hypersexuality and "decadent" druggy hedonism.'

Another reason house started in Chicago was that Steve Dahl, a shock-jock radio DJ in the city, was an anti-disco campaigner. In the summer of 1979, he famously launched his 'Disco Sucks' campaign, hoping to banish it from local radio, saddened that his beloved white rock music was being marginalised by both AM and FM radio. In July that year, hoping to fill seats at their Comiskey Park stadium after a lacklustre season, the Chicago White Sox baseball team asked Dahl to organise a Disco Demolition Night, the climax of which was the detonation of a crate filled with disco records. White Sox officials had hoped for a crowd of 20,000, about 5,000 more than usual, but instead, at least 50,000 – including tens of thousands of Dahl's listeners, most of whom had brought disco records with them to be burnt – packed the stadium, which eventually resulted in a riot.

'Steve Dahl reigned as the King of Rock in the late seventies, so he hated disco,' says Jesse Saunders, one of the first Chicago DJs to develop a house sound in the early eighties. 'It was the opposite of everything that he stood for. Back then, if you were gay, gay-friendly, or different to the status quo then you were considered not good enough for the rock movement. So Dahl decided the best way to get people to conform to his "Godliness" was to destroy the culture they lived and breathed. It was a bold statement to basically say, "We don't like blacks, the gay community, or anybody who sympathises with them and their music." Not only disco records were brought in, after all, but funk and soul records too. But Chicago was and is to this day a very segregated city, and that gives you a perspective of the landscape and the motivation for those followers of Steve Dahl to do what they did.

'Around the time of Disco Demolition I was combining all of these great genres together that I loved – new wave, reggae, funk, disco, and classic rock - into a sound that could bring everyone together. I was making pause button remixes on a cassette deck for about five years at this point, extending the breaks and highlighting various sections of the record that weren't being utilised to enhance the frenzy on my dance floor. Then with Disco Demolition the best thing happened, because the death of disco signalled the birth of house music. Being that the purpose [of Disco Demolition] was to destroy the ideal of this love and coming together for the lovers of disco, it was an epic fail. House music has grown to be a million times bigger than disco, and the LGBT and black communities in Chicago have thrived because of this music. It has become a way of life, and Chicagoans embrace their homegrown creations with a passion like no other. Just like New Yorkers hold their hip-hop dear, so do Chicagoans with their house music.'

Gay clubs had always been first with the next iteration of dance music, and London was no different. Gay clubs had been there at the advent of disco, been there as the New Romantic and electro scenes developed, and throughout the early eighties, when London's club one-nighters defined the culture, the best places were nearly always the gay clubs, which invariably had the best DJs. That's one of the reasons Mark Moore had such a keen sense of what was going on. It was also one of the reasons why he found it so easy to move from playing records to making them.

Actually, the process of that transformation was another happy accident for Moore. Rhythm King had recently opened their offices, as part of Mute Records, in the Harrow Road, not far from his mother's new council flat. Moore would visit regularly, to hang out and take records to play during his DJ sets. As well as borrowing records he was also taking imports in to them, recommendations for them to license, and records by UK artists such as the Beatmasters and the Cookie Crew, Baby Ford, Taffy and Renegade Soundwave. So, the label started signing bands that Moore had suggested, and having some chart success with them. Unofficially he became their on-off A&R man, which eventually led Rhythm King to ask him to think of recording something himself. Moore said he had a loop, a sample actually, from Rose Royce's classic 1979 disco tune 'Is It Love You're After?' that he thought might make a good track, and so he set to work. Rhythm King put him together with Pascal Gabriel, a Belgian producer who had earned a reputation for doing innovative remixes for Soft Cell and Yello, and a few weeks later they had 'Theme from S'Express'.*

'I love the Rose Royce record, but my favourite part had always been the arpeggiated synthesiser sound at the beginning, and I'd always thought it would be great if the whole record was like that,' says Moore. 'Don't get me wrong, the original is a brilliant record, but I wanted that bit to just go on and on and on and on. "Theme from S'Express" was obviously heavily influenced by hip-hop, and by the fact that people were sampling James Brown breaks and looping them, but I wanted to do the same thing with disco. Which hadn't been done before. I acted in exactly the same way as a hip-hop producer would have done, but instead of just using a loop of "Funky Drummer" I went with Rose Royce. I loved the futuristic, acid house feel of it. I wanted the Rose Royce song to go on and on and I wanted to build a collage over the top of it. So, the record was just as influenced by hip-hop, and by the likes of Double D and Steinski, as it was by house music. I loved all the house records coming out of Chicago, but I didn't want to just copy them. I wanted something that was me, which is why it doesn't sound like a typical house record, and it doesn't sound like a typical disco record. It's also got some of the ethos of my punk roots – nothing is forbidden! Anything goes in the pot. In those days you could clear samples for £250. We did a white-label version and all the London DJs were playing it for six months while Rhythm King cleared all the samples.'

---

* Gabriel was the Belgian I was with when I was stabbed, as I described in Chapter Three. After our altercation, we became good friends, ran a market stall together, and once clubbed together to buy a car, even though at the time I couldn't drive. He was always the designated driver, and I was always the navigator. I had the left-hand side of the car, he had the right, and we co-existed like Harry H. Corbett and Wilfred Brambell in the sixties TV sitcom *Steptoe & Son*. Our co-ownership ended when we knocked over a cyclist in Covent Garden.

Forgetting the cost of the samples (minimal), the record cost £500 to make.

Lyrically the record is banal, deliberately so. '"I've got the hots for you" was definitely a comment on the crassness of disco lyrics,' says Moore. 'I wanted the record to be ironic as well as cool.'

Acid house records weren't scaffolded by language, they were upholstered with drum machines.

'Theme from S'Express' is a truly postmodern record, something of a recursive masterpiece, destined to repeat itself for ever. An anthem four minutes from stern to stern, it is the sound of joyous, semaphoring exuberance. The reason the record was so immediately engaging was because it was always arriving, rushing forward, like continuous foreplay. One of the fallacies of acid house was that it was a series of multiple orgasms, whereas in fact it was like any other kind of dance music: the constant state of anticipation. A crashing carnival of noise, it uses the intro of 'Is It Love You're After?' and weaves in a series of samples (borrowings from records by Gil Scott-Heron, Debbie Harry and Stacey Q) that make you feel as though the record is never going to start, let alone end. As it announces itself, you feel as though you're approaching the brow, about to peer into the vast valley below, which in some respects wasn't so far from the truth: some of the illegal raves during the second summer of love attracted twenty thousand people drawn by the promise of twelve hours of music, laser displays, swarms of artificial smoke, giant projector screens, bouncy castles, Ferris wheels and big dippers. And of course, an awful lot of Ecstasy.

Moore seemed to regard sampling as a kind of absolution, a way of mixing himself a more tolerable future. As an avatar of acid house and the sampling revolution – where it was first understood that as a DJ you could simply be a compilation of encounters with other DJs – Moore stands as a creator of one of the era's most memorable reference points, but the record was bigger than he was, which is exactly as it should have been.

It's not like he hadn't been building up to this. *My Life in The Bush of Ghosts* by Brian Eno and David Byrne had made him want to buy

THE SECOND SUMMER OF LOVE

a sampler, and *The Idiot* by Iggy Pop had made him want to buy a drum machine, while his love of disco derived from going to funfairs back when he was in his teens. 'Disco was ingrained in me,' he says.

Listen to 'S'Express' and the sources sink out of earshot, even if the mode of inspiration remains in place. As often happens with records that are the result of wholesale sampling, input begat output, with the output winning. Like a lot of dance music the era produced, 'S'Express' was all sensation, all about a vibe, a body thing. Horn-rimmed critics had been blathering on about the 'mindless' nature of pop ever since the mid-fifties; now, maybe they had a point. Here was modern pop, searching for transcendence through repetition.

Strangely, the record isn't technically acid house, even though it became so closely associated with the genre.

'The record obviously became a big acid house tune, even though it isn't officially an acid house track because we didn't use a 303,' says Moore. 'Danny Rampling was one of the first supporters of it, as he used to come down to my night at Heaven. The first time he heard it when I played it there, he came up to me and said he had to have it to play himself. So I gave him a cassette of it, before we even had a record, and he started playing it on Kiss FM. Colin Faver also played at Heaven, and he played it on the radio while it was still only on cassette as well. Thanks to Danny it became a Shoom anthem. I think it became a popular acid record because it's got a great sense of fun and abandon. As a friend of mine said, you can hear the drugs in it.'

Ecstasy had changed what people looked like. 'It's quite endearing looking back,' explains Haçienda DJ and author Dave Haslam, 'but no one knew how to dress. People were thinking, "Do we wear shoes or trainers with this music? Do I wear a T-shirt?" The look of acid house was almost anti-fashion, a bizarre mix of Mediterranean beach bum, hippie student, and nascent football hooligan: T-shirts and baggy trousers, ponchos and dungarees, and bandanas and sweat bands. Ecstasy and acid house became the great levellers.'

'Acid house changed the whole landscape of clubbing,' says Moore. 'It changed the whole mentality. Previous to acid house you would dress up to the nines to go clubbing, but it soon became pointless to dress up because your clothes would be ruined by the end of an evening, just covered in sweat. So everyone started dressing down when they went out. And because acid house was so intrinsically linked to Ecstasy, the euphoria levels obviously went up, so it was like New Year's Eve every night, for twelve hours. It was an intensity that got ramped up by the drugs and the music. Clubbing beforehand had been more elegant and more aloof, but now it was tribal, more pagan. It was more religious, as going to club was like going to worship. The clubs that I used to go to were very elitist, and now it was suddenly hug your neighbour. It got slightly hippie, although having said that, getting into Shoom was just as difficult as getting into Blitz. Suddenly all ravers were equal, but some were more equal than others.

'Image for us wasn't important, it was just second nature. We never had a stylist, had never really heard of them. The first time I heard about someone having a stylist was when Judy Blame did Neneh Cherry for "Buffalo Stance". We would just turn up for *Top of the Pops* with bin liners full of stuff to wear that we'd bought in Oxfam. We'd rummage around in the bags and make it up as we went along. "Hey, why didn't you wear this?" Having said that, I did start to feel that after a while it was beginning to become a bit faceless with some of the bands, who didn't try hard enough. I suppose image-wise, S'Express were vibing off the whole rare groove thing, so we looked like a cross between Sly and the Family Stone and the Jackson Five cartoon show. A few people incorporated this into their look, but mainly it was baggy.' (Conflictingly, Moore also had a towering, dawn-of-rock'n'roll pompadour, which gave him a matinee idol sheen.)

Moore's analysis is correct. What soon became apparent with dance groups at the time was that it didn't really matter what they looked like, because no one was watching them anyway, as they were too busy dancing. Moore and his friends may have spent the previous eight years or so bouncing around the pinball of London clubland, driven by sartorial narcissism as much as a hedonistic narrative, and yet when S'Express became pop stars, they sort of didn't. If you think of many of the British DJ acts who became successful at this time - MARRS, Bomb the Bass, S'Express themselves - can you describe what they looked like? The instantly realised generation of ravers - genuine ravers, not the ones your parents always colloquialised - who were throwing out their fancy club gear and dressing in T-shirts, beads and bandanas, were too busy clutching their water bottles and trying not to fall over to look at anyone who might have been on stage. Hold on, was there even a stage? Saliently, 1988 was the year bands became records, and where success was now suddenly predicated on an ability to move the crowd rather than an ability to smile or sneer provocatively for someone's camera. There were no stars involved, no heroes, egos or BPM satyrs. In an inversion of Thatcherism, the cult of the individual was dead. If your head was above the parapet then you were probably doing something wrong or hadn't taken enough drugs. The records that became popular in nightclubs in 1988 may as well have all been white labels, or been deliberately disguised (which is what Northern Soul DJs used to do to protect the source of their bounty), as nobody cared about anything but the noise, the sound, the groove, the beat, the stuff working its way around your brain and into your body. After all, if you had taken enough drugs, you ceased to notice that a lot of the music sounded suspiciously like broken car alarms.

The difference between disco and house was remarkably simple: whereas a good disco record introduced itself and then took you on a wild journey, with plenty of highs and deliberate lows, and bits that encouraged you to point in all kinds of strange directions, house seemed to just take you from A to B with the least amount of fuss. House always sounded like the so-so record you might hear between two great disco records, something that sounded as though it never really got out of third gear. It contributed to a continuum, with the peaks building towards the end of an evening rather than the end of a single song.

In the noughties, as EDM started to creep its way around the globe, the DJ would start to replace the rock star as the evening's entertainment, but before the age of the DJ as king, as shaman, MC, bandleader or conductor, the acid house DJs were seen as facilitators first, and personalities second.

The appeal of acid house was its ability to hold a room, no matter how big it was. It didn't seem to matter how big the venue was, or how big the field was, as the 'oneness' experienced by the crowd was apparently limitless. The music was from the heart and the drugs lifted the soul, turning the cathedrals of dance into vast pagan citadels where the crowd moved as one. Raves became these egalitarian mini-festivals, yet there was a formality about them which made each experience little different to the one before. Many critics described the experience as child-like, principally because of the infantile way people behaved, but then that was the point. The equitable nature of those enormous gatherings couldn't take away from the fact that the original, smaller clubs had more of a pure spirit about them.

London's Shoom was small, full of smoke, and felt like a deliberately contrived space. The squelchy, serrated sounds greeted you as you entered the room, followed by a swirling mass of heaving flesh. It seemed almost like some kind of controlled experiment, to see how people behaved in completely proscribed circumstances. The experience wasn't free form at all, but rather an environment that precluded error or the influence of extraneous factors. Danny Rampling would always start his sessions at Shoom by playing Barry White's 'It's Ecstasy When You Lay Down Next to Me', which would be his call to the dance floor. The beats would begin at 95bpm, and then move up to 100, 105, 110 and 115 before finally hitting 120, which was the optimal house tempo. Unlike the London clubs of the early eighties, Shoom wasn't a petrie dish of cultural experimentation, it was just dancing. A lot of dancing.

Moore was also one of the featured DJs at Shoom. 'Often it was so chaotic you couldn't really see in front of you, you couldn't really talk to anyone. So, a lot of the time you just spent on your own, dancing, alone ... You'd have people in their own world, doing that mad trance dancing, oblivious to everyone else ...' And all shouting 'Aciiiidd!' to anyone who approached them. 'Initially it was a lot like *The Night of the Living Dead*, with all these zombies, but then the drugs kicked in and everybody got friendly.'

Because the genre had so few genuine stars, the music papers ignored it at first. Helen Mead was a writer at the *NME* at the time, but she couldn't get her editors interested. 'Everybody knew what was going on in the clubs except for the people on my neighbouring desks at the *NME*,' she said. 'Taxi drivers, the girls I'd buy my sandwiches from at lunchtime. But the people that I worked with were totally dismissive. They just did not get it. And there was no attempt to try and get it.'

But when the tabloids got involved, manufacturing the kind of opprobrium that they reserved for wild and untamed youth, the *NME* decided it needed to express a view, too. But by then, it didn't matter what the music press thought, as the nation's youth had decided to take matters into its own hands (along with a small bottle of water and a couple of pills).

Acid house revolutionised the UK's nightclub scene almost overnight, as dancing and drugs replaced drinking and dressing-up as a raison d'être for going out. And this was national, it wasn't just about London.

· · ·

Up until Mike Pickering opened his Nude night in 1986, focusing primarily on house (and hiring Graeme Park in the process), Manchester's Haçienda was considered to be a bit hit-and-miss. But when acid house started to spread around the country in 1988, all of a sudden it was boom time. 'There wasn't anyone in the Haçi for the first five years, it was dead,' said the Happy Mondays' Shaun Ryder. 'But it always felt like an important place where you knew things could happen. [Acid house] is when everything changed. When life suddenly went from black and white to Technicolor, when we first got the E.'

'Acid house seeped into areas outside of music and clubbing,' says Mark Moore, today. 'Even football hooliganism disappeared for a while, because they were all taking Ecstasy and hugging each other in the clubs. Suddenly everything had changed, and people were talking to people they hadn't talked to before, because they weren't in their tribes. Suddenly people were having gay friends who might not have had gay friends before. Maybe they even started having black friends. Generally it did a lot of good, and made people far more accepting.'

'Theme from S'Express' went to Number One on the UK singles chart in April, where it stayed for two weeks, not that Mark Moore was especially fazed by this ascendency.

'Pretty much everyone did want to be famous, but then a lot of us had come out of punk, so we thought, "Yeah, being famous, what a load of nonsense,"' says Moore. 'We were very nonchalant about the whole thing. Also, in my little pond in those days, which was the clubs we all went to, there was probably a thousand of us, maybe two, so in my pond I was playing to a thousand people at Heaven, and yet no one else had heard of me. In my own bubble I was already famous, but when we had a hit with "S'Express" the bubble just got a little bit bigger. So, I kind of took fame in my stride. A lot of people in the pond were famous in their own heads anyway. Whenever one of us actually did something it was just an extension of that. I remember talking to Tim Simenon from Bomb the Bass about how we'd forget we were famous, and we'd go out and people would ask us for our autographs, which we found very odd. It would throw us. Someone came up to tell me they'd bought the record, and I said, "Oh, that's so nice, how did you hear about it?" And they looked at me strangely and said, "It's Number One." Obviously, I enjoyed it, as did the rest of the S'Express girls. It didn't become a tedious circus until much later. We loved it.'

The dance revolution sparked by acid house continues to this day, as electronic beats remain the driving force of the music industry, and of pop music in general. Mark Moore was there at the outset, and he talks about those days without a hint of ennui.

'Acid house probably had far more of an impact than a lot of other youth cultures,' he says, as if repeating a catechism, 'but the problem is most of the other ones had better looks. So whenever someone does an exhibition or a book, this period never comes out of it as well as the others. Punk, glam, hip-hop, New Romantics, they all look so much more interesting, even if they only burned for a few years. Culturally the impact of acid house is huge because we're still feeling it now, because most music these days is dance orientated, and it all started back then in the late eighties. There was also no manifesto. Most youth cultures have unwritten manifestos, but we didn't have one, other than loving your neighbour.'

1989

Speaking Truth to Power

'Fight the Power' by Public Enemy

When Spike Lee decided he needed an anthem for his film *Do the Right Thing*, there was only one phone call he was going to make: to Public Enemy's Chuck D. After a few false starts, the director green-lit 'Fight the Power', a song that not only defined the film, but also defined the global power of hip-hop in 1989. The genre had come a long way since the Sugarhill Gang's 'Rapper's Delight'. So much so that some said Public Enemy sounded like they came from another planet.

> *'The United States is like one big jail for black people, because we're locked into a mentality and a mindset that limits our potential. It has us against us.'*
>
> *– Chuck D*

By the end of the decade, the huge success of 'Back to Life' by Soul II Soul, 'Ride on Time' by Black Box, 'Voodoo Ray' by A Guy Called Gerald and 'French Kiss' by Lil Louis was a signifier that the charts could soon be almost completely urban, as the entertainment world turned into one big dancefloor, powered by BPM on both sides of the Atlantic. But it was the seismic success of Public Enemy's 'Fight the Power' that told the world that rap had not only come into its own, but that it owned the future.

Originally recorded as the theme for Spike Lee's *Do the Right Thing*, 'Fight the Power' might be Public Enemy's greatest song, their 'Anarchy in the UK'. The song is as relevant now as it was then, a record that has continued to resonate down through the ages, a symbol of black power throughout the nineties, and a recurring top-note throughout the Black Lives

Matter revolution of 2020. It is as uncompromising now as it was then.

'I wanted [the track] to be defiant, I wanted it to be angry, I wanted it to be very rhythmic,' Spike Lee told *Time* magazine. 'It was written to be an anthem,' the group's leader Chuck D explained, 'and it was written at a particular time that needed an anthem.'

The decade would end with the domino collapse of the Eastern Bloc, the last knockings of Thatcherism and pro-democracy protestors demanding political reform in China. Elsewhere, Iran placed a $3m bounty on the head of *The Satanic Verses* author Salman Rushdie, Tim Berners-Lee produced a proposal document that would eventually become the blueprint for the World Wide Web, and the Hillsborough disaster, one of the biggest tragedies in world football, claimed the lives of ninety-six Liverpool FC supporters.

This year, Fox started broadcasting *The Simpsons*, Sony would buy Columbia Pictures, and Rolling Stone Bill Wyman married his eighteen-year old girlfriend Mandy Smith (whom he'd been dating – some would say raping – for nearly six years). The decade had seen such a cavalcade of different types of music, and yet it was dance music in all its many forms that would start to shape the cultural bedrock of the next ten years, even as pop started to fracture some more – begetting grunge, Britpop, the Spice Girls and a seemingly never-ending stream of urban sub-genres. If rap had started the decade as a novelty, by the end of the eighties it had turned into the major musical lingua franca of the time, a genre that would become more encyclopaedic and more fragmented with each passing year.

Nineteen-eighty-nine is not generally afforded the kind of respect shown for the more well-known and oft-celebrated 'seminal' years in popular music. In the pantheon of pop you'll find 1954 (the year Elvis Presley recorded 'That's All Right'), 1963 (Beatlemania), 1966 (Swinging London), 1971 (rock's golden year, at least according to the journalist David Hepworth), 1976 (punk), 1977 (punk again), 1981 (the year of the Great British Single: 'Ghost Town' by the Specials, 'Tainted Love' by Soft Cell, 'Don't You Want Me' by the Human

League, 'Mama Used To Say' by Junior Giscombe, 'Ant Rap' by Adam and the Ants, etc.) and 1995 (Oasis v. Blur).

But 1989?

A quick scroll back through your musical memory and you'll probably think 1989 was the anodyne year of Bobby Brown, Paula Abdul, Milli Vanilli, Phil Collins, New Kids on the Block and Jive Bunny. The biggest news in the music industry was Michael Jackson being christened the 'King of Pop' after receiving the *Soul Train* Heritage Awards (at the age of thirty-one). Think again, however, and 1989 not only produced more than its fair share of classic hits, it also showcased the variety and diversity of pop in a way that had actually been reflected in the charts for the last ten years.

There was the funky falsetto Electro Pop of the Fine Young Cannibals' 'She Drives Me Crazy', the Londoncentric beats of Soul II Soul's 'Keep On Movin', the proto grunge of the Pixies' 'This Monkey's Gone to Heaven' and the zietgiest-y Mancunian groove of the Stone Roses' 'Fool's Gold'. Elsewhere you had the Daisy Chain hip-hop of De La Soul (complete with Yacht Rock samples from Steely Dan and Hall and Oates) and the adult reportage of Lou Reed's extraordinary *New York*.

Hip-hop had certainly come a long way since 'Rapper's Delight'. In 1979, rap was still thought to be something of a novelty, but by 1989 the genre had almost become predominant. It had moved through the heavier rock-influenced work of Run-DMC and the Beastie Boys, and the start of the golden age of gangsta rap and West Coast rap, to a point where it was becoming the dominant sound of pop. By the end of the decade, pop's aperture had become hip-hop's aperture.

In ten years, rap hadn't just become the sound of the street, it had also become the sound of that boulevard of mediated street credibility hankered after by every white middle-class teenage boy since rock'n'roll first kick-started the generation gap back in the mid-fifties. Gang culture was just as attractive to the white suburban homies of the late eighties as it had been to the grammar school fans of the Rolling Stones back in the sixties, or indeed the Clash in the seventies. What better way to exaggerate your street credentials than by immersing yourself in hip-hop?

Suddenly it was not enough to simply like hip-hop to appear cool, you had to look the part, too, by wearing baggy shorts and T-shirts, accompanied by basketball shoes and a baseball cap, either worn backwards or at a cocky tilt. For a while there was even an appalling Madison Avenue name for this new breed of wannabes, a word that highlights the vast chasm between what was acceptable in 1989, and what is acceptable now: *wiggers*. Insulting and as unconscionable as this term is, at the time it was nevertheless indicative of what was happening in the culture at large.

And there was no one the white, teenage suburbanite liked more than Public Enemy, a hip-hop group whose album *It Takes a Nation of Millions to Hold Us Back* had recently made them the most famous hip-hop group in the US. Their rebellious intent was signified by their bad-boy logo: a b-boy in the centre of a sniper's crosshairs.

In one respect, the end of the eighties mirrored the beginning of the sixties, echoing the famous put-down to Brian Epstein, the Beatles' manager, by Decca's senior A&R man, Dick Rowe. The band had auditioned for the record label on 1 January 1962, at their recording studios in London. A month later, Epstein received a rejection letter from Rowe: 'Guitar groups are on their way out, Mr Epstein,' was the airy reply.

If you glanced at the charts on either side of the Atlantic in December 1989, you could have been forgiven for thinking that Rowe's asinine comment had finally come true. Hip-hop had become the new orthodoxy. In October, Public Enemy had even graced the pages of the *NME*, with the cover line 'Public Enemy. The greatest rock'n'roll band in the world?' It was the kind of endorsement that had previously been the preserve of the Rolling Stones, the Who, the Clash and U2. Not a bunch of MTV-unfriendly black militants with scant regard for the white rock canon.

But it wasn't the music that was important.

'Rock'n'roll is there to be studied and learned about,' Chuck D told the *NME*'s Danny Kelly. 'Rap has closer links to rock'n'roll than to any other music. What is rock'n'roll? It's the projection of attitude, not the delivery of sound. Attitude! Rap acts have that attitude, that character, that rock bands used to get across to the public. They just haven't learned to project it.'

Oh what a dream it was, to be a hip-hop rebel. To wear your baseball cap in a jaunty, perpendicular fashion, or a monogrammed beret along with your impossibly opaque sunglasses. To sport a lot of jewellery, and an oversized pocket-watch, hanging around your neck like a portable breast plate.

· · ·

The decade had already witnessed various stages of hip-hop's coming of age: in 1983 KDAY became America's first true hip-hop radio station; in 1985 the Fat Boys appeared in a Swatch commercial; the same year, the Chicago Bears recorded 'Super Bowl Shuffle'; in 1986, Run-DMC teamed up with Aerosmith for an inspired locker room version of their old hit 'Walk This Way', while in the same year the Beastie Boys released *Licensed to Ill*, a rap record made by three middle-class Jewish boys who used to be in a suburban punk band ('Three idiots create a masterpiece,' according to *Rolling Stone*); in 1987, Theo Huxtable rapped on *The Cosby Show*; and a year later, *Yo! MTV Raps* made its debut, making VJ stars out of Dr Dre and Ed Lover.

A new hegemony couldn't have come at a better time, at least if the UK charts at the end of the year were anything to go by. If the decade had proved it had over-delivered in terms of diversity and quality, it certainly wasn't on show in the final Top Twenty of the year. If the Number One wasn't bad enough – a lackadaisical version of 'Do They Know It's Christmas?' produced by Stock Aitken Waterman featuring an enervating list of chuggers including Cathy Dennis, Lisa Stansfield, Sonia, Cliff Richard and Big Fun – the other high flyers included Jive Bunny, Jason Donovan, Bros, New Kids on the Block, the Christians, Wet Wet Wet and

Jeff Wayne. If one of the spurs of the creative spirit is the fight against mediocrity, there was certainly a lot to choose from as the decade tumbled to a close.

The US charts weren't much better, swamped by the likes of Phil Collins, Tayler Dayne, Cher, Michael Bolton, Milli Vanilli, and Jody Watley. On this occasion it really did feel as though mediocrity was a genre in its own right.

Of course, while hip-hop may have been at the forefront of the culture, bizarrely the music industry still didn't afford it the respect it deserved. This year, Will Smith, who was still known as Jazzy Jeff's partner the Fresh Prince, was nominated for a Grammy for the pair's crossover hit 'Parents Just Don't Understand'. Even though the pair would go on to win the award, Smith decided not to attend the ceremony because this inaugural rap performance at the awards was not going to be televised.

'We chose to boycott,' he said at the time, calling the rebuff a 'slap in the face ... You go to school for twelve years, they give you your diploma, and they deny you that walk down the aisle.'

His partner said, looking back, 'To put it bluntly, a lot of the Grammy committee were old white men that didn't understand this brand-new genre. At the time, hip-hop was just starting to break out of the mind-set that it was going to die next year.'

This would be the last year that hip-hop was treated this way by the industry, and by 1990, ten long years since the success of 'Rapper's Delight', hip-hop was everywhere – on MTV, on the radio, in commercials, on network television, all over. Whether you wanted gangsta or gimmicks, whether you wanted music for your head, your heart, or your feet, there was a hip-hop for you. It was all hip-hop.

Public Enemy's 'Fight the Power' was certainly all hip-hop, and if it did less than a lot of contemporary rap records to shape the future of hip-hop, it arguably had the more lasting impact. The group would hit many speed bumps, but their legacy would be huge.

Art that feels like the product of an unlikely journey is frequently presumed to have authenticity at its core, and yet the genesis of 'Fight the Power' was no different nor more complicated than the genesis of Barry Gibb's 'Grease' or Aha's 'The Living Daylights': it was a title song written to order.

Alive to the needs of the time, and fresh from the success of *She's Gotta Have It* and *School Daze*, in the autumn of 1988, Spike Lee was in the process of planning his latest movie, *Do the Right Thing*, an angry portrait of racial tension in Brooklyn's Bedford-Stuyvesant neighbourhood, colloquially known as Bed-Stuy. He needed a title song for the film, something grand, something epic, a big bad tune that people would take with them when they left the movie theatre.

So he called for Public Enemy, rap's unofficial prophets of rage. He invited them for lunch in an Indian restaurant in Greenwich Village, and tried to convince Carlton 'Chuck D' Ridenhour and several other members of the group to record a hip-hop version of 'Lift Every Voice and Sing', the traditional song which was known universally as the black national anthem.

Perhaps unsurprisingly, Chuck D wasn't convinced this was such a good idea.

'[Spike said he needed] an anthem to scream out against the hypocrisies and wrongdoings [of] the system,' he remembers, and he knew that wasn't it.

Band member Hank Shocklee wasn't convinced either. 'It was heated,' he recalls. 'I'm saying, Spike, kids don't listen to "Lift Every Voice and Sing". Open this window, stick your head outside and listen to the sound you hear coming out of cars and boxes. It's the spirit of the streets that you wanna convey.'

Chuck D says there were problems from the off. 'Spike wasn't a hip-hop fan. He came from the jazz background, and a lot of them are real musicians and therefore they look down on hip-hop.'

In the end, a snippet of Branford Marsalis playing 'Lift Every Voice and Sing' can be heard over the opening credits, before the screen explodes with Public Enemy's eventual contribution to the film, 'Fight the Power'.

Perversely, the year's most significant song had its roots in an old Isley Brothers' song from 1975. While the venerable R&B group had reinvented themselves with their 1973 album *3+3*, and had experienced huge success by mixing the customised balladry of Todd Rundgren ('Hello It's Me') and Seals and Crofts ('Summer Breeze') with commercial funk like 'That Lady' and 'Live it Up', the lacquered medallion men weren't shy of making the occasional political sideswipe. 'Fight the Power' was one of those.

'We decided not to be passive, to take a stand,' said Marvin Isley, in 1976, when discussing the song. 'We don't close ourselves away like some entertainers do – we listen to the radio, read the newspapers and generally get into what's happening out there.'*

The Isleys may have provided the title, but Chuck D's major lyrical inspiration for the song came from an X-rated track by the rapper Blowfly, called, with typical MC imagination, 'Rapp Dirty' (aka 'Blowfly's Rap'). Little more than a pornographic jingle – imagine Chuck Berry's 'My Ding-A-Ling' adapted for teenage hip-hop fans – its ribald nature made the Public Enemy leader think: 'In one line Blowfly was acting out the role of a KKK

---

* The Isley Brothers didn't have a particularly antagonistic public profile, although Danny Baker says that when he requested an interview with them when he was working at the *NME* in the late seventies, he was told that they weren't ready yet to talk to white journalists; which was odd as by this stage in their career they had already been in the industry for over twenty years.

'They had been around for ever but their radical phase was in full flood, sort of like early sixties George Carlin v. early seventies George Carlin,' Baker told me. 'They had obviously undergone some sort of political change hinted at only visually on *3+3*, although the previous album *Brother Brother* had a quite brutalist cover. I don't recall being particularly shocked or affronted. It was of a piece with stuff like The Watts Prophets and Last Poets I think and possibly they needed to distinguish the new Isleys from the "Motown" Isley Brothers – something the press were reluctant to do. The influx of younger band members clearly must have had an influence. I recall that it wasn't "we aren't ready to talk to white journalists" but rather "we don't talk to white journalists any more". Not sure how long that lasted.'

grand wizard, saying something like "I'm the grand wizard of the Ku Klux Klan, nobody mess with me, Motherfuck you and Muhammed Ali." That line always stuck with me because if you talk about Muhammed Ali, you gonna make a black person mad. I just decided to flip the script, kind of an ironic thing.'

This chimed with one of the pivotal moments in Lee's film, when a trouble-making b-boy criticises a local Italian restaurateur for not having any black faces on the pizzeria's wall of fame. This flashpoint encouraged Chuck D to ruminate on the invisibility of black icons in contemporary US culture: 'Most of my heroes don't appear on stamps,' he said.

In the finished lyric, Chuck D calls Elvis Presley a racist and John Wayne a redneck.

When Shocklee first heard the lyrics, he blanched: 'I was like, "Whooo! You said that?" Chuck never worries about anything. I love Chuck's spirit. I'm the one that was always like, "Well, I'm not sure about that one, Chuck. I mean, there's a lot of Elvis fans out there."'

For Public Enemy, Elvis would briefly become as much of a totemic hate figure as he did for the Clash, back in 1977. Chuck D has always said that he wanted his band to be a hip-hop version of the Clash, a gang with intellectual heft who weren't afraid to stick their heads above the parapet. In fact, their whole image was built around the idea of rebellion. Chuck D had first seen the Clash at the New York club Bonds, during their famous seventeen-night run in 1981, supported by Kurtis Blow.

'I had great respect for Joe Strummer,' he said. 'How he used his music – incorporating a lot of black music like hip-hop and reggae – was very different from the guys who invented rock'n'roll.'

As a younger man he had been far more circumspect – 'I thought they were a bunch of people that were whining about their existence ... I didn't think their problems were as severe as black people's problems' – but he eventually came to respect the Clash for their latent idealism. 'They talked about important subjects, so therefore journalists printed what they said, which was very political. We took that from the Clash, because we were very similar in that regard. Public Enemy just did it ten years later.'

If they learned anything from their British prototypes, it was the art of mythmaking. 'Like the Clash, the story of Public Enemy was bigger than the music, at first,' says Chuck D. He understood that songwriters needed to be faster than media, and that technology and musical instruments were tools as well as toys.

Like the Clash, Public Enemy always liked to think of themselves as being on something of a war footing, primed to respond to even the slightest criticism (this included the pseudo-paramilitary image). Chuck D calls this period Public Enemy's 'war years', obviously putting himself centre stage, as Joe Strummer used to do.

'You take the most hits, you get the most scar tissue,' he said to the journalist Dorian Lynskey in 2015. 'That's cool. I got no regrets on that. We battled the mainstream, we battled our company, we fought every goddam minute.'

Like Strummer, Chuck D grew up in a middle-class family, in the black suburb of Roosevelt, Long Island. He could smell injustice at a thousand paces, and he knew those injustices would help form the DNA of Public Enemy's material.

Chuck D started the group in 1985, when he met William Drayton (later Flavor Flav) at Long Island's Adelphi University.* A part-time DJ and amateur agitator, he developed his MC skills while making deliveries for his father's furniture business. Two years later came their debut album, *Yo! Bum Rush the Show*. It was relevant, politicised, memorable – and looked towards the future, by adding a heavy rhetoric to their sound. This was urban folk music, as Public Enemy quickly developed an ability to deliver urgent messages connected to current events. 'Public Enemy is

---

* Flavor Flav's career would take an odd path, and he would go on to appear in many reality TV shows, including *The Surreal Life, Strange Love, Flavor of Love, The Farm* and *Celebrity Wife Swap*.

the security of the hip-hop party,' said Chuck D. This was rap with its fists in the air.

'We knew hip-hop moved every two, three years. We knew in the nineties the new thing was coming in.'

So the band's records became like an alternative version of CNN. Inspired by the Clash, he wanted his band to be as skilled in reportage as beats.

'What's going on with Thatcher? Why is Nelson Mandela still in prison? That type of shit. I felt confident. I was in a group. If I was on my own and it was all swirling around my head, I'd have been loony.'

And unlike a lot of entertainers, who think that ideologies – or at least their passionate espousal of them – could easily transfer to office, Chuck D knew he was a more effective band leader than a politician.

'Hell, fucking no!' he said when asked if he had ever considered a career in politics. 'I'm a culturalist. I'm damn near a fucking hippy. The closest I would be to any office is cultural ambassador.'

At the end of his interview with Lynsky, he removed his baseball cap, rubbed his shaved head and sighed. 'Life is a fight, man. In the middle of the smoke, you fight to breathe.'

Time has a way of turning heresies into sacred cows, and so it is with 'Fight the Power', an anthem that became a hymn. The record was a sonic Molotov cocktail, while the music was driving, constant, liquid. The record bludgeoned you with its sheer spectacle. 'Every instrument is a drum,' James Brown used to say, and 'Fight the Power' is a mess of beats, a song that sounds like a car being rocked by a crowd from side to side. It's an assault, a tidal rhythm, one that simply doesn't let up.

'The drums had to feel like African war drums,' says Hank Shocklee, who actually produced it. 'But instead of us going to war, it had to be like we were already winning the war. This needed to say, "I'm angry, but I'm not mad to the point where I want to destroy everybody. Instead I'm charged with the energy of overcoming something."'

281

'Me and Chuck then built up the track. It was a totally different process from today, when cats listen to a finished track then put rhymes on top - that separates emotion and content. All the samples had to work with Chuck's emotion. We had to find something from all our hundreds of records to fill a second, and it all had to be done by ear, without computers or visual aids.'

If Little Richard had once been described as sounding like the last man on Earth singing the first song ever written, Chuck D sounded like an angry, disgruntled newsreader.

Shocklee has a brilliant way of describing the song's belligerent lope. 'It's easy to make a dope beat,' he told the *Guardian*'s Ben Beaumont-Thomas, 'where the kick and snare are keeping the groove together. But "Fight the Power" doesn't have that. You can't tell what the kick and the snare are doing. They're creating a backdrop, but it's not pronounced, it doesn't swing. It's more of a head-butt, reminiscent of a Black Panther rally, a put-your-fist-up kind of vibration. If a song has swing, it makes you move from side to side, that's a different emotion, all about celebrating something. That's what set "Fight the Power" apart: it wasn't trying to be groovy. The groove couldn't be so hypnotic that you'd get lost in it, since then you'd lose what the song was about. It would be a good song, but not an anthem.'

Like 'Rapper's Delight' ten years previously, 'Fight the Power' was a kit-bag of samples. There were over twenty on the record - Sly Stone, Wilson Pickett, Branford Marsalis, Syl Johnson, James Brown, Bob Marley, Rick James, Trouble Funk, and even the Isley Brothers themselves (the central loop alone was made up of ten different samples). The verses - such as they were - sounded far more inventive than the chorus, while the record needed all the extraneous noise to make it so effective - it needed to sound like a history lesson as well as a call to arms.

Twenty-five years after the record's release, Chuck D was asked how he felt about it. 'I feel like Pete Seeger singing "We Shall Overcome",' he said.

SPEAKING TRUTH TO POWER

'Fight the Power' was the sound of the street, the sound of the urban experience. Up until 1989, if I had wanted to hear the sound of New York - a relatively modern sound of New York, not the one imagined by Ella Fitzgerald in 'Take The A Train' or 'Lullaby of Birdland' - I would have opted for 'Peaches en Regalia' by Frank Zappa or 'Crosstown Traffic' by Jimi Hendrix (swiftly followed by Lou Reed's 'Walk on the Wild Side' or 'Let's Clean up the Ghetto' by the Philadelphia All Stars): the first because it sounds like a traffic jam (Zappa described the album it came from, *Hot Rats*, as 'a movie for the ears'), and the second because the lyrics seem to deposit you right on the corner of 50th Street and Sixth Avenue, right opposite Radio City. Many New York punk songs evoked the city sensationally - the Ramones' '53rd & 3rd', for instance, or Blondie's 'In the Flesh' - and yet most of them treated the city as a metaphor. And while 'Fight the Power' was as metaphorical as you wanted it to be, it actually *sounded* like the city (even though *Do the Right Thing* was obviously set in Brooklyn).

New York itself had changed in the ten years since the Sugarhill Gang first colonised pop radio. Back then, Manhattan was the urban jungle, the no-go city. Fast forward ten years and gentrification was well on its way to turning Gotham into a retail/condo theme park, a place the poor and the disenfranchised could no longer afford to live. The culture was starting to move to the boroughs, and specifically to the vast conurbation of Brooklyn, an area only marginally smaller than Los Angeles or Chicago. Brooklyn was where the liberal white elite moved when they could no longer afford the Upper West Side, where the artists and hipsters moved when they could no longer afford the lofts in SoHo, or the basements in the East Village, and where Hispanics and blacks traditionally rubbed up against Ukranians, Italians and the Hasid.

The borough was also the setting of *Do the Right Thing*.

'I knew I wanted the film to take place in one day,' says Spike Lee, 'which would be the hottest day in the summer. I wanted to reflect the racial climate of New York City at the time. The day would get longer and hotter, and things would escalate until they exploded. I'm a New Yorker, so I knew that after ninety-five degrees the homicide rate and domestic violence goes up - especially when you get that week-long or so heatwave.'

This was the film where people stopped calling Lee the black Woody Allen. He had turned himself into a figure about whom everyone felt they needed to have a view, and there was a lot to have a view about.

'I'm a black man and I want to make movies about black life,' he said in the film's productions notes. 'One of the biggest lies going is that no matter what race, creed or religion you are, it doesn't matter: we're all Americans. That's a lie, always has been. Just ask the Native American Indians. I want people to feel the horror at the end of the movie. I want people to know that if we don't talk about the problems and deal with them head on, they're going to get much worse.'

Spike Lee's third film takes place in Bed-Stuy on the hottest day of the year. Sal (Danny Aiello, who was nominated for an Oscar for his performance) owns a pizzeria which, because of its location, is only patronised by blacks; Mookie (Spike Lee himself), is the pizzeria's delivery boy. Sal's walls are covered with photographs of famous Italians - DeNiro, Pacino, Stallone, Sinatra, Travolta - something that Buggin Out (Giancarlo Esposito), the area's most militant preacher of black awareness, takes objection to. In the intense heat, this fracas starts off a chain of events which eventually lead to an untimely death.

Technically, structurally, dramatically, this was Lee's most accomplished film to date. Coming after the shambolic *School Daze* (a leaden allegorical musical which examined the frictions between two black frat houses, the Wannabees and the Jigaboos), *Do the Right Thing* proved that his skills as a director were exemplary. With a metronomic pace he takes us through the sweltering Brooklyn streets, eavesdropping on the inhabitants and tabulating the swelling tension (in one particular instance, a drama unfolds when John Savage, playing the yuppie owner of a recently gentrified local apartment, accidentally scuffs the box-fresh sneakers of Buggin Out).

Lee's forte at the time was social realism, and here characters come and go in a most uncontrived fashion, the soundtrack intruding only when it ought to (which in Public Enemy's case, is a lot). Filmed in a documentary fashion not dissimilar to *She's Gotta Have It*, you feel like you're really there, walking by the Bed-Stuy brownstones as Ruben Blades, Public Enemy and Latin hip-hop fly out of the windows.

But the movie isn't about atmosphere, training shoes or even pop, come to that, it's about race. The leisurely way the film unfolds leaves you completely unprepared for the finale, even though the racial tension has been increasing, ratchet-by-ratchet, like the heat, minute-by-minute. For a determinedly anti-racist film, during those last few minutes the emotions become blurred, and some critics felt that Lee became swept up in a torrent of black rage; did Spike Lee support Louis Farrakhan, or was his name – and the emotions which arise from the mere mention of it – just another shock tactic, just another entry in the index of radical black buzzwords which flew about the movie like confetti?

According to Terence Rafferty, writing in the *New Yorker*, Lee was 'clearly willing to sacrifice some political clarity for the sake of movie-style power. In order to make himself heard, he has chosen to adopt the belligerent, in-your-face mode of discourse that has been the characteristic voice of New York City in the [Mayor] Koch years. Spike Lee's movie isn't likely to cause riots (as some freaked-out commentators have suggested), but it winds up bullying the audience – shouting at us rather than speaking to us. It is, both at its best and at its worst, very much a movie of these times.'

Roger Ebert, who at the time was one of the most influential critics in America (in 1975 he had won the Pulitzer Prize for distinguished criticism), was unequivocal. 'Everywhere I go, people are discussing it,' he wrote, the day it was released. 'Some of them are bothered by it; they think it will cause trouble. Others feel the message is confused. Some find it too militant, others find it the work of a middle-class director who is trying to play street-smart. All of these reactions, I think, simply are different ways of avoiding the central fact of this film, which is that it comes closer to reflecting the current state of race relations in America than any other movie of our time.'

Several New York film critics slammed the film and fanned the flames of racial divide with their first takes, at least according to the director.

Lee's anger is something that has never really left him.

'I'll tell you my least favourite reactions to the film,' he said in 2014. 'The reviews of David Denby and Joe Klein saying that black people were going to riot after seeing this film. That they [black people] weren't intelligent enough to make the distinction between what's happening on screen and what happens in real life – so they would come out of theatres and riot all across America. You can Google it. Blood was going to be on my hands, and I was going to be personally responsible for David Dinkins not being the first African-American mayor [of New York City], because the primary was that September. That still bugs the shit out of me. I know people might read this and say, "Spike, move the fuck on," but I'm sorry - I can't. They never really owned up to that, and when I think about it, I just get mad. Because that was just outrageous, egregious and, I think, racist. I don't remember people saying people were going to come out of theatres killing people after they watch Arnold Schwarzenegger films.'

Perhaps predictably, the film didn't incite riots that summer, and instead cemented Spike Lee as a major league talent. Even though it wasn't nominated for Best Picture, he got an Oscar nomination for the screenplay, and Danny Aiello received one for Best Supporting Actor. The Library of Congress went on to call it 'culturally, historically and aesthetically significant', and in 1999 it was selected for preservation by the National Film Registry.

The furore surrounding the film continued throughout the year, where it got to the stage that it became even more of a cause célèbre than it was intended to be. Even though the film was released in the middle of July it was still the subject of heated editorials in the end-of-the-year op-eds in newspapers on both sides of the Atlantic. And as 1989 tick-tocked into 1990, it was still all that many critics could talk about.*

'Fight the Power' quickly became a leitmotif of *Do the Right Thing*, and as Lee was editing it, he continually dropped the song into more scenes; when Chuck D first saw a rough cut he was shocked by how many times the song appeared (fifteen plus). Branford Marsalis called the song's use 'the greatest marketing tool in the world'.

Public Enemy's success was more pronounced than the success of many of their contemporaries, as they took punk's shock value and married it to the manufactured rebellion of early rock'n'roll, when the parents of pop consumers genuinely thought their children had become co-opted by the devil himself. The band's sound design and their sense of menace were perfectly calibrated, their militant mien as attractive as it had been with the Clash over a decade earlier. While Public Enemy were the logical extension of a genuine musical revolution, challenging every

---

* Barack and Michelle Obama saw the movie on their very first date. 'He was trying to show me his sophisticated side by selecting an independent filmmaker,' said Michelle. His options at the time would have included *Batman, Honey, I Shrunk the Kids* and *The Karate Kid III*. 'It's a good thing he didn't take her to see *Driving Miss Daisy*, or Michelle would've got rid of him after the first date,' said Lee. 'One and done.'

Do the Right Thing famously lost out at the Oscars the following year, as the Best Picture award instead went to *Driving Miss Daisy*, a very different interpretation of black emancipation. In 2019, Lee won the Oscar for Best Adapted Screenplay for his work on *BlacKkKlansman*, although the director had had his sights set on a Best Picture nod. Interviewed backstage at the ceremony, Lee, who by the time the journalist had got to him had already swallowed six glasses of champagne, was not best pleased that his film had been beaten by *Green Book* – in which, in a kind of inverse mirror to the 1990 winner, a roughneck bouncer played by Viggo Mortensen drives a black pianist played by Mahershala Ali on a tour of the Midwest and the Deep South.

'I'm snakebit,' Lee said. 'Every time somebody's driving somebody, I lose.'

preconception, their rock'n'roll outsider status was as old as Chuck Berry.

On 9 May, though, Public Enemy moved the dial in a way that would have been anathema to the Clash, the Sex Pistols or indeed any fully paid-up member of the newly established liberal punk elite.

In an ill-considered interview with the *Washington Post*, the band's 'minister of information' (basically a glorified PR spokesman), Richard 'Professor Griff' Griffin, said, among much other incendiary nonsense, 'The Jews are wicked. And we can prove this,' before going on to say that they were responsible for 'the majority of wickedness that goes on across the globe'.

Chuck D called up various rap journalists across the US – David Mills at the *Washington Times*, John Leland at *Spin*, and RJ Smith at the *Voice* – to try and encourage them to drop the story, but to no avail. Some said he was threatening, but whatever he did, it didn't work.

In a flash, the auguries of agitprop rap had revealed themselves to be slack-jawed bigots, and even though Griffin wasn't exactly Chuck D, his words sent shockwaves through the media. He compounded his crimes with some equally abhorrent remarks about the gay community, and so six long weeks after the *Washington Post* interview, Chuck D begrudgingly fired him from Public Enemy. Griffin's remarks made the band look puerile, and yet they contributed to the increasing noise that swirled around *Do the Right Thing*.

The year would end, as would the decade, with hip-hop's hegemony creating as much controversy as ingenuity. Its attitude and character would continue to recalibrate the music industry, as hip-hop slowly became one of its most dominant voices. And yet, if you listened closely you would have been able to hear the scratchy sounds of cheap guitars being tuned up from South London to Seattle, and from Manchester to Williamsburg. If you put your finger in the air you could feel the winds of change swapping direction right in front of your face, as the pendulum swung once again, this time from the turntable to the fretboard.

To wit: at the end of December, the band that would soon become Blur were still performing as Seymour (their name inspired by the title of a J. D. Salinger book), while Noel Gallagher was still a roadie for the Inspiral Carpets. It would be another two years before he started priming Oasis (who, appropriately, were named after a leisure centre in Swindon) for Britpop supremacy.

Nineteen-eighty-nine was also the year that Jarvis Cocker first had the idea for 'Common People', having met a girl a few months earlier at St Martin's School of Art who wanted to move to Hackney to live with the little people. Paul Weller would wind down the Style Council this year, too, dusting off a Gibson Firebird and reacquainting himself with the works of Steve Winwood. Nirvana had just released their debut album *Bleach* and were a year away from welcoming Dave Grohl as their new drummer.

U2 meanwhile were still staggering around the globe on their *Lovetown* tour, knowing they had 'to go away and ... dream it all up again,' as Bono said onstage on one of the last dates of the tour. Soon they would be in Berlin's Hansa Studios, burrowing away at the European angst of *Achtung Baby* (they would arrive on 3 October 1990, on the last flight into East Berlin on the eve of German reunification).

By deciding to record at Hansa, U2 hoped to catch some of the magic dust left behind by David Bowie after he used the studio in 1977, although their decision wasn't based on the changing geopolitical fortunes of Europe as much as any existential crisis or creative funk.

Europe was soon to be unrecognisable. Russian leader Mikhail Gorbachev's decision to abandon Soviet hegemony in Eastern Europe would cause colossal shock waves throughout the Eastern Bloc countries, which predictably resulted in the opening of, and then demolition of the Berlin Wall, the singularly most important metaphor of the decade. This was a *fin de siècle* moment ten years too soon, a moment that managed to embody a litany of seismic events, from the collapse of the Iron Curtain to the resignation of Margaret Thatcher, from the release of Nelson Mandela to the death of Ayatollah Khomeini.

Grunge, Britpop and the growing pains of a united Europe all contributed to a shift away from the commercial density of the eighties. Guitar pop seemed to be rearing its head again.

Not long to go now.

Epilogue

Popism

'There was never any respect for what we did. We went to the Royal Albert Hall one evening for an awards show – we were being awarded something for a dance mix of one of Bananarama's hits. But that wasn't credible enough for all the DJs in the audience with their funny hats and whistles, so they pelted us when we went on stage to collect it. I got a can of urine that hit me on the shoulder.'

– Mike Stock, from Stock Aitken Waterman

Of course, while the eighties were broad, and catholic in taste and styles, and in many instances often quite radical, elsewhere there had been a narrowing of the pop mainstream, something which was at odds with the genuine legacy of the decade, and which occasionally even overshadowed it.

Towards the end of the decade – before those cheap guitars began ceremoniously tuning up – both UK and US pop started to become terribly homogenised. The US charts gradually became the home of the power ballad – Quarterflash's 'Harden My Heart', Mr. Mister's 'Broken Wings', Foreigner's 'I Want to Know What Love Is', Scorpions' 'Wind Of Change', Starship's 'Nothing's Gonna Stop Us Now', Bon Jovi's 'Never Say Goodbye', REO Speedwagon's 'Can't Fight The Feeling', Heart's 'Alone', Journey's 'Don't Stop Believin' etc. – and the UK charts were colonised by the kind of pop which was seemingly being developed almost exclusively for the teenage and pre-teen market – A-ha, Nick Berry, Five Star, Mel & Kim, Rick Astley, Bros, Kajagoogoo, Kylie Minogue, Jason Donovan, Sonia and Brother Beyond.

This particular genre – the noise made by diffusion boy bands – was one that was often respun when people looked back at the eighties, the type of pop that chimed with the other filigree top notes of the decade's more throwaway culture: Cabbage Patch Kids, Rara skirts, Ghostbuster toys, Yuppies, Filofaxes, cocktail bars and shoddy postmodern architecture. The chief perpetrators were the production collective Stock Aitken Waterman (abbreviated as SAW), the English songwriting and record-producing trio consisting of Mike Stock, Matt Aitken and Pete Waterman.

Their forte was a kind of watered-down hi-NRG, with an urgent instrumentation and a sloppy beat, a beat so indecisive that anyone could dance to it (including those who very much couldn't dance at all). This evolved into a fairly generic type of synthpop, where the trio would first write a song, then record it, and then finally bring in a singer (or similar) to perform it. Their assembly line technique produced hundreds of hit singles for the likes of Rick Astley, Kylie Minogue, Bananarama, Sinitta and Hazell Dean, as well as the kind of micro-celebrity whose main claim to fame was attending West End parties, and then being photographed doing so.

Snubbed by the music press and the broadsheet critics (the *Guardian* called them 'Schlock, Aimless and Waterdown'), their system was really no different from the one employed by Motown in the sixties. It was certainly as successful. At one point in 1987 they had five simultaneous Top Twenty hits all of which were constructed at PWL (Pete Waterman Limited) in South London, a studio-cum-business HQ where every wall was covered with gold and silver discs – there was a Formula One racing-car in the foyer, and a Skyhawk guided missile suspended from the TV lounge roof.

Like many people in the music industry in the eighties, they measured their art strictly in terms of their popularity.

'We're the renegades of Pop!' said SAW, the same year. 'You may laugh, but we are! The record companies hate us and the *NME* hates us and everyone in between from *Black Echoes* to the average Smiths' fan hates us. Mostly they hate us because we're fucking BIG. We sell loads of records to *real* people. Let me tell you about the average *NME* reader – long coats, shop in Camden market, listen to the Smiths on their own ... They think we're aliens! We make loads of money selling records to people who aren't like them. We've sold 30 million records since we started ...'

And it really was a system, one that would soon be employed by producers all over the world, from Manchester to Sweden, and from Los Angeles to Milan. Soon, pop singles would start to be written and produced by committee (by the mid-nineties, it wasn't unusual to find a dozen co-authors of a successful hit single), as certain technologies like Auto-Tune and vocal pitch correction software meant that almost anyone could make a record. Pop became more of a commodity than ever before, as the dark, emerging shadow of Simon Cowell started reimagining the consumer as the performer. On the one hand you could say that this - the talent contest - was the natural endgame of the atomisation of pop (where literally everyone had the opportunity to be a star), but on the other hand, all the records sounded the same: emotive but without feeling, passionate but predominantly manufactured.

However, it is not Stock Aitken Waterman who we always re-member when we think of the eighties, not any more, at least.

The eighties have been relentlessly consumed and repackaged, and as we've steadily grown away from it, so the decade's magni-tude has increased. It is no longer the decade that taste forgot, no longer the ugly problem child in the narrative arc of post-war pop. These days the eighties is as much a part of our recent culture as the fifties, the sixties, the seventies or indeed the nineties, while its influence is immense. It's impossible to imagine Lady Gaga without mentioning Madonna, and the same goes for Empire of the Sun and Depeche Mode, Justin Timberlake and Michael Jackson, Haim and Gloria Estefan, or even Bruno Mars and the Police. Think of Fischerspooner, Ladytron, Little Boots, La Roux or Calvin Harris, or dip into indietronica, electroclash, chillwave or synthwave - and the eighties are never very far away. The Weeknd wouldn't have happened without the eighties, nor would any song on the *Drive* soundtrack. And what about Billie Eilish?

The percussive world we now live in is solely due to the techno-logical developments of the time, too, and the global rave of EDM obviously has its antecedents in the decade of house and trance. In the early eighties, as the world of dance and pop was starting to splinter, and as the underworlds of club music began to capture the imagination of those critics who had previously been besotted only with post-punk ideologies, so they began lobbying for more dance coverage in the music press, more dance music on TV, more dance music everywhere. Now, in the twenties, we all live in a world of dance, a world awash with BPM, and it feels completely normal. So, while the atomisation of pop has created a kaleidoscopic plane of sub-genres, there is perhaps more of a singularity now than ever, a singularity driven purely by dance.

Is this the legacy of the eighties? The relentless rhythm of mass-market EDM? Or is it the TV-advertised handbag pop of SAW? Could it be the limitless synthpop of 2021 - the neoclassical, electronic cabaret or scary art pop? Or could it simply be ambient dub or Afro Trap?

You know what? I think it might be them all.

Acknowledgements

First and foremost I'd like to thank Lee Brackstone for commissioning the book, for his wise counsel, and for being such a generous and benevolent editor. He has made this a much better book because of his laser-like attention to detail. Thanks also to the wonderful Jonny Geller for negotiating the deal. Thanks are also due to Afrika Bambaataa (who I seem to remember I first met in a council flat in Camden in 1984), Sarah Bedford, Neville Brody, Barbara Charone, George Chesterton, Jerry Dammers, Corinne Drewery, Alan Edwards, Mark Ellen, the late Tony Elliott, Matthew Freud, Martin Fry, Bob Geldof, Harvey Goldsmith, Duncan Hannah, David Hepworth, Trevor Horn, Terry Jones, Nick Logan, Mark Moore, the late Prince, Bruce Springsteen and Bernard Sumner. The following publications have been extremely helpful: *Dazed, Esquire, The Face, Financial Times, British GQ, Guardian, i-D, Independent, Manchester Evening News, MarketWatch.com, Mojo, NME, The New Yorker, New York Times, Q, Qz.com, Record Collector, Rolling Stone, Daily Telegraph, The Times, Uncut, Vanity Fair, The Word.*

· · ·

The following books have also been invaluable:

Bang! A History of Britain in the 1980s, Graham Stewart (Atlantic, 2013)

Chapter and Verse: New Order, Joy Division and Me, Bernard Sumner (Bantam, 2014)

Designer Boys and Material Girls: Manufacturing the 80s Pop Dreams, Dave Hill (Blandford, 1986)

Encyclopedia of Pop Culture, Jane and Michael Stern (Harper Perennial, 1992)

Everybody Dance: Chic and the Politics of Disco, Daryl Easton (Helter Skelter, 2004)

Generation Ecstasy: Into the World of Techno and Rave Culture, Simon Reynolds (Little, Brown, 1998)

Glory Days: Bruce Springsteen in the 1980s, Dave Marsh (Pantheon, 1986)

The Haçienda: How Not to Run a Club, Peter Hook (Simon & Schuster, 2009)

I Want My MTV: The Uncensored Story of the Music Video Revolution, Craig Marks and Rob Tannenbaum (Dutton, 2011)

Last Night a DJ Saved My Life: The History of the DJ, Bill Brewster and Frank Broughton (Headline, 1999)

The Last Party: Britpop, Blair and the Demise of English Rock, John Harris (Fourth Estate, 2003)

Le Freak, Nile Rodgers (Spiegel & Grav, 2011)

Mad World, Lori Majewski and Jonathan Bernstein (Abrams Image, 2014)

The Mojo Collection, Ed. Jim Irvin and Colin McLear (Canongate, 2003)

Prince, Matt Thorne (Faber & Faber, 2012)

The Rap Attack: African Jive to New York Hip Hop, David Toop (Pluto Press, 1984)

Rip It Up and Start Again, Simon Reynolds (Faber & Faber, 2005)

Substance: Inside New Order, Peter Hook (Simon & Schuster, 2016)

Time Travel, Jon Savage (Chatto & Windus, 1996)

24 Hour Party People, Tony Wilson (Channel 4 Books, 2002)

Uncommon People: The Rise and Fall of the Rock Stars, David Hepworth (Bantam, 2017)

Yeah Yeah Yeah: The Story of Modern Pop, Bob Stanley (Faber & Faber, 2013)

Picture Credits

Preface: Getty/Lex van Rossen/MAI
Intro: Getty/Photoshot
Chapter 1 – 1980: Getty/Laura Levine
Chapter 2 – 1981: Getty/Chalkie Davies
Chapter 3 – 1982: Getty/Kevin Cummins
Chapter 4 – 1983: Getty/Kevin Cummins
Chapter 5 – 1984: Getty/New York Daily News Archive
Chapter 6 – 1985: Getty/The Washington Post
Chapter 7 – 1986: Getty/Stephen Wright
Chapter 8 – 1987: Getty/Time & Life Pictures
Chapter 9 – 1988: Getty/Tim Roney
Chapter 10 – 1989: Getty/David Corio
Epilogue: Getty/Terry O'Neill

Index

INDEX

EPILOGUE

Parsons, Tony, 68
Paul, Billy, 46
Peel, John, 22, 102
Penman, Ian, 102
Pet Shop Boys, 6, 14, 134, 206, 223
Petridis, Alexis, 16, 136
Petrie, Daniel, 45
Petty, Tom, 239-41
Philadelphia All Stars, 47, 283
Phillips, Julianne, 184
Phuture, 247
Pickering, Mike, 263
Pickett, Wilson, 282
Pigbag, 99, 109
Pink Floyd, 119, 235
Pixies, the, 28, 273
Plant, Robert, 17, 148
Police, the, 30, 45, 297
Polsky, Ruth, 123
Pop, Iggy, 226, 259
Pop Group, 99
Portishead, 68
Positive Force, 43
Prefab Sprout, 13, 15, 25
Presley, Elvis, 16-18, 41, 147, 153, 158, 162-3, 170, 207, 228, 239, 245, 272, 279
Pretenders, the, 14-15, 151
Price, Simon, 68
Prince Buster, 79
Prince, 6, 13-14, 30, 171, 206, 219-41, 247
promo videos, 104n
Public Enemy, 6, 13, 30, 271, 274-88
Pye, Ian, 196-7

Quarterflash, 295
Queen, 19, 53-4, 79, 206, 248

Rachlin, Chip, 155
Rafferty, Terence, 285
Raghip, Engin, 72
Ramones, the, 41, 146, 252, 283
Rampling, Danny, 247, 249, 259, 262
Ranking Roger, 80
Reagan, Ronald, 15, 51, 169, 178-9, 181-2, 232-3
Reed, Lou, 6, 123, 273, 283
R.E.M., 6-7, 13, 19, 26, 188
Renegade Soundwave, 256
Reni, 29
REO Speedwagon, 295
Replacements, the, 19
Revolution, the, 227
Reynolds, Simon, 255
Richard, Cliff, 30, 275
Richards, Keith, 195
Richie, Lionel, 6, 51
Ridgeley, Andrew, 206
Rihanna, 150
Rimmer, Dave, 122
Robinson, Joe, 39
Robinson, Sylvia, 39-41, 45
Rock, Chris, 228
Rodgers, Nile, 27, 42, 53-4, 101, 152-3, 160
Rodgers, Paul, 17, 27, 42
Rodriguez, Rico, 69
Rogers, Kenny, 51

Rogers, Susan, 229-30, 234
Rolling Stone, 18-19, 28n, 152, 155, 171, 174, 180, 202, 232, 235
Rolling Stones, 18, 25, 52, 206-7, 223, 227, 274
Roosevelt, Franklin D., 178, 183
Rose Royce, 257
Rose, Axl, 25
Rosenberg, Liz, 157
Ross, Diana, 51, 150
Roth, David Lee, 11, 148, 179
Rotten, Johnny, 101, 157, 252
Rourke, Andy, 200, 207
Rowe, Dick, 274
Roxy Music, 90, 95, 107, 252
Rundgren, Todd, 234, 278
Run-DMC, 13, 55, 273, 275
Rush, Jennifer, 30
Rushdie, Salman, 272
Ryan, Michael, 232
Ryder, Mitch, 180
Ryder, Shaun, 263

Sabino, Rob, 153
Sade, 12, 14, 103
Sallon, Philip, 253
Saunders, Jesse, 255
Savage, John, 284
Savage, Jon, 96, 198
Savage, Ronald, 57n
Saville, Peter, 133-4
Schneider, Florian, 128n
Schneider, Fred, 156

308